# FUN HOUSE CHRONICLES

# FUN HOUSE CHRONICLES

by

Linda B. Myers

**Fun House Chronicles**
Copyright © 2016 by Linda B. Myers
All rights reserved.

*Published by*
Mycomm One
Port Angeles, Washington, USA

Printed in the United States of America

*Cover design by* introstudio.me
*Interior design by* Ruth Marcus, Sequim, WA

Paperback ISBN: 978-0-9838158-7-7
Library of Congress Control Number: 2016903171

Typeset in Minion.

For updates, news, blog and chatter, visit www.LindaBMyers.com

## DEDICATION

To Mom, Dad and Roger

## AUTHOR'S NOTE

My mother and father both ended their days in long term care facilities, one with physical and the other with mental ailments. Shortly thereafter, my husband entered a care facility. Four years later, he died there. For more hours than most, I've sat in those hard visitor chairs watching the comings and goings of staff, residents, and families. Some were appealing, others appalling.

My novel *Fun House Chronicles* is the result. It is about a woman who enters a nursing home and how it affects the people around her. There is hope and humor as well as sorrow here. I'd like to think this story can help support you or a loved one as you travel your own journey.

# TABLE OF CONTENTS

## FUN HOUSE CHRONICLES

## ONE

## FUN HOUSE CHRONICLE
# Mealtime

"*Get me down to dinner, you goddamn bitches.*" *Gladys announces she's ready to eat.*

*The cognitive residents share one end of the dining room, each with three tablemates. They gossip, tell tall tales, and gripe about the afternoon's entertainment, especially if the Belly Dancing Grannies performed again. One resident might introduce another's brittle ankle to a lightning quick swing of her walker, but otherwise meals pass uneventfully.*

*The more helpless residents eat in the war zone at the other end of the dining room. Some manage on their own in about the same way toddlers do. Others are spoon fed. After each meal, bits of food cling to the popcorn ceiling and to the staff. Eying an aide's scrubs, the physical therapist says, "I see squash was on the menu tonight."*

*Most aides are patient with their old charges. The youngest among them chirp like song sparrows, filling old ears in great need of idle chatter. They share their stories about two-timing men and frizzy ends and what little Bobby did yesterday. Some even seek counsel from the residents who have seen more and done more. These may be the only solid relationships they've ever had with the elderly. It will end, of course. These old people will die. Experienced aides grow wary of exposing their hearts.*

*The day passes by, and mealtime begins again.* "Get me down to dinner, you goddamn bitches."

L ILY GILBERT countersank a pie plate of beer under her border of hostas. Tucking a dove gray tendril into her scrunchie, she knee walked to the end of the row and sank another plate in the rich earth then filled it with flat Coors. That made four plates, one at each corner of her backyard garden. It had been a disappointment this year, suffering slugs the size of bear scat. "Just crawl in and drown, you slimy little bastards."

Getting down on her knees was not as easy as it used to be, but it sure as hell beat getting back up. She steadied the flat blade of her hoe on the soft ground, grabbed the handle and hoisted herself upward. Her foot slipped off the side of her Croc, and she nearly toppled because she was standing on the blade of the hoe. After regaining her balance, she worked the clog back on, picked up the beer can and her garden gloves, and limped back into the house.

She never felt the small wound on the bottom of her foot where the blade, fresh from the dirt and manure, had nicked her skin.

· · ·

"Mother, you nearly died," Sylvia Henderson said to Lily in the hospital days later as she smoothed the sheet where Lily's leg should have been. She still couldn't bear to touch the stump itself. "Another infection could kill you. You just can't live alone any longer."

"Who says I can't?" Lily, skin grayer than her hair,

was entrapped in a web of tubes and wires. Surgeons had removed her leg bit by bit battling the infection that raged from her foot upward. A nurse called it a galloping amputation. Now the leg ended at the knee.

"Who says you can't?" Sylvia had gathered all the data she needed to win this argument. "Damn near every doctor this side of the Rockies."

The two women locked eyes. Lily's were crusted and yellow from the pain meds. Sylvia knew her own would be fiery red from lack of sleep, but she'd hidden the puffiness with a generous application of light-toned concealer.

"Then why don't you come live with me?"

Sylvia had to be realistic for them both. She stiffened her spine yet another notch. "We've talked about this before," she said and counted on her fingers. "I have no nursing skills whatsoever. I run a business so I can't be with you all the time. We'd fight like two cats, and you know it. Besides, there's Kyle."

"Lucky for you."

*That's the first time she ever said there was anything lucky about Kyle.*

. . .

Eventually, they compromised. Sylvia agreed that Lily could go back home to live if Lily would accept caregivers round-the-clock. Sylvia was thrilled to have an action plan, some way to move forward at last.

She decided it would take three full time caregivers plus visits from home health nurses. How hard could that be to arrange? Her mission was one-third accomplished when Lily's housekeeper, Aurora, agreed to be the morning

3

caregiver. Lily already liked the scrappy Latina, and Sylvia knew she was reliable.

For the others, Sylvia imagined excellent women with stellar credentials, superior references and the soothing touch of Clara Barton. She soon learned that, at least in Washington, a home care aide doesn't need training so there was no certification to guide her choice. Besides, at what Lily could afford, Sylvia would be lucky to find someone with no known felonies plus a regular pulse. Sylvia finally hired a student from the community college for the night shift. Lily would be asleep unless there was a problem, so the girl didn't need to pass all of Lily's rules for sainthood. But finding someone for the afternoon shift was a horror.

"Tell me what type of person you would like," Sylvia asked her mother in the colorless hospital room, hoping to interest her in the task.

"A cabana boy. Italian, maybe Spanish."

"Come on, I'm serious."

"I'm not?"

"You're not."

"Okay, a fashionable woman in her forties, well educated and attractive, one who knows me and won't steal me blind. Why, that sounds like my daughter. But, of course, she's too busy."

By the time Lily came home from the hospital, Sylvia had managed to hire a quiet woman who'd never been farther from Edmonds, Washington than Tacoma. Lily fired her before the day was out because, "She just crept around making me nervous." The second hire lasted almost a week before Lily fired her for being too bossy. The third, according to Lily, couldn't cook worth a damn.

Next, in desperation, Sylvia hired a male Certified Nursing Assistant. Lily took one look at him and said no goddamn wet-behind-the-ears boy was going to handle her hoo-haws, and if Sylvia thought that was such a spiffy idea, she could let him handle hers. Sylvia was so non-plussed she hadn't thought to ask what a hoo-haw was.

"Lily doesn't realize this is no picnic for me either," Sylvia lamented one evening to her husband, Kyle. "She hates getting weak, but I hate it, too." Your mother is always supposed to be stronger and wiser than you. But Lily was frail now. She'd lost muscle tone quickly in the hospital so her lithe athletic build seemed a thing of the past. Lily would always have the high cheekbones and sculpted features of a genuine Nordic beauty, but her lovely skin, soft as suede, now hung looser on face and body. It didn't return to its natural pink blush but stayed as pale as ash.

Lily looked old.

Of course, Sylvia hated to see her mother lose ground for all the emotional turmoil it caused them both. But there was a practical reason, too. The more Lily failed, the harder she was to handle.

Finally, a miracle applied for the job. Sylvia prayed that this one, this Jessica Winslow, would take it. She approved of the attractive young woman as soon as she met her. Jessica was dressed in a respectable blouse and slacks for the interview, her natural curls and not so natural blonde streaks were neat, her only visible piercings were in her ears. She was younger than Sylvia, maybe mid-thirties, and looked strong enough to help Lily should she fall.

"You sure you don't want coffee, too, Mother?" Sylvia asked as she handed Jessica a delicate cup with a matching saucer at the beginning of the interview.

"You should know by now I prefer tea in the afternoon," Lily snapped while she gave Jessica the once over. "You have any candy?"

"I have some gummi bears," Jessica answered, diving for her purse.

"Now you know you shouldn't have those," Sylvia intervened then said to Jessica, "Mother is a diabetic, you know."

Jessica had not been an official caretaker before but said she felt up to the Activities of Daily Living, government-speak for meal prep, dressing, bathing, transferring, and toileting. She wasn't wild about cleaning, though, not with her own house and barn to keep up.

Sylvia quickly assured her. "The morning woman, Aurora, does most of the cleaning. And it's just mother, so there's never really much mess. She's quite tidy, aren't you, Mother?"

"Sylvia, I'm seventy-six years old. I know how to behave." She unlocked her wheelchair brakes and pushed herself slowly to a room at the end of the hall, leaving her daughter and Jessica to their coffee.

There was a brief but very pregnant pause until Sylvia said, "Mother is a little peevish these days."

"Losing her leg, her freedom…it must be hard for her to stay positive. Hard for you, too."

"Yes," Sylvia said. "I'm not sure which one of us is losing the most strength."

• • •

Jessica Winslow stopped for groceries and two fifty pound bags of oats after her interview, fretting about the cost of feed for humans as well as horses. When she thought about the job as caregiver, she was excited. She wanted an afternoon shift, and this one was three to eleven. That gave her mornings to tend the horses and even filled in her lonely evenings.

"It's not going to be easy," she said to the talk jock on the car radio even though he always ignored her. "Sylvia strikes me as wound pretty tight."

God help the wrinkle that mussed those linen trousers or the fingernail that split. The woman even had a personalized notepad imprinted with *Suggestions from Sylvia* in elegant type. "Don't think I want to receive too many of those suggestions."

On the other hand, the mother was a tough old bird. She could tell that Lily knew just which of her daughter's buttons to push.

When Jessica got home, there was a message from Sylvia on her voice mail offering her the job. Had there even been time for her to check references? Personal caregivers must be hard to find, especially those who want the second shift.

*Add to that I'm not a crack head, and I have more teeth than tattoos. What's not to like?*

• • •

Lily was more than peevish. She was pissed. After a lifetime of independence, she was stuck in a goddamn wheelchair. She had been good to her body, other than a few youthful escapades involving unsafe drugs and unsafe sex. *And what sex isn't unsafe considering all the problems it leads to?*

Her body had let her down anyway, long before her mind was ready to push up daisies. The only vice she hadn't reined in was a sweet tooth, the single characteristic she shared with her son-in-law Kyle. But it was never out of control enough to cause diabetes.

Although she wouldn't admit it to Sylvia, Lily knew the next infection would likely kill her. Or, worse, strip her bit by bit. The other leg? Her hands? Eye sight? It was all possible. She'd be left with two options for the future: suicide or a nursing home. Door number one or door number two. Behind either, the Grim Jokester sat in wait.

## TWO

FUN HOUSE CHRONICLE
# The Tumbleweed

*Ken lived unfettered as a tumbleweed. He loved racing cars and racy women, longed for that something that was just out of reach. He inhaled, ingested, or injected every type of vice, and everyone fell in love with him when he landed in his final lock-up, the small town nursing home.*

*He haunted the halls in the small hours, providing company for the other night prowlers. Sometimes he would simply disappear to the chagrin of the administration, and buzz down to the local steak-and-egger in his electric wheelchair. Or to Safeway to get a cherry pie to share with other residents. He always had a story, and even the overworked nurses stopped long enough to listen to him tell it.*

*It took a lot of time, fight and pain to finally stop his big old heart. When his next of kin was found and informed, her first question was, "Where's his wallet?"*

*Everyone at the nursing home is glad that's one final pain Ken missed.*

JESSICA BELTED out Kenny Chesney's song about shift work as she drove to Lily Gilbert's house on the first day of her new job. She was off key because she no longer had a CD to sing with. Ed had taken them all out of her Toyota and put them in his truck. It was one of the minor reasons Jessica thought of him as Ed the Evil these days.

That morning she'd taken Folly for an extra long run in the woods before feeding the horses. He wasn't used to her being gone so she was feeling guilty about leaving him alone. The cocker/dachshund mix was a rescue dog they called their cockadock. He loved a good snuffle through the undergrowth, especially if it resulted in a rancid treasure even raccoons rejected. Ed had left this little dog when he left her, so Folly had to make do with her inferior toss of a stick or pine cone.

*See? Ed the Evil.*

She pulled into Lily's driveway, arriving early to give herself time to get oriented. Sylvia had told her that the morning woman would show her the ropes. Aurora, a rotund Latina, was cleaning silver when she arrived. After they introduced themselves, Jessica asked, "Getting ready for a party?"

"No. No more parties. Sylvia will take the silver now." The two exchanged a sad glance but said no more about the gleaming tableware.

For the next half hour Aurora brought Jessica up to speed on everything from petty cash to medical equipment. Finally Aurora finger combed her raven hair, shrugged on a baggy sweater, picked up a tote bag and went out the door with a cheery, "Buena suerte."

*Good luck?*

. . .

Lily heard the new girl walk down the hall toward her bedroom. She was lying down but alert, with an old afghan in a jumble beside her where she had tossed it. *Jessica. That was the name. Blue eyed blond. Irish if the freckles don't lie. We'll just see how long this one lasts.*

Jessica peeked into the room, and Lily saw her grin. *That smile's broken a heart or two.* "Well, come in if you're coming."

Jessica entered and put a small bag of candies on the nightstand. "These are sugar-free. Not as good as gummi bears. But pretty darn good. My horses like them, and they know about these things. What can I do for you first, Mrs. Gilbert?"

*I can't be bought that easily, my dear, not with a bit of candy. It was clever, though. Maybe there's actually somebody home behind those baby blues.*

Lily pointed to a velvet-cushioned boudoir chair. "Pull that a little closer and sit down. And for heaven's sake, call me Lily."

Jessica did as instructed. "Tell me about yourself, Lily. I need to know –"

Lily interrupted. "Here's what you need to know. I'm older than God and less predictable. I'm not cute. I hate cute so do not confuse me with *The Golden Girls*. I would prefer never to be given anything with kittens or teddy bears printed on it. I like junk food when I can get it, but I don't smoke and rarely drink, although that doesn't make me holier than any thou. I have been a waitress, a florist, a picture framer, and a hundred other things. I did them all well, else why the hell do them? People often don't like me, and I just as often don't care. If you want to work for a pushover, please leave. If you're willing to stand up for yourself and not pity me, stick around."

Jessica nodded, then continued the statement she'd started. "– more about your medical condition."

"Oh, that." Lily reviewed the whole picture for Jessica. She'd struggled for years with neuropathy, brought on by diabetes. Her nerves were damaged, so her lower extremities were numb. "I stopped driving when I could no longer feel the accelerator."

"Probably a wise decision," said Jessica.

"Wasn't my decision at all. I terrified Sylvia so bad tearing out the driveway that she hid the keys from me. I told her to sell the damn car if that's how she felt about it. And by God, she did."

"Another wise decision." Jessica chuckled.

"Yep. Sylvia's got more piss and vinegar than it appears at first. Anyhoo, I couldn't always tell where my feet were on stairs either, so I even had trouble with the front stoop."

"Good thing your bedroom isn't a loft."

"Or that I'm not a roofer."

"Or an aerialist."

Lily realized how long it had been since someone had laughed with her about losses that otherwise made her cry. Jessica was earning points. "Let's see, what else? Oh yes, since you will occasionally see me in my altogether, you better know I have acute cellulitus."

"Cellulite?"

"No, not dimpled thighs. Cellulitus. It's fluid build-up in the numb areas. Looks ugly and leads to infections I can't feel. It's dangerous because my immune system is screwed up by the diabetes." Lily tried for nonchalance, but she was terrified her body would become a live trap. If this girl was to be her caregiver, she'd better hear it all. So Lily even admitted to her newest problem. "Since the amputation, I've been feeling phantom pain. As if I didn't have enough of the real McCoy."

"How did you lose your leg, Lily?"

"A slug got me."

"Someone shot you?" Jessica's eyes opened as wide as blue moons.

"Not that kind of slug." Lily explained she was in her garden killing slugs when she stepped on the hoe. "It was coated with cow shit at the time."

"Fertilizer is better on dirt than it is on feet."

Lily brightened. "Do you garden?"

"Only when I have to."

"Well, in this job, you may have to. My garden is important to me." *Not much else is anymore. Except Sylvia.*

"I guess I'll survive. What happened next? With your leg, I mean."

"At first, I thought I had a cold. But I kept getting weaker, having chills. Sylvia says I was fuzzy headed, more so than usual. About the time I turned yellow as a lemon peel, she rushed me to the emergency room. The sepsis nearly killed me. I finally beat it, but not before my leg was amputated at the knee."

"Will you be getting a prosthesis?"

The question intrigued Lily. "I came home too weak for the sawbones to even consider an artificial leg."

"Well, maybe we can get you in good enough shape for the sawbones to reconsider."

*Okay. Sylvia might have gotten this one right.*

· · ·

Jessica was preparing dinner in the obsessively clean kitchen, wondering if Aurora picked up every crumb with tweezers. She wasn't a stellar cook, but she could handle the basics. As long as Lily liked stew or baked chicken or meat loaf, she'd stumble through well enough.

Lily was parked in her wheelchair at the kitchen table, having a cup of tea and watching her every step. As the day had progressed, Jessica found Lily to be as inquisitive as a cat. She was fairly sure she would never be fired as long as there was more to any tale she was telling. So Jessica began telling her own story, doling out installments like Scheherazade.

"I board horses, give riding lessons and show my own Paso Finos," she said while chopping a red pepper for a salad. She carefully wiped up the seed that fell to the floor.

"Paso Fino…past their best, right? That pretty much describes me."

"It doesn't mean they're past their best. It means fine step. A Paso Fino horse is a very smooth ride. They prefer a kind of speed walk to a trot." Jessica dried her hands, then took her wallet from her purse and removed a photo for Lily's inspection. "That's me with Latin Lover."

"The horse or the guy? They're both gorgeous."

"The horse. The guy is Ed, my husband. Well, he was my husband," Jessica said, her voice catching just the slightest bit.

Lily peered up from the photo. "Touchy subject?"

It was inevitable that Lily would hear the story of Ed the Evil. But not now, not yet. Jessica wasn't ready to reveal that much of herself. Her old charge might decide she was in less need of care than her caregiver.

. . .

Sylvia sat at her mahogany desk in her home office. She was trying to work, pasting a love seat in front of a fireplace then dragging it into the floor plan's bay window. She sat back against the lumbar support in her ergonomically designed chair and frowned at the monitor. She clicked on the love seat, turned it slightly and pasted an end table to its right. With a sigh, she saved her work and closed the program. She really couldn't concentrate while she hovered near the phone waiting for a call from the new girl.

If she wasn't all goosey about that, it would have been a wonderful afternoon of blessed quiet, the first time to really concentrate on her work in weeks. She just couldn't help holding her breath, waiting for whatever would hit the fan.

She wondered where Kyle was at the moment. His real estate business was tricky right now so he was always out with some prospect or other. Sometimes he got a listing for a house that she was hired to stage. It was always fun to work together. That hadn't happened in a while.

Her glance meandered over to the photos nearly buried under fabric swatches on her desk. There was the studio shot they'd had taken for their twenty-fifth. They were still handsome people thanks to the sensible diet and exercise program she managed for them both. Goodness knows what he might do on his own without her to watch over his taste for sweets. With her help, Kyle was still slender, sporting that little bit of gray at his temples which helped dignify his boyishness.

She had bigger breasts and wider hips than when she was young, of course. But it wasn't unattractive, especially if she were clever about the clothes she chose. She favored suits that highlighted her small waist.

Thinking of their youth, she rummaged under the swatches until she found the small snapshot of them both from design school, what, twenty-six years ago? Twenty-seven? *We look too young to be so sure of each other.* Kyle was the first person she'd ever met who liked her just the way she was. He didn't try to change her. And that thought bounced her right back to life with her mother.

When she was a little girl, she'd wanted riding lessons. She'd requested English style, loving the look of the proud ladies on their jumpers. But her mother bought her Western lessons instead so she would be at home on trail rides anywhere in the country. Sylvia fancied the grand plie of ballet over the shuffle step of tap dance, but Lily laughed at the little pink tutus. Sylvia loved her mother without question, but they were as different as lady fingers and molasses cookies. Their prowess at irritating each other grew as the years went by.

"I like to follow the rules," she'd once said to her mother.

"And I like to flout them," Lily had answered.

Lily was a time bomb at home just waiting for another infection to explode. She'd no doubt need a nursing home one day. That fact filled Sylvia with a burning knot of dread that even Prevacid couldn't touch. She knew that in the end she'd have to be the bad guy and say when it was time.

She hoped Lily's finances would allow her the best care choices. Sylvia wanted every nickel to go to her mother's welfare, not to her own inheritance. She'd even asked Aurora to clean the silver that had been her great grandmother's, the antique samovar, teapot, bowls and tray. She'd sell it all when the time came that cash had more value than legacy.

Lily would be as hard to transplant as a wildflower. When it happened, she'd give up on life long before she died. Sylvia shuddered and willed the bubbling grief to still before it overflowed. Then she replaced the photo, blew her nose, and stared at the phone.

She'd waited to get the "I quit" call from Jessica all afternoon. She'd just have to call her mother herself.

"Hello?" Lily answered.

"Hi, Mother, how are things going?"

"Fine, dear, but would you mind calling a little later?"

"Well, okay. Are you all right?" Her mother was never too busy to talk these days.

"We're having dinner. Jessica made me oyster stew! I haven't had it in years."

"Oyster stew? You hate oysters."

"No, dear, I just hate them raw. And that's the only way you ever serve them."

*Maybe I'll just go kill her now. No jury of my peers would convict.*

**THREE**

**FUN HOUSE CHRONICLE**
# Glossary

*N*ursing home trade speak can be irreverent, offensive, even morbid. It's not spoken in the public lounges or resident rooms. But when the staff lets it rip in the privacy of their break room it is not for the faint of heart.

Chrissie suffered a direct hit on her first day, fresh from her Certified Nursing Assistant classes. A coworker welcomed her to the job, calling the nursing home the Departure Lounge. Over time she learned a dying patient was CTD (Circling The Drain) or ART (Assuming Room Temperature) or FTD (Fixing To Die).

A Code Brown or Code Yellow meant incontinence, depending on the source of the leak. Seniors were Raisins, and the ones who used walkers or wheelchairs were Creepers. Gardening meant tending to those in a vegetative state.

It went on and on. And it appalled Chrissie. At least it did until the night when, attending to a patient blowing vomit and diarrhea simultaneously, she heard herself call for help with an OBE (Open Both Ends).

Now Chrissie understands the language is a way to cope with ongoing trauma and death. These days, she goes about the wiping and cleaning a far more tolerant servant in God's Waiting Room.

CLARICE HAGADORN avoided being drawn into the lives of a bunch of sad old sacks. *Life can be depressing enough without that, thank you very much.* Still, the morning news was damned irritating. The dingleberries at Madrona Park Assisted Care had announced they'd no longer take Medicaid patients. They were looking for other facilities to take their current handful of long term residents.

"I don't understand. How could something this horrible happen?" asked Lia when Clarice arrived at work that morning. Lia looked up from the newspaper spread open on her reception counter. The Indonesian's soft brown eyes looked troubled.

Clarice explained. "A state law passed that denies facilities the right to take in private pay patients then evict them when they go on Medicaid."

"That sounds like a good law." Lia's brows puckered in concern. "Doesn't it?"

"It's well meaning. But it scares the crap out of some places."

"Why?"

"They don't want Medicaid people if they aren't profitable. Now they have to find loopholes. Some claim they can no longer meet the patient's needs. Some are dropping their Medicaid contracts so they can evict patients they already have, and carry on with only a private pay clientele. That's the Madrona Park route."

"But that's cruel! It's these people's home. Where will they go? Just out on the street? Who'll take care of them?"

Clarice didn't know the answers, so she hated to be confronted with the questions. As the bookkeeper for a nursing home, she knew how thin the profit line could be.

"Care facilities are in a bind. We all need to make a buck to survive." She shrugged at Lia then trudged on to her office. After hanging her windbreaker on the peg behind the door, she flopped into her desk chair and turned on her computer. She forgot Madrona Park when she remembered the joy of losing another half pound that morning.

Six months ago, Clarice had been 70 pounds overweight. She was tall so she carried it well, and her job at Soundside Rehabilitation and Healthcare Center was sedentary enough that she could do it in comfort. Still, drop a pen and let it roll under her desk, she was in trouble. She was only forty-two, but she was as out of shape as someone twice her age.

Then their gung ho administrator, Jeff Parkinson, had come up with a new torture. Office staffers were to take turns handing out food trays to residents who didn't eat in the dining room. Jeff believed it was good for everyone, not just the nursing staff, to get to know the residents. It was part of his from-our-family-to-yours-because-we-care bullshit.

To handle the multi-level meal cart, Clarice had to get her back in shape for bending and lifting. That meant another fucking diet. The day Jeff circulated his memo, Clarice snuck into the rehab room to weigh herself while the residents were gathered in the activity room listening to the AccordiAnnes butcher polkas. She was appalled when she tipped the scale at 240 pounds. She gasped so loudly that Babs Sloane, the Activities Director, heard her and came to see if a pipe had burst.

"No, no, everything's fine…just stubbed my toe," Clarice said, quickly turning so Babs wouldn't see her tears.

She turned her head away from Lia, too, passing behind the reception desk and scuttling into her own office. *To be caught crying would be the icing on the cake. The no fat, no sugar, no taste cake.* Being fat is public enough as it is. Everyone could tell she had security issues since obesity is as obvious as a clown's shiny red nose.

Dieting was nothing new to Clarice. She'd lost weight before, always regaining those pounds and more. But this was the first time she was living alone, not counting the two Burmese cats, Kit Kat and Hershey. Dick Head had divorced her years ago. And her son Cole was off at college. Dieting might be easier now that she wasn't cooking for anybody else.

Before that brief flicker of hope could die out, she'd emptied her dish of Werther's Originals into the wastebasket and placed an online order with NutriSystem. She needed portion control, but she damn well wouldn't go to any groups. *My name is Clarice, and I'm fat as the Hindenburg.*

That had been six months ago. She was down almost 40 pounds. She still was heavy, but the other staffers had started saying things like, "Did you get a hair cut?" and "Are those new glasses?"

Clarice kept a list on her home computer of things she noticed as she lost:

– *My pants are getting longer.*
– *My boobs stick out farther than my midriff.*
– *The bus seat next to me isn't always the last one taken.*
– *Kit Kat and Hershey can't fit on my lap together.*

She glanced around to be sure nobody was looking her way, and rummaged inside her blouse for a moment. Then

she emailed herself an addition to her list:
– *With your bra hooked in the smallest position under-wires poke you in the armpits.*

⸪ ⸪ ⸪

Jeff Parkinson, the administrator at Soundside Reha-bilitation and Health Care Center, was taking inventory of his progress toward a smoother operation. All in all, he was pleased. In his first months on the job, he'd made changes that settled major staffing issues.

"You want a latte, Jeff? I'm making a Starbuck's run," Lia called from the reception desk.

"Make it a decaf, thanks. Iced with two percent." A few months ago, Lia hardly spoke to him, much less offered to be the coffee mule. Of course, he couldn't pat his own back too energetically about his success with the staff. It was in no small part due to their disgust with his predeces-sor. The numbskull hadn't done the slightest thing from their point of view. On day one, Jeff revised the rules. He allowed CNAs to work four long days so they could avoid paying for day care or buying gas on a fifth day. The new policy was an instant hit.

Next he began giving the Certified Nursing Assistants bounties if they brought in friends to take the CNA course. Because they liked him, they actually did it. Now Sound-side trained enough CNAs to fill its own needs and to staff one of the other centers in the CompreCare Group. Hap-pier CNAs made for happier nurses and, in theory, happier residents. He wasn't naïve enough to think they all loved him, but he doubted they called him a JAFA, their term for 'Just Another Fucking Administrator.' Jeff could almost see his star rising in corporate eyes.

Jeff's good mood was shattered when he finally found the time to scan the newspaper. He grappled daily with the crisis in costs for long term care, so he wasn't really surprised by Madrona Park's plan to boot out their Medicaid residents. He even knew of one place that got around the law by sending some to the hospital and refusing to take them back. They had the stones to call it 'dumping.'

Jeff had no stomach for such conduct. He'd never offload Soundside's lifers. *We can even take in one of the displaced seniors from Madrona Park. CompreCare corporate doesn't have to know as long as I keep Soundside operating in the black.*

Jeff patted the short hair around his prematurely bald spot, wiped his glasses with a lens cloth, and left his office to take a stroll around the halls before Lia got back with the coffee.

Clarice was covering for Lia at reception, and Jeff said hi but she apparently didn't hear. He wondered if something was different about her, a new hair style or some such. But he forgot about it as he prepared to greet Gladys, the resident most likely to tell him to go to hell.

\* \* \*

Clarice was vaguely aware that someone had spoken to her, but she had just made an amazing discovery. When she sat down at Lia's chair, she crossed her legs. Crossed her legs! It had been ages since she'd actually put one knee right over the other. As soon as she could she'd add to her list:

– *I can cross my legs like a girl.*

She stayed chipper the rest of the day, right up until the Staff Benefit Committee meeting. As a rule, Clarice skillfully dodged committees, but Lia had nominated her for this one.

The chairwoman was the Activities Director, Babs Sloane. She was bouncy as one of the physical therapy balls, scuffed and worn but always on the move. Her kinky tight perm made her head look covered with pubic hair, but nothing could be lower maintenance. Babs not only sported an almost unbearably sunny disposition, she could pinch the polish off a penny. As the bookkeeper, Clarice knew Babs performed miracles with almost no budget at all.

Babs convened the committee in the staff break room where she placed six stacks of baskets on the lunch table. Meanwhile, Clarice eyed the two committee members who were new hires.

Dominic, a line cook, was a zit-faced lad who looked like a porcupine with all that gel in his hair. It was just a little less spiky than his attitude, but kitchen help was notoriously hard to hire. Alita was a brighter bulb from the housekeeping staff. The teenager looked sweeter than an animated Disney heroine. Little birds and furry critters probably gathered round her to dance and sing while she worked.

Addressing the newcomers, Babs began the meeting. "This committee is responsible for staff parties and other rewards."

*It's destined to fail because nothing pleases everyone.* Clarice couldn't imagine partying with, to pick just one, that miserable bastard from maintenance, and she assumed many staffers felt the same about her.

"We need a real bash this year," Rick Peters said. He was sitting across from Clarice where he'd maneuvered himself next to Alita. He was one of the few single male aides, and Clarice had heard rumors he'd sampled more than his share of the female staffers. Small wonder. He was a poet's dream of square jawed, tousle haired, brown eyed, killer grinned perfection. *Jesus, the kid even has dimples when he smiles.*

Babs said, "Rick is right. Today we need to focus on the yearend holiday party. I know it seems a long way off, but you can never start raising funds any too soon." She explained she wanted each of them to visit stores around town to ask for gift donations. They should give an empty basket to each who agreed to fill it. Soundside would display them and any visitor could bid on them. The profit would fund a party for the whole staff.

"Will people really buy them?" Lia asked.

"Of course! Family members like to tip people who care for their loved ones, but we're not allowed to accept gratuities. An auction gives them a way to do something nice for us all."

"What's in it for the stores?" asked Alita.

The bookkeeper in Clarice voiced a cynical opinion. "They give at wholesale but write it off at retail."

Babs raised an eyebrow briefly then returned to her usual sparkle. "And they receive such wonderful publicity. Now, everybody take four baskets. We'll meet again soon to see how you've done."

Clarice knew that, at the end of the day, Babs would be getting most of the baskets filled herself. Another person might say the hell with it. But that person would not have the can-do spirit of an Activities Director.

"I really like your new glasses," Babs whispered to Clarice. "They make you look younger."

**FOUR**

**FUN HOUSE CHRONICLE**
# Robert

*R*obert *yelled from his room, "Hey! Hey, nurse."*
*Nurse Mary Beth seldom responded to such tactics.*
*After a time, Robert upped the ante. "Hey! Hey, nurse.*
*Get in here."*
*No response.*
*"Goddamn it! Get in here."*
*No response.*
*Finally, Robert did a wheelie out of his room,*
*careened down the hall, and rolled to a halt inches from*
*the unflappable nurse. She was at the meds cart prepar-*
*ing evening dosages.*
*"Nurse! There's no call girl on my bed," Robert raged*
*in indignation.*
*"As far as I know, there is no call girl on anyone's bed,"*
*said Nurse Mary Beth, preparing an insulin injection for*
*52A.*
*"Well, I needed you."*
*"I am not a call girl, Robert. I am a nurse. I don't*
*make as much as a call girl. I believe you mean a call*
*light."*
*Nevertheless, the old man in 48A yelled, "I want a*
*call girl on my bed, too," as did those in 50A and 56B,*
*passing the chant on down the hall.*

LILY FINISHED the breakfast tray that Aurora had brightened with a rosebud from her garden. Then she read the morning paper, including the article about Madrona Park residents. *Poor old buggers. Next they'll be set out on the curb for Waste Management to pick up.*

It put her in the perfect frame of mind for her own drama. "It's Nurse du Jour Day," she grouched as Aurora helped her onto the commode. Nurse du Jour was Lily's term for the home health nurses who came three times a week to search for wounds on her remaining leg. They unwrapped and cleansed it, then rewrapped it in creams, ointments, gauze and a compression bandage. At the slightest sign of trouble, Lily was prescribed more antibiotics.

She was terrified they'd find a new patch of telltale redness or sniff out a fetid odor. Lily took her angst out on them, hating that they never stayed on schedule and that it was rarely the same nurse twice in a row. "Knowledge of my medical woes is lost as the baton is passed," she'd complained to the service's management.

Today's nurse didn't arrive until well into Jessica's shift. The florid woman tried to appear upbeat, but she was frazzled. No doubt her feet hurt along with her back from the physical exertion of handling the infirm. And she'd run out of gauze pads and Eucerin cream.

Lily aimed a stage whisper toward Jessica. "Thank God there's an upside to neuropathy. Since I can't feel much below my knee, she can't make this process painful."

After the nurse left, Lily finally relaxed. She said to Jessica, "You must have some kind of sonar or something."

"Why's that?" Jessica asked while she pulled sheets from the linen closet and carried them to the bedroom.

The bed always needed to be changed following the leg cleansing even if Lily felt too drained to get out of it.

"When Nurse du Jour is here, you know I'm on edge."

"On edge. As in rabid? Bitchie? Snide?" Jessica shook out the clean bottom sheet.

"Okay, okay. But you don't disappear. You stick like a burr." While she spoke, Lily rolled over on her side with her back to Jessica and inched away to the other side of the bed.

Jessica lifted the fitted corners of the used bottom sheet on the side Lily vacated then rolled it like a carpet against Lily's back. "The nurses teach me tricks so I do a better job with you. Like how to change the bed while you're in it. And I watch to learn how to wrap your leg in case a nurse doesn't show up one day." She placed the clean sheet down on the exposed part of the bed and rolled half of it against Lily. "Besides it doesn't take sonar to know you're on Orange Alert where infection is concerned."

Lily chuckled. "My husband used to say Orange Alert when he was beginning to feel frisky."

"That's not what Homeland Security means by it," Jessica answered while Lily turned back toward her across the rolled sheets, ending up on top of the clean one.

"No. But they don't have the fun Harmon and I had."

"What happened to your husband, Lily?" Jessica pulled the used sheet off the other side and rolled out the clean.

"Oh, becoming a widow is an old sad story," Lily said, centering herself in the newly made bed.

Jessica placed the top sheet and a light blanket over Lily, then sat on the green velvet boudoir chair. "Well, it might help me with my new sad story. I'm learning how to be a widow, too. There, it's out. For great periods of time, I can almost pretend that Ed the Evil is just off on an extended road trip."

Lily recognized it in Jessica's face, that emotional ache relentless as a stone in your shoe. "But words like *widow* or *deceased* or *alone* make the whole thing real again. All right then," Lily said while Jessica invaded the Kleenex box. "Let's talk about Ed another time, whenever you're ready. In the meantime, I'll tell you about Harmon. I've been without him for, oh, forty-five years so my wound is hardly fresh. Still, it seems impossible that it's been so long."

Jessica gave a mighty nose blow before asking, "He died, in what, the mid sixties?"

"In Vietnam. The name Harmon means soldier in some obscure language, and he sure as hell lived up to it. He was blown from one end of Dong Ha to the other."

"Sylvia must have been a baby. You couldn't have been much more than a child yourself."

"A flower child at that. Harmon's parents hated that he married 'a drugged out hippy chick.'" Lily used her index fingers to draw the quote marks in the air. "Our love was entirely too free for them. They wanted no part of me. They disowned him and little Harmony, too."

"Harmony?" Jessica looked confused.

"That's Sylvia's first name. In the sixties we thought that kind of thing was groovy. But she always hated it. Sylvia is her middle name in honor of her great-grand-mother. I never thought we'd actually use it, but it's all she ever answered to. I finally had to give up on Harmony."

Lily looked across the room seeing nothing but her past, although she felt Jessica's warm hand close gently over her own knotted fingers. "Harmon's family hoped he'd come to his senses one day, forget all about us and return to the fold. Even after he died, they still disowned their granddaughter."

"How could they do that?"

Lily was no easier to win over than a feral cat, but she was beginning to trust Jessica with secrets she didn't even tell her daughter. "I've certainly wondered the same thing. Of course, I wouldn't have made it easy on them to get to her if they tried. I was plenty angry."

"You had every reason to be outraged. Imagine not wanting a granddaughter."

"I've mellowed now. I can see that maybe they just didn't want to chance more pain. Losing their only son must have made it too hard to start all over again with a grandchild. Whatever their reasons, Sylvia and I were on our own."

"What about your own parents?" Jessica reached for another Kleenex.

But Lily wasn't listening. Jessica's interest in the story had reminded her of telling fairy tales to Sylvia all those years ago. The little girl listened intently, but demanded that Lily retell each tale without anyone burning in ovens or being eaten by wolves. Sylvia wanted happy endings for everyone back then and still did, which was why she was so ill-prepared for –

"Lily? What about your parents?" Jessica asked again.

Lily left Sylvia's story and came back to her own. "I was estranged from them, too, what with all those anti-war demonstrations. They booted me out long before I met Harmon, and I never looked back, even when I could have really used them. Especially my Mom since I hardly knew which end of a baby to diaper when Sylvia came along. But somehow Harmon and I muddled through.

Even enjoyed it."

"Do you still miss him?"

Lily could hear the hope for a magic bullet in the question. She wished she had one, but no such thing existed. "You never forget that kind of loss, Jessica. But along the way, it gets less painful. Living life day to day is the only way I know to make that happen. Never underestimate the importance of a daily grind."

"I keep imagining what life would be like if Ed had lived." This time Jessica took the whole Kleenex box and held it on her lap.

Lily understood the feeling all too well. "I know. It's like characters in a good book. You want to know what becomes of them after the author says the end."

"I'm afraid my story ended too damn abruptly. That I won't have any more chances."

"Oh, my dear. Other loves, responsibilities, sorrows will seep in, but you have to be open to them. To let it happen." Lily patted Jessica's hand. "Soft hands. Feels like there're no bones in there at all. You're still so young...Do you want to tell me what happened to him?"

"Another time, I think." Jessica's eyes were as red as her nose. "I should begin dinner now."

"It's just as well. I'm tired, Jessica. I think I'll catch forty winks."

"Good idea." Jessica replaced the tissue box on the nightstand and moved the chair back from the bed. She started to leave but looked back and said, "Thank you, Lily." Then she turned off the light and left the room.

Alone, Lily's thoughts wandered back to the newspaper article about old people being evicted from an assisted care facility. It was a short trip from their plight to the gremlins

31

waiting in her own future. She'd been quick with advice for Jessica, but could she apply it to herself? Was she open to living life in a new situation?

Maybe it was better to end it now with suicide. *If I were really serious, how would I go about it? A plastic bag over my head might work. But surely my body's need for air would ignore my brain's command, and I'd rip the bag off.*

To experiment, she put a pillow over her face. In a matter of seconds, she tossed it aside, gasping. *Okay, suffocation is out.*

She decided to catch those forty winks after all. And think about life or death another day.

\* \* \*

Sylvia patted her lips with her linen napkin and said to her husband Kyle, "Jessica Winslow seems to be working out."

"Jessica Winslow?" he asked, grinding sea salt onto his salad. Sylvia had recently decided it was better for them since it was organic, without additives. Sea salt had replaced Lite Salt on their table which, in turn, had replaced iodized salt. Kyle had once complained that he paid the price when she read health news. She'd said nonsense, she was merely concerned for their overall fitness.

"You remember, the afternoon woman. It's been a month, and Mother hasn't fired her yet."

"Then Ms. Winslow should apply for sainthood," Kyle said with conviction. He had received his own poor report card from this mother-in-law many years before.

Since Sylvia had a temporary respite from the personnel business, she had time to investigate the care facilities in the immediate area. Her current system of round-the-clock caregivers was a house of cards that would collapse sooner or later. One of two things would happen: Lily would suffer a critical infection, or she'd run out of money to pay for the care. Either way, they needed a back-up plan. And since Lily wasn't doing it for herself, Sylvia had to step in.

She'd begun her search with the precision of a war admiral. Kyle would be briefed every step of the way. His willingness to listen was one of the things she loved most about him.

Adding a dollop of low fat sour cream to her baked potato, Sylvia began her report. "I looked into nursing homes online today. Medicare lists facilities by state. It tells you how big a place is, if it's not-for-profit, whether it takes Medicaid, stuff like that."

"Some sure look nicer than others when you drive by them," Kyle said. "A few look like the Bates Motel."

"Assisted care units are usually newer, but they don't all have RNs round the clock. Some states may required it, but Washington doesn't. That's a deal breaker. So a nursing home is her best option when the time comes." Sylvia tried to keep her voice steady. She was up to this. This was a job that needed to be done, not a death sentence for her mother. It was a way to prolong life, not to expand misery. *Oh, Mom.*

She cleared her voice and asked, "How do you like this chicken? It's a new recipe."

"It's different. Is this…a prune?" Kyle looked concerned, as if the shiny black lump on his plate might actually be the thorax of a beetle.

"Yes, the sauce is made from different dried fruits."

"Oh. Well, then. Very nice with this Pouilly-Fuissé."

"To select a nursing home, you can click on a bunch of quality measures like nurse-hour-per-resident ratios. And here's a nice phrase: infection containment."

"Does that mean they wash their hands between patients?"

"And they don't share thermometers."

"They better score well on all measures, or Lily will give them a run for their money."

On the contrary, Sylvia had discovered that not all nursing home attributes were important to every patient. For instance, Lily might want a private room, but never be able to afford it, so the availability of one was not an issue. But food quality and room cleanliness were critical. "You choose what matters most to you. A place's total rating isn't as important as going through each individual criterion on the list."

Finances were an issue, of course. 24/7 health care at home was unbelievably expensive. Sylvia had offered to help, but Lily had hissed like a wild cat. If Lily went to a nursing home from a hospital, Medicare could provide for a while. After that, she'd pay thousands each month until her money was pretty much gone. Only then would Medicaid kick in.

"I thought I'd look only at places that take both private pay and Medicaid patients. Then we won't have to put her through a second move when her money runs out."

Kyle nodded his agreement. "One move will be hard enough on both of you." Then he frowned for a moment. "Seems to me there was an article about this in the paper a week or two ago. Something about kicking people out?"

"I'm sure there are places that might do that sort of thing, but we'll be more selective than that. I've narrowed the search to four facilities I'll visit on Mother's behalf." As Kyle sprinkled more sea salt on his chicken, she said, "Careful with that, dear. I'm just thinking about your blood pressure. And save room for dessert. I found a recipe for cheesecake made with fat free cream cheese."

As she straightened the kitchen following the meal, Sylvia imagined a cozy facility where loving nurses eagerly catered to the beloved's every whim. Luscious, nutritious meals were served, and duffers sat together happily reminiscing when they weren't watching movies or playing parlor games. She thought it important to show up unannounced at the nursing homes on her list, instead of alerting the management in advance by making appointments. Soundside Rehabilitation and Health Care Center was one of the four that had made her final cut. But she experienced a brief pang of worry. *Will my mother make theirs?*

**FIVE**

**FUN HOUSE CHRONICLE**
# Butt Cracks

*H*is wife hasn't seen Charlie's privates since the day he entered the home, and certain sightings were never a daily occurrence. Like the backside of his scrotum.

Male wheelchair jockeys can be plagued with pressure sores, so Charlie has dressings changed each morning before rising. Hands-on treatment in the end zone is a sensitive balancing act for both nurse and patient. Too much antiseptic spray is like sticking a firecracker under his balls and lighting it. But if the area is handled too gently, then a man may do what men do. So Charlie and the Nurse keep up a running patter for distraction.

MONDAY

Charlie: Most women want paid a lot more to do that.

Nurse: Considering where my hands are, you might not be a smart ass just now.

TUESDAY

Nurse: Men have these loose parts just hanging out there looking to get hurt.

Charlie: That's not what they're looking to get.

WEDNESDAY

Nurse: If you don't stop making fun of the Seahawks, I swear I will hurt you.

*Charlie: Maybe we should skip the scrotum exam this morning.*

*Between the washing and the dressing, there is a period when the medication must dry. The Nurse comes around to sit in Charlie's vacant wheelchair and talk to him face to face. They discuss fishing and bowling and her granddaughter's college choices. Then she finishes the chore, dressing the wounds for another day.*

*His banter makes her job easier; her banter makes his life easier. They are intimate partners in a way that his wife and he have never been.*

SOUNDSIDE WAS third on Sylvia's hit list. She liked that Rehabilitation was part of its name. It was hopeful. Like coming in didn't mean you'd never go back out. *Oh, who the hell am I kidding?*

The first person she met as she squared her shoulders and marched through the sliding glass doors was Gladys. "Hello! How are you today?" Sylvia asked with unnatural cheer.

Gladys had settled like putty into a wheelchair. She was as toothless and squinty-eyed as a pirate with the sailor's mouth to match. "You bitch!"

Sylvia looked behind her to see who could have angered the old dear. Seeing nobody, she realized she was the bitch in question. "Excuse me. I do beg your pardon." She backed away then pivoted to approach the reception desk where a small brown woman wore a name tag that identified her as Lia.

"I see you've met Gladys," Lia said, looking up from the stack of mail she was metering. Her teeth were dazzling white in her round face. "She's often our reception committee. Aren't you, Gladys?"

"Goddamn!" Gladys drooled from a mouth that was a gummy hole.

It was a troll's leer or maybe a smile. Sylvia couldn't tell. She fought down revulsion as she watched the ancient begin a slow journey down a long hall, pulling herself along with two slippered feet at glacial speed.

"How may I help you?" Lia asked and Sylvia turned her attention back to the receptionist.

*She's what? Filipina? Indonesian? Pretty. Upbeat. Smiley. A receptionist at a nursing home should be. Of course. But how is that possible in this...this...hall of horrors?*

Sylvia untied her tongue. "I would like to speak with someone about my mother. Here. About her here. About my mother living here in your facility." She stopped when she realized she was babbling.

"Of course. I'll get Jeff Parkinson, our head administrator. Please have a seat."

Sylvia plucked a Soundside brochure from a counter rack and took a seat in the lobby. She was not surprised that the sunny floral chair coverings were actually vinyl. From the two facilities she'd visited so far she'd learned that, no matter how pretty from a distance, the furniture had tough, heavy duty surfaces resistant to incontinence. Lobbies always smelled like bleach or carbolic or whatever these places used to disinfect. Her eyes watered, maybe from disinfectant, maybe not.

She'd also learned that newer facilities were built with administration offices to the front, surrounding an ostentatious entrance. Actual resident rooms were far away and out of sight. Few occupants were limber enough to drag themselves all the way to the front, so visitors were protected from the cries and odors that emanate from forlorn old people. People like Gladys. All in all, Sylvia preferred it that way.

But Soundside was not new. It was small enough for residents and staff to exist cheek by jowl. Sylvia heard a triumphant, "Bingo!" from down the hall, followed by a burst of cheering and booing. The jovial sounds temporarily soothed her anxiety.

*Maybe it won't be so bad.*

But she knew she was whistling past the graveyard and wasn't that an awful choice of phrases considering the circumstances.

\* \* \*

Jeff Parkinson saw a handsome, smartly dressed woman pretending to read the Soundside brochure while she waited for him in the lobby. If he had to choose one adjective to describe her, it might have been sleek. Her dark brown hair, unobtrusive make-up and suit were flawless, unlike most visiting family members who appeared far more harried. She could have been a lawyer or some kind of state official, except nobody actually read the pap in that brochure unless they had a relative in imminent need.

When she lifted her face toward him, Jeff recognized the look. Her stormy brown eyes had the haunted expression of The Family Member. Enough tears had been shed, feelings rubbed raw, hope pinched out to finally push The Family Member through those sliding glass doors. This lovely woman's emotional needs were no doubt as debilitating as her loved one's physical needs.

Jeff hoped he could make her see the good that could be done even in a place that housed so much sorrow. He introduced himself then invited Sylvia to the privacy of his office.

As they entered, she said, "I'm here about…"

"You're here about…" They spoke simultaneously. Jeff smiled, and indicated his guest chair. He took the other one. This was no time for the buffer zone of his desk.

"Yes, about my mother. She's currently living at home, but I'm not sure how long she can manage." Sylvia placed her purse first on her lap, then down on the floor. She smoothed her skirt until it covered both knees.

Jeff knew she was nervous, maybe even frightened. They all were, the ones who had to confront the inevitable. "It's never pleasant to contemplate changes like this. Please know we can help you and your mother through it with as little trauma as possible." He noticed Sylvia was having trouble keeping her hands still. While he spoke, she fingered a paper clip holder on his desk, moving it until it was equidistant from the stapler and the tape dispenser. "Why don't you tell me about your mother."

And Sylvia did, from the first infection to the galloping amputation to home care. "Right now, caregivers are with her round the clock. Except for when she fires them." Sylvia aligned the business card holder with the stapler.

"It's nearly always best for somebody to be at home as long as possible. But it is wise to know your long term choices before you have to make them. Would you like to take a tour while we talk?"

Sylvia kicked over her purse as she stood. Jeff picked it up, handed it back to her, and they stepped out of the office.

"This area is administrative services which includes marketing, social services, and so forth. You've already met Lia. And here is our bookkeeper Clarice." The little receptionist smiled again. She was dwarfed in size by the other woman passing by who merely nodded.

Leaving the reception area, Jeff took Sylvia past the Central Nurses Station and offices for the Intake Specialist and the Director of Nursing. Everything was orderly and efficient until they arrived at an office that looked like terrorists had bombed a craft store. Baskets, colored papers, balls, fabrics, and silk flowers were piled in every corner of the room.

*I really must ask Babs to organize just a bit more,* Jeff thought as he introduced her to Sylvia. "Our Activities Director has projects going with the residents all the time."

"Oh yes! Providing entertainment is a must," Babs enthused while she straightened a stack of dog eared books. "It keeps everyone active and connected with each other. We have programs for all levels of ability and cognition."

Jeff walked on and Sylvia followed. He glanced sideways and noticed she was keeping her gaze on the floor. The Family Member always feared images that would haunt forever. And that pained Jeff, his inability to help her. There was so much positive that he wanted to share to soothe her fears. He wanted to hold her and tell her that her mother might find solace here even before she herself did. He sighed at the enormity of the task and knew he didn't have the words. No one did, not really. So he carried on in the rehearsed tone of a public speaker.

"Soundside is a constant care center, not an assisted care center. We have a full nursing staff, with at least one RN on duty 24/7. To support them, we have LPNs, aides, and specialists in physical, occupational and speech therapy. Our rehabilitation center can help with recovery of all kinds, including strengthening your mother, post amputation."

"That would be good." Sylvia said.

*Does she look a little brighter? No, those eyes are just shiny from unshed tears.*

Finally, Sylvia brought up money, a subject The Family Member rarely handled gracefully. "After Medicare runs out, my mother will be able to pay her own way for a while. But Medicaid will be necessary down the road."

"That's very common, Mrs. Henderson. Our social worker can help you with all the paperwork around the time of transition."

"But, I saw…well, you wouldn't evict her or anything like that, would you?" They had moved to the doorway of a spacious room that looked like a gymnasium invaded by a team of seniors painfully lifting weights.

"Absolutely not. That will never be the policy as long as I am here at Soundside." *Damn that Madrona Park story.* "We have many Medicaid recipients who call us home, and we're proud to fill their needs."

Jeff could see her relief, at least until she watched one old woman using parallel bars to shuffle a miniscule step away from her wheelchair. Sylvia paled. Newcomers were so often shocked by the frailty of old people trying to recapture lost ground.

\* \* \*

*This Jeff person is perfectly pleasant and all, but these fossils look more like they're being tortured than restored.* Sylvia's attention was drawn to an old man, mouth agape and skeletally thin. A speech therapist helped him form vowel sounds, and cooed about his progress.

"His moans sound just like moans to me," Sylvia said, sorrow rising like floodwaters.

"But Mrs. Henderson, just days ago he couldn't follow her at all," Jeff answered, then moved along down the hall. "Progress may be slow, but it is progress nonetheless. We try to give people back the ability to live a peaceful life. That often means relearning skills they have lost, like Mr. Jenkins is doing."

Jeff stopped at the doorway of a room filled with a dozen residents. They were playing the Bingo game that Sylvia had heard from the lobby. Several clutched their cards and waited eagerly for the next call. Others were asleep in their chairs, collapsed as though their bones had been sucked out of their skin. One old man leered at Sylvia and raised a hand to touch her, but she sidestepped him as they passed.

"They enjoy each other's company," said Jeff.

"My mother won't want any part of it."

"A lot feel that way when they first get here. But once they get comfortable, most join in."

Sylvia would rather have a colonoscopy than continue this tour much longer. It was a horror show with the whole staff pretending these relics could ever be happy again. Things got worse when they toured the resident rooms. Some were spartan if they housed short term residents recovering from hospital stays. But others had massive accumulations of kid's drawings, family photos, crocheted throws, and entire zoos of stuffed animals. Each door was decorated with a cartoon cutout of a squirrel family in swimsuits carrying surfboards. The cartoon balloon said "Summer! Everything is Beachy Keen!"

*Goddamn hilarious.* "My mother would just d…" Sylvia stopped herself in time.

It was the third nursing home she'd visited, and she could take no more. No more wizened old people bellowing their rage or resigned to sobs or stoically waiting to die. *How can this be endgame for my mother?*

Sylvia abruptly stopped the tour, thanking Jeff for his time and telling him she had just remembered another appointment.

\* \* \*

Jeff watched her walk away, her heels tapping a staccato rhythm on the linoleum. He had seen The Family Member go through this before. Maybe she would be back, maybe not. He hoped he had helped her decide on Soundside. In the meantime, he returned to his office to put his desktop back in order, just the way he liked it, with the paper clip holder right next to the stapler.

Now to deal with Jimbo. One of the local garden centers had presented Soundside with fifty bird feeders and bags of seed. A feeder was to be hung outside each residential room. But Jimbo, the maintenance supervisor, had made it clear that he felt his job ended with repairing wheelchairs and opening clogged drains, for crying out loud. He took umbrage at installing hooks, hanging feeders and filling them with seed. "Bird seed leads to bird shit," he'd muttered when Jeff assigned the task a month ago.

Jeff knew that may be true, but he cared deeply about good relationships with other organizations. *Get a gift, use a gift. Or you might not get another.*

He composed a terse memo to Jimbo, strongly suggesting the job be done no later than month's end.

\* \* \*

Clarice felt like an enormous Red Riding Hood delivering baskets for staff party donations around town. The very worst was the Village Fudgery. Maybe Babs was taking a shot at her weight by assigning it to her. *Oh for God's sake, this is Babs we're talking about.*

Clarice made a mental note to add to her weight loss list:

– *Obesity is no longer the excuse for your paranoia.*

The Village Fudgery caused her angst. She felt like an alcoholic forced to enter a favorite old watering hole. She went after lunch one day, when she was as full as she ever got. She waited until no one she knew was anywhere near to see her enter this heaven. The sweet aroma of chocolate and coconut and burnt sugar hit her like a nuclear blast, weakening her resolve along with her knees.

"Why, Clarice! We wondered what happened to you," said Gert, the leathery string bean that owned the shop. "George, come out here and look at our Clarice!"

"Hi, Gert…George." Clarice was embarrassed by the fuss. George, the actual candy maker, at least had the decency to be round as a bobber.

"Now we see what happened to you. You're melting away!" he exclaimed. "Quick, Gert, give the lady a truffle before she disappears."

"NO!" Clarice even startled herself. "I mean, no thank you. They're delicious, but they're off my list for the time being."

Clarice explained the staff project, and before she left the couple promised a basket filled with fudge, assorted chocolates, nuts and chews. The next hurdle would be to avoid bidding on the basket herself.

It was raining when Babs called the next meeting, water pounding the windows of the break room. To the staffers who groused about the weather she chirped, "At least we won't have to water our lawns." Clarice wondered if Babs had any idea how annoying she could be.

All in all, eighteen stores had promised to fill baskets. Since Dominic had done nothing, Babs nominated him to help her gift wrap them when the time came. All other team members seconded the motion. As they stood to go, Clarice couldn't help but notice that Rick and Alita left together.

\* \* \*

Jeff looked out his window as an ambulance pulled into the nursing home's circular front drive and parked under the portico. It did not have a siren shrieking and lights ablaze, nor was there urgency in the motions of the emergency medical technicians. That meant it wasn't here to rush a resident to the hospital. It was bringing one of Madrona Park's throw-aways to live at Soundside.

Jeff smoothed what little hair he had, straightened his glasses and hurried to the lobby to greet Alvin Jacobs. "How do you do, Mr. Jacobs. Al," he said extending his hand. "I'm Jeff Parkinson, the head administrator. We hope you will be at home here at Soundside."

Small obsidian eyes embedded in a face as round and massive as a grizzly peered back at him. The man made a sizable mound on the gurney. Jeff imagined it was an easier way to transport such a giant than in a wheelchair. Al looked around the lobby from the gurney rolling his head slowly side to side. "Nothing special," he announced. "But then, neither am I."

Gladys, wide-eyed with excitement, pulled herself upright from her chair to peer at the new resident. "That's a goddamn bear!" she shrieked.

Alvin Jacobs made a deep rumbling sound that could actually have been an ursine growl. But it resolved itself into a laugh. The big man finally extended a massive hand to the administrator. Jeff grasped it, then nearly flapped back and forth as the bear shook it. "Maybe I'll be okay here after all. Madrona Park can go to hell."

Jeff had to agree.

**SIX**

**FUN HOUSE CHRONICLE**
# The Judge

*N*orman *was a district judge, respected more than liked. But dementia is a great equalizer, and now the judge is sentenced to life in the nursing home.*

*He is given to howls and whoops day and night. He can be a bully, striking out at aides, but at other times he is mellow, making the contented moans of a large dog who has found the right spot in the sun.*

*One day, a very young aide confided to the nurse that she was worried about Norman. "He's speaking in tongues," she said.*

*The nurse went to listen for a moment and said, no, Norman was merely singing "Mairzy dotes and dozy dotes and liddle lamzy divey."*

*The girl had never heard the nonsense song from Norman's childhood. In this instance of the very young caring for the very old, she didn't realize that he was actually happy. To her credit, she learned the words, and can sometimes be heard singing to other residents as she showers them or changes their sodden bedding.*

As SPRING gave way to summer, the bond between Jessica and Lily blossomed as profusely as her garden. But today Lily was decidedly glum as she sat in the wheelchair on her backyard patio, watching Jessica do the chores she would have loved to do for herself.

*A garden is full of ways to kill yourself. And you can enjoy the fragrance while you're at it.* Bulbs, roots, leaves, or blossoms of belladonna, foxglove, hyacinth, yew, even bleeding heart could be pulverized into powder to create a deadly cup of tea. Anybody who ever read English cozy mysteries knew that. But Lily didn't know the proper proportions. And were apricot pits also somehow involved? *I'd probably just puke it all up or give myself a case of the trots. Or go into a coma for years and –*

"That's the last of the sunflower seeds," Jessica interrupted her perverse reverie. While Lily woolgathered, her caregiver had filled the bird feeders, swept up the empty seed casings below them, and poured sugar water into a bright red feeder, all the while dodging a pair of Anna's hummingbirds that dive bombed her head. Jessica used the hose to fill the bird bath and then handed a watering can to Lily. "Get to work."

Lily could still douse the geraniums and petunias, pushing her wheelchair from planter to planter, deadheading the spent blossoms as she went. She couldn't reach her impatiens in the shady border next to the house, so Jessica gave them a drink, pulled a few weeds, then set fresh slug traps with a can of Coors. Finally, she stood, stretched her back and wiped sweat from her forehead. "The slugs shouldn't get all the refreshment around here. How about we break for a couple of cold ones?"

"Whatever," Lily sulked. She heard the screen door slam as the younger woman went inside to the kitchen fridge.

Jessica returned with two small bottles of Diet Coke, then flopped down into a deck chair next to Lily. They both were shaded by the oversized patio umbrella. Jessica took a swig, gave a less than ladylike burp, then looked around the yard. "I have to admit it looks gorgeous."

Most days, Lily agreed. In fact, she considered her garden the best part of herself. Twenty-five years ago when she'd purchased the house, the yard was a sloping, weedy lawn. Over time, she'd planted rows of rhodies and photinia to screen out the neighbors, and converted the slope into a rockery with multiple flowerbeds from her property line to her patio. It was a color riot, dozens of varieties and heights bobbing wildly in the breeze. Woodland skippers, tortoiseshells and other butterflies fed here although Lily saw fewer of them now than in years past. Too fragile for the modern environment. *Just one more goddamn loss.*

Lily said, "It looks gorgeous? Quite a review from someone who thinks a garden should be nothing but oats and hay." She knew she was being cantankerous but couldn't help it, even when Jessica shot a perplexed look her way.

"You feeling all right, Lily?"

"I'm fine."

"You seem a little...upset."

"I said I'm fine. Let's change the subject." *If I keep acting this way maybe I can get her to shoot me.*

For a time they both watched two plump robins splash with such vigor that the birdbath was nearly emptied. Then Jessica said, "I imagine Sylvia likes to garden, too, right?"

"Are you kidding? Get her hands dirty intentionally?

Touch a bug?"

"All rightie then," Jessica said. "I'm done picking the subject. Got anything you *would* like to talk about?"

"Oh hell, I'm sorry. I'm a miserable old bat."

"Yes, you are. Now what's wrong? Maybe I can help."

"You've heard the phrase, sick and tired of being sick and tired? I feel like that a lot these days."

"But Lily, you're getting better. You just have to give it time –"

"Don't sugarcoat it, Jessica. As they say, there's no gold in the golden years. I have to pretend enough as it is with Sylvia. She actually believes that a nursing home will be just hunky-dory down the line. She's been paying them visits."

Lily felt tears well up, irritating her all the more. "Crap." She pulled a bedraggled tissue from her sweater pocket. "I don't really blame her, you know. I've never done right by her. She always wanted a proper home, but I raised her like a nomad. I never did what she wanted. I was a lousy mother."

When Lily stopped to wipe her eyes, Jessica said, "I think you have her fooled, Lily. She seems to like you well enough."

"Oh, I know that. But we piss each other off. She wants everything so perfect, including me. Like that's going to happen. You know she's an interior designer, don't you? Hell, I never gave her an interior to design other than apartment walls for cheap posters."

"So she has lots of room to go wild now."

"Honey, I know you're trying to make me feel better, but I disappoint her all the time. I shouldn't have done that so often when she was a kid. And I shouldn't do it now when we have so little time left. But a nursing home? I just

51

don't know how I can handle that."

Jessica gave her an intense stare. "Tell me."

*Well, what the hell. She asked for it.* "I've been thinking it's about time to cash in my chips."

"What?" Jessica sat up straight so fast she knocked over the Diet Coke.

"You know what. Buy the farm, eat my gun, off myself."

"You crazy woman! Don't even joke about that," Jessica snapped while she mopped up the spill.

"Maybe I'm not joking, and maybe I'm not so crazy." Lily saw a red blush of anger work its way up Jessica's neck, but she didn't back off. "I'm sick and old and I'm only going to get sicker and older. It's a logical option for anyone in my shoes to consider. Or should I say shoe?"

"Well, consider it if you have to, but don't do it. You can't just give up. Promise me. You're the one who told me you have to be open to new things."

Lily didn't really want her caregiver to feel anger or fright. Lily already felt enough of that for both of them. So she yielded. "Well, you don't have to worry. Whether I want to or not, I don't think I can. It would be one more example of putting my own feelings ahead of Sylvia."

"It would break her heart, and you know it." Jessica paused then added, "And besides, I'd have to look for another stinking job."

After a moment, Lily chuckled. "Well, we can't have that."

The tension broke, but like a blister it left touchy skin behind. An afternoon breeze rustled through, and soon the coolness sent Lily back indoors. She asked Jessica to fill the birdbath again before she came in, after she put the pop bottles in the recycling bin.

There was really nothing more to be said.

* * *

Following the tour of Soundside, Sylvia rushed home and down the stairs to her basement workroom. The Fabric Forest, Kyle called it since piles of upholstery and carpet swatches oozed out like living tendrils, pushing his part of the office further and further into a corner.

"Selling real estate just takes listings. I require actual samples," Sylvia said on the rare occasion that he complained. "So I need the most space."

She intended to dig into her current project of redecorating a law firm. While waiting for her computer to boot up, she grabbed a stack of curtain fabrics and moved it off the monitor. Holding them, Sylvia thought how much nicer these rich fabrics were than the ones that littered the Activities Director's office. Her tears began plopping onto the frilly sheer on top, creating salty stains.

"Damn it all to hell and gone," Sylvia cried. As long as she could remember, Lily was capable of causing her pain even if she didn't mean to. And it wasn't going to get any easier.

All the years of Sylvia's childhood she'd been hauled along Lily's erratic path, one city to the next. She was almost twenty when her mother had made her final move to Washington state. A lot of years ago. *She finally got stopped when she had no mainland left.*

Sylvia had no memory of any other relative, just an old photo of her father in his uniform. "Maybe Daddy will find us in Chicago," she'd said to her mother as a very young child on the way to another new home.

"Sylvia, you know that isn't going to happen."

"But maybe it was all a mistake and he isn't really dead and he's looking for us everywhere."

Lily had said nothing for a long time then told her, "The army makes mistakes. Lots of them. If it helps you to believe he is alive, then that's what you should believe."

Sylvia had believed it until she grew old enough to know that the only thing at the end of a rainbow is a big pot of disenchantment. That was about the time Lily had left Paul, the only other man that little Sylvia thought could have played the part of Daddy.

Now mother and daughter had reversed roles. Lily would have to travel the road that her daughter chose. Sylvia was unprepared for how hard making choices for her mother would be.

When the phone rang, Sylvia cleared her throat and answered, "Henderson Interiors." She knew that whoever was calling would never have guessed that the very together Sylvia Henderson was feeling overpowered by circumstances she couldn't handle.

That night in bed, she confided her fears to Kyle. She put down the magazine article about Georgian architecture that she had been trying to read. "I just feel so guilty about making choices for my mother."

"Of course you do," Kyle said as he removed his socks and deposited them into the hamper. "It's the human condition."

"Guilt?"

"Certainly," he continued as he got into bed and put on his reading glasses. "You will feel guilty to put your mother into a care facility. But you will feel guilty if you leave her at home and she gets another infection that kills her." He pulled up the covers and snapped on his reading light.

"You'll feel guilty if you butt into her freedom so much that her last years are miserable, and you'll feel guilty if you butt out so much that she tries to do more than she can, and ends up with no last years in which to be miserable." Kyle leaned over and kissed her on the cheek. "You simply can't win, my love. So take a deep breath, realize that you are a good daughter doing the best you can, and that this is going to be one of the hardest chapters in your life. But you will live on to smile again." He opened his book on French vineyards.

"Well, that's comforting. Glad to know that guilt is a universal."

"You wouldn't want anybody else to miss out on all this fun."

She smiled at him. "Good night, Sweetheart. Thanks for the advice. Sometimes you even sound like you know what you're talking about."

* * *

Jessica drove home mourning for Lily. It was almost midnight when she got to her ranch house and let her dog Folly out of the kitchen for a late night run. Feeling restless herself, she walked out back toward her barn. A spotlight mounted on its peak augmented the quarter moon, but it was still dark as she came up to a pasture fence. He must have heard her footsteps on the gravel because as soon as she arrived at the rails and put out her hand, he was there.

"Evening, Latin," she said to the stallion. At just fifteen hands Latin Lover was not a big horse, but he was a half ton of pure pleasure as far as Jessica was concerned. He was a champion show animal, as comfortable on trail rides as in the ring. But these days his primary business was siring foals. He had colts and fillies from mares all over the Pacific Northwest, many of them now champions in their own events. As his fame for producing athletic, sweet tempered champions grew, so did his stud fee. Jessica had told Lily, "He's the perfect employee. He keeps me in business, works for hay, and loves his job."

Latin Lover had a spacious box stall in the barn but he preferred the outside, rain or shine. Jessica obliged him that freedom on mild summer nights. In the daylight he was as dark as blackstrap molasses, showing glints of mahogany only in the brightest sun. Now in the dimness, Jessica could only see him as a ghostly form. He accepted an ear scratch, gave her a low whinny, then moved away into the shadows again.

"Sure, leave me here in the dark. That's what guys are good at." Sadness for Lily's situation apparently had a ripple effect.

*The little lady loses the Mister and then the ranch.*

It sounded like the plot of a made-for-TV movie. But it could be a true story for Jessica if she wasn't very careful. Just the thought of failure made her as breathless as if one of the horses had kicked her in the gut. No matter how hard she worked to keep her home and her business, without Ed's income it was touch and go.

"Ed," she whispered. "Why wouldn't you listen to me? Why didn't you stay home that night?" If anyone answered there in the night, she didn't hear.

From the day she'd met Ed, she'd never given another thought to life without him. It was inconceivable, but it had happened. He was there, all sassy and passionate, then in a losing battle between tires and ice, everything changed forever. Jessica would carry on, of course, because she loved this twenty acres of land. The animals depended on her to rise from her bed each morning when all she really wanted was to hide in despair. Their needs pulled her through the worst of days.

And now this tetchy old woman, this Lily, was inching into the 'pull her through' category as well. She was like a battle scarred soldier, incapable of self-sufficiency but still a proud old warrior. They were both fighting their way through the dark. Jessica realized how much they were counting on each other.

Folly jumped up to nuzzle her hand. She patted him and turned toward the house. "Here's the plan, Folly. I'll tell her about Ed the Evil tomorrow. She'll like that. And I have to get so I can talk about it. It's time. But right now, it's time for bed."

As Jessica and her cocker/dachshund mix walked back to the house she realized she felt a little better. She was looking forward to introducing her lost love to her new found friend.

\* \* \*

The next day, Lily appeared to be in a better mood. She told Jessica she fancied a game of Scrabble. Jessica was pleased her old charge was willing to keep her mental skills honed, so she rummaged around the top of the guest room closet where Lily said she'd find the game. She did, under Clue, Sorry and Chinese checkers, the remnants of Sylvia's childhood.

Jessica put the Scrabble game on the kitchen table. While Lily opened the box and turned the little wooden tiles upside down, she prepared a plate of sliced Braeburn apples and Tillamook white cheddar. Then she sat down and soon discovered that Lily could trounce her every time. "I struggle to come up with *ZOOM* and you slaughter me with *ENZYME*," Jessica bristled. Lily clearly relished a win, so they played most of the afternoon.

It was during the third game that Jessica finally told Lily about Ed the Evil. But she apologized first. "I can't talk about him with old friends or even my parents. They all want me to recover faster than I can. You've been through it yourself, so it's easier to talk to you. But, Lily, you're my patient, and I really shouldn't burden you."

"Piffle. I've told you I'm nosey. Besides I didn't know him. I won't suffer like your parents do."

"When he died last fall in —"

"No! I don't want to start with Ed the Dead! I want to know about the living one. The Ed the Evil one. Start at the very beginning."

Jessica was so grateful for the chance to remember better days that she reached over and hugged her confidante, knocking over her letter tray in the process.

"Good," said Lily. "I didn't like that selection anyway. I'll take more and you start talking."

So Jessica began.

"I first saw Ed ten years ago, when he was twenty-eight. It was at a horse show over in Moses Lake. I didn't own Paso Finos then, couldn't afford them. But I trained a couple fillies for their owner and rode them in competition for her. Anyway, I noticed this man leaning against the fence, looking at those fillies. And, oh Lily, talk about your shock and awe! I went weak in the knees and in the head at the same time.

"I'd seen taller men, more handsome. Dated my share of them. But this guy…he was like kindling to me. He had that weathered cowboy look, dark skin with sun bleached hair. Eyes the color of thunder clouds, laugh lines around them. A nose that had been broken once kept him from being too pretty. I knew right from the get-go that he had nothing better to do with those bulked up arms than put them around me."

"Holy camole," Lily muttered with a theatrical shiver.

"You know what I did? I hit on him! Strutted up to him, working it for all it was worth, and said, "So...you like my girls?""

"Sounds like a bad Mae West."

"Is there any other kind? Anyway, he turned those blue-gray eyes on me, all surprised like, looked me up and down and said, 'I have to admit. Your girls look just right to me.'

"And then I said, 'We are talking about the fillies, right?' He laughed and said, 'Oh, man. I am in a whole lot of trouble here.'"

"Great beginning," Lily said enthusiastically. Jessica thought she meant her story until Lily started a new game with NYMPH.

"That's eight billion points. Go on with the story. And don't skip any of the sex bits."

"The sex bits are none of your business, but believe you me they were ample and amazing. After a time, it was too hard to live apart, so he moved to my side of the Cascades. We bought an old house and large barn with enough pasturage for a couple dozen horses. I started boarding and giving riding lessons.

"For our wedding, Ed bought me the most wonderful present. He purchased a foal from the woman who owned the Paso Finos. That's how I got Latin Lover. Through the years his stud fees have paid for a lot of oats."

She sighed at the pleasure of sharing these memories. "They were fabulous years, Lily. Story book stuff. My business grew. I even bought a couple mares from my friend when she decided to sell off her stock. Ed shared the barn chores with me when he was home, but he was usually on the road."

"Doing what?"

"His main job was hauling RVs from the manufacturers to their new owners."

"I never heard of a job like that," Lily said, slapping down the word NOSEY on the Y in NYMPH.

"He worked long hours at it and made good, steady money. Ed owned the truck and picked up fifth wheels in the Midwest, delivering them here. Or Canada. He could usually get a trailer to make the trip back, too."

"Sounds like a fine time, being paid to be on the move," Lily said as she filled her tray back to seven letters. "I'd have liked a job like that."

"Things were okay until fuel prices shot up. Hard on independent truckers. Hard on everyone," Jess conceded, while playing SPOIL. "Fuel was the reason we began to fight. He felt he needed to drive more to make up for earning less. So he started driving nights. And in bad weather."

"The male need to provide?" Lily suggested while frowning in concentration at her tiles.

"The male need to be an asshole. We could've gotten by on boarding horses for a little while, until he found other work." *How can I be so angry with someone I miss so much?*

"Then he must have liked the job, Jessica."

Jessica glanced up to see if she was being criticized, but Lily's eyes were on her tiles. "You're right, he did. Even though I hated it, he wouldn't listen. The more I bitched, the more he laughed at me."

"Is that why you call him Ed the Evil?" Then, with a sharp intake of breath, Lily lowered her voice as if someone else in the empty house might overhear. "Or did he play around while on the road?"

*Nosey is right.* "No, not as far as I know. I would have known how to fight that." She looked at her tiles, but the letters made no sense to her. "One night the weather in the Cascades had me worried sick. The passes were treacherous. I pleaded with him to wait it out before making the trip. I told him it was evil to make me feel so bad, but he just laughed it off.

"A couple days later, he had an *Ed the Evil* decal pasted to the side of the truck. The letters were made to look like chrome pipes. Big joke, huh?" She looked up and smiled wanly at Lily. "Before he headed out again, he told me he'd have an *Ed the Evil* tattoo by the time he got home."

"Did he get one?"

"Didn't get the chance. His truck and the trailer jackknifed on Snoqualmie Pass. They told me it was a patch of black ice."

Lily said no more, just added *UST* to one of Jessica's *O*s, emptying her tray on the final play. She beat Jessica by more than 100 points.

*So much for the sisterhood of widows.*

* * *

Jessica went along pretty well until a memory of Ed leapt out to stab her. *It's like living in a slasher movie.* But tonight she felt calmer than usual. She wasn't so plagued

61

by sorrow, and her financial fears had apparently gone to bed. How she had enjoyed talking about Ed with Lily. Instead of making her miss him all the more, it had felt good, like allowing fresh air to get at a wound in order to heal it.

She was too jazzed to sleep. Folly curled up with her on the sofa, snoring lightly as she watched a late, late showing of *High Noon* and ate Cheerios out of the box. Folly pushed against her in his sleep with his short doxy legs, trying to create more space for himself. Some doggy dream caused his feet to twitch. *Maybe he's thinking about Ed, too.*

"Do not forsake him, you nincompoop," she yelled at Grace Kelly for waffling in the movie.

She and Ed had made love just about anytime, anywhere the mood hit. They'd even christened a couple of those new trailers before he delivered them to their owners. But their favorite time was in the early morning, snuggled into a warm bed in a cold room. They called it grappling before grapefruit, and what a sweet way to begin the day. Ed said he was glad she was a morning person.

Now Ed was Ed the Evil, and he was no more. His side of the bed was always cold, and he was never in Billings or Spokane on his way home to her. She remembered what Lily had said about loss and living day to day to get over the pain. She was doing her damnedest to move forward, but the empty bed was nearly unbearable.

In the end, Gary Cooper lived, but Ed was dead. She pushed the dog off the sofa, put him out to pee one final time, then back in to sleep some more. She padded into the bathroom, turned on the shower, and took two aspirin while the water warmed.

Jessica stepped into the shower and let the water loosen her weary muscles. She worked six hours in the mornings with the horses before her eight hour shifts with Lily, so she always felt fatigued. But tonight, she thought about the many times she and Ed had started the morning together in this very spot, how he would run the soap over her breasts and down to the secret, private areas. Without him, she must soap herself alone. With the help of warm water and warmer memories, she came.

*Daybreak is lonely for your mourning person, Ed.*

SEVEN

FUN HOUSE CHRONICLE
## Spouses

*Esther visits the old man every day. She is elderly herself, so the drive is hard on her bones, and her vision isn't what it used to be. She brings news of their son's job and the grandchildren's school plays and, when she can think of nothing else, the weather. She bakes little surprises to tempt his old palate. But he is so wintered in his own despair he offers nothing in return but complaints and bitterness. When the time comes that she must leave, Esther slowly shuffles to the door. He follows in his wheelchair, enraged that she is leaving, yelling down the hall, "Go on, then. Get out of here, goddamn you, go on." But, the next day she is back, with another story, another treat.*

*A few rooms away, George comes each afternoon to join his wife for dinner. He makes sure her dress and sweater match the way she always liked, and he brings bits of costume jewelry from home, pinning a favorite brooch to her bodice. He combs her hair, and pats her cheek, telling her the worst old man jokes in the world to hear her giggle like she used to as a girl. Pushing her chair, he proudly escorts her to the dining room. She has no memory of who he is or what's been lost, but he remembers it all.*

*For these spouses, is this duty or is this love? Or are they one and the same?*

LILY HAD learned the one thing she couldn't discuss with Jessica was suicide. While it occasionally amused her to hear Jessica squawk like a bantam hen, this was not a fitting subject. She needed to confront it on her own. Lily waffled back and forth on the subject, depending on her mood.

On the one hand, she didn't want her daughter bereaved by an act Sylvia would never understand. Suicide defied the natural order of things, and nothing in Sylvia's life argued with tradition. Besides, if you decide on suicide, you never have a chance to decide on anything ever again.

On the other hand, it was unnatural to keep a body going in pain or on machines longer than it wanted to go. Lily had heard it said that suicide is the coward's way out, but she thought it took enormous courage to get out of the way when you were a burden to others. *Maybe I could float away on an iceberg like an old Eskimo.*

For now, Lily decided to put thoughts of suicide on hold. It had dawned on her that she had the method at her disposal when the time came to make the decision. She had a store of insulin in the fridge. She could use it to overdose. Her glucose level would topple, she'd get sleepy, slip into a diabetic coma and pass away. *The end.*

Simply knowing she had a way out comforted her, and allowed her to postpone any decision. Her sense of urgency waned. Thinking about it weeks later from the nursing home, Lily realized that this had been a pivotal moment in her life. When the time came that she needed her stash, Lily was too weak to take matters into her own hands.

She began sleeping in late and waking up hazy. Aurora, who was there in the mornings to see it, asked, "You up too late, Ms. Lily? Maybe play board games with that student all night?"

"No, just in the afternoons with Jessica."

"Then spooky movies, maybe? All these kids like zombies and devils." Aurora crossed herself.

"Nothing scary, Aurora. No vampires or aliens. I'm just a little too tired to get up this morning."

"Okay, Ms. Lily. You stay put. I give you a nice warm cloth for your face."

\* \* \*

Jessica was alert as a sentinel after Aurora talked to her at their shift change on Monday. But the home health nurse didn't find infection or any other problem. Lily denied there was an issue, grumbling about her caregivers to Nurse Du Jour. "They're just scaring each other like a couple of kids telling ghost stories."

For Jessica, the real give away that something was sapping Lily's strength happened in the late afternoon. She beat Lily at Scrabble. She demanded to take Lily's temperature, and it was running slightly high. Jessica knew exactly what to do. She called Sylvia, Lily bitching all the while that she should not upset her daughter. Sylvia said she'd contact the doctor.

After a tense half hour, Sylvia called Jessica back. "I talked to the doctor through his office manager, not person to person, of course. There's an enervating virus going around with symptoms like Lily's. The doctor can work her in first thing Wednesday morning, but in the meantime, count on the old tried and true. Aspirin, liquids and bed rest."

"Okay. I'll be sure she gets it." Jessica looked at the old woman sulking in her bed. "At least I'll try."

"And be extra careful with the blood monitor. If she's fatigued, it would be easy to give her too much insulin."

Jessica didn't want to add her own worry to Sylvia's, but she couldn't help it. "The home nurse saw nothing to worry about. But still, I wish the doctor could see her sooner."

"I wish he could, too. But it's hard enough to get her to go to a doctor she knows, much less rush her to one she's never met. So we'll wait. It will give us time to work out transportation. I have no idea how to get her into my car."

Jessica said she'd look into Paratransit or city buses that could handle wheelchairs. Then Sylvia asked to speak with her mother. Jessica handed the phone to Lily who hissed, "Why'd you have to make her fret?"

Jessica got the aspirin from the medicine cabinet while she eavesdropped on one side of the conversation.

"Hello?…Yes, dear….Yes, dear…No, you don't need to come…I'd like to nap…please don't worry…no, dear… I'm fine…really…bye-bye." Lily handed the phone back to Jessica to hang up, and said, "She's such a worrier, that girl."

"Hmmm. Her mother is infection prone and is feeling fatigued and the doctor can't see her today. Nope. No reason for your daughter to worry that I can see. Now take these." Jessica handed her the pills and a small glass of water.

"Don't you start siding with her, little missy. Now go away, and let me sleep."

When Lily awoke just before dinnertime, Jessica was relieved to report to Sylvia that her mother looked perkier and was even bossier than usual. "No, I didn't think that was possible either." They laughed in mutual relief.

When Jessica came on shift the next afternoon, Lily's temperature had spiked. Her skin looked yellow. Not able to reach Sylvia at home or on her cell, Jessica called an ambulance.

"I don't want to go," Lily protested weakly. "If I felt any better, I'd really give you hell about this."

"If you felt any better, I'd be more worried for the EMTs than you." Jessica tried to sound lighthearted, but she was frightened to the bone.

Lily was whisked away to the ER. Jessica followed in her Toyota, but by the time she ran into the hospital lobby from the parking lot, Lily had disappeared behind a wall of officialdom. Jessica handed over Lily's insurance card at reception, but could not pry information out of them. She was not a family member. She was told to wait.

She sat with nothing to do but jiggle a leg and fret. She looked around. The hospital in this little Puget Sound town was no big city trauma unit. The injuries weren't bullet holes or knife wounds. Those waiting their turns had an assortment of sunburns, bee stings and tennis elbows. Jessica tapped her foot and bit a thumbnail. *My loved one should go ahead of your loved one. Oh God how I hate to wait.*

Time crawled. Finally, a massive male nurse lumbered out from the inner sanctum. He bellowed, "Someone out here named Jessica?"

Her heart skipped a beat. Then she leapt out of her chair, crossing the lobby with the speed of a gazelle. "Me! I'm Jessica."

The nurse peered down at her. "You're Lily Gilbert's friend? God help you."

"Why?" *Had she...is she...?*

He explained that Lily was back there yelling at the whole staff. "She told me to haul my fat ass out here to get her friend Jessica right this instant, and then just maybe she'd settle down. Just maybe."

"Ah. Yes. That sounds like Lily."

"Reminds me of my granny, well, except she's the wrong color and all. Come on with me."

At last Jessica joined the old warrior in the ER examination room. Lily might talk tough, but she looked as delicate as her namesake, huddling on the gurney and shivering in the air conditioning.

"You're cold, aren't you?" Jessica said softly, unfolding a second blanket that was at the foot of the bed. She tucked it around Lily, then leaned down and hugged her. "Let's just pretend you're sitting in the sun, working me like a slave in your garden. You know, happy thoughts."

The two friends clung together, holding hands. Neither spoke for a long time, one sick with infection and the other sick with worry. Finally Jessica muttered, "Sometimes I wished to hell I smoked."

\* \* \*

The jacquard drapes for the law firm's lobby were beautiful, no doubt about it. Sylvia was pleased that this group of lawyers had enough pizzazz to want something other than Business Suit Gray or Beyond Boring Beige.

The vertical stripe tone-on-tone fabric was a deep brick red, and a drop dead color coordinate for the floral pattern in the chairs. But hanging the wide expanse of material was taking forever, and she really didn't want to pay her workers overtime. She was on a ladder herself, helping arrange the freeform valance, which is why she didn't hear the cell phone tucked in her briefcase an office away. When she finally checked her messages, she rushed to the hospital, head and heart both pounding. The parking lot was full, of course. *Why would a goddamn hospital need lots of visitor parking?* Fuming, she circled and circled like a carousel before finally waiting for someone to exit the front door of the hospital. She stalked an old couple in her car like a motorized shark, until they tottered to their own vehicle, then sat inside apparently memorizing the Bible before they finally backed out and drove away. Waiting, she thought she'd go crazy.

Jessica's last message said her mother had been admitted to intensive care. Sylvia had been that route before with Lily, so she knew exactly where to go once she finally entered the hospital. She found Jessica all alone in the ICU waiting room, an area not much larger than a wide spot in the hall.

*So who the hell owns all those cars out there?* A piece of Sylvia's mind refused to focus on the important stuff. She was surprised Jessica was still there since she wasn't in with Lily. She must have something she needed to discuss. *A complaint? A pat on the back? Couldn't it wait?*

Apparently, Jessica just wanted to report what had happened. "We were over an hour in the emergency room before a doctor could see her. Then another hour before they cleared a room in the ICU for her. By then, she was very jaundiced, certainly exhausted."

"Infection," Sylvia nodded, trying to appear in control. *Is my mother dying? Is my mother dying?*

"I'm not family, so I can't enter intensive care, and Lily's too sick now to demand it." Jessica was visibly distraught, but Sylvia could think of no comforting words to calm her. If she could, she'd use them on herself.

*But why is she so upset? She doesn't think I blame her, does she?* "You did nothing wrong, I'm sure, Jessica. You and Aurora take good care."

Jessica looked confused. "I know that. But she's my friend. I'm frightened for her."

*Her friend?* Sylvia finally got it. That's just what the caregiver was becoming to her mother. Jealousy zapped her like an electric shock. *They share stuff I'm not part of. This isn't the time for that. Think about Lily.*

It was hard to stay on point when her head felt stuffed inside a bubble, disconnecting her from her surroundings. She distractedly straightened a pile of pamphlets entitled *Senior Services in King County*. Then she spread them into a perfect fan on the end table. She stopped fussing when she saw that her hands were trembling and preferred not to have Jessica notice. She wished the hospital's framed artwork wasn't in such soothing tones, maybe something brighter and happier.

*Concentrate.* "I guess I better go see what I can find out."

"Please come let me know how she's doing. I'll wait."

"I'll be back soon to meet Kyle. He's on his way. Um, that's my husband."

"Yes, I know."

"You do?"

"Lily told me."

"Oh." *Because you're her friend. What dirty linen did Lily air about Kyle? Stop it.* She stood and walked away to find her mother.

The medical staff had been slow to diagnose a lymphedema-induced infection during Lily's last hospital stay. The amputation had followed. Maybe this time they'd be quicker to take action, knowing what they could expect. Sylvia mumbled a prayer or a mantra, she wasn't sure which.

Sylvia stopped outside her mother's door to gather her wits. She finger combed her hair and smoothed her blouse. Straightening her back and donning a smile, she entered the private ICU room. Lily was sleeping, surrounded with monitors and two IV drips, one with nutrients and the other with antibiotics. Sylvia sat on the sturdy side chair for a time, looking at the silent woman. She observed how slack the skin on her mother's hands had become, veins crisscrossing their backs like blue highways. She gently clasped one of those old hands, remembering when Lily would twirl her little girl around in the air. Strong hands that held her tight when there was nobody else.

"It's way too soon to let go, Mom," she whispered, knowing it always would be.

She sat beside her mother, and arranged the water bottle, kidney shaped plastic bowl, hand sanitizer, and tooth brush on the bed tray. Tomorrow she would have Jessica bring over some personal things.

"Let's see." She extracted her *Suggestions from Sylvia* notepad and began a list. Reading glasses, magazines, hair clips, a nightie, the crème she used to soften the wrinkles around her eyes. She thought for a moment. *That old afghan she loves, but it's certainly seen better days. No, I'll get a new one instead.*

Making a list made her feel better. When she slipped out to go back to the waiting room, Kyle was there speaking quietly with Jessica. He was tall and as slender as a marathon runner, and had folded himself down into one of the low chairs that hospitals think are comfortable. His skin looked slightly florid to her, but then, maybe it was just the contrast to Lily's pallor. Maybe he'd been working out when she called him.

When she approached, Jessica stood with a questioning look. Kyle unfurled himself, taking Sylvia in his long, welcoming arms. He held his wife until her resolute spine finally allowed her to relax against him. She rested there, drawing enough of his strength to recharge and pull away.

"She's sleeping now, but we should be there when she wakes up," she said to Kyle, then turned her attention to Jessica. "Thank you for staying. We are indebted to you for acting so decisively on my mother's behalf. You truly are her good friend. But I think you can leave now."

"Will you call me with an update?"

"Of course. And don't worry. We'll pay you for the whole day."

She hadn't meant it to sound crass, although she saw the hurt cross Jessica's face. But Sylvia had more immediate concerns as they left the caregiver behind, shutting her out of the ICU.

* * *

The doctor came to Lily's room on his evening rounds. He explained to Sylvia and Kyle that another amputation wasn't an issue, that there was no open wound. Lily was starting to respond to the antibiotics. Nonetheless, it took eight days before the infection was vanquished. Sylvia was at the hospital as much as possible, and she saw to it that Jessica was allowed in, too.

Friends from town and the Garden Club sent flowers and cards. But Lily was aware of little of this, with medications that held her floating on a cloud of her own. Sylvia watched as her mother became a far older, far weaker woman. Too weak to return home, too weak even to fight about it.

Sylvia made the decision that the hospital should release her to a nursing home. The doctors agreed, and in an unusually candid moment, one of them even suggested that, as prone to infection as Lily was, she should never again be out of the reach of registered nurses.

Sylvia had done her homework and believed she was prepared. But she learned that regardless of the homework anyone does, by the time you need a care center, you take the one that will take you. She had preferred another place, one both bigger and newer. But her preference had no beds available when Lily needed a room. Sylvia had no choice but to instruct the hospital to deliver Lily to Soundside.

*One way or another, Mom, we're always letting each other down.*

\* \* \*

Lily remembered little about the hospital experience, except the misery that aged her daughter's face. The ambulance ride to the nursing home had been almost pleasant, like bounding along on a swiftly moving ship. But waking up that first afternoon clear of drugs and in mental control? Well, surely that was the brink of hell.

An insistent keening had awakened her. She realized she'd been trying to soothe it by whispering, "Hush, baby girl, everything's all right." But Sylvia wasn't there.

Lily finally grasped that the crying came from whoever was on the other side of the curtain that separated this room in two. With massive effort, she rolled over on her side, away from the noise and faced the window. She noticed the empty feeder hanging lifeless just outside. It made her think about the rich mix of birds that populated her garden at home.

Soundside. She'd been told that was the official name for this Puget Sound nursing home, but Lily thought of it as the Fun House. Patrons entered with a shiver of dread, a prickling to the spine, the expectation of unknown paths and infinite madness. Specters leapt out, floors swayed, nothing could be trusted.

Grief enclosed her like shrink wrap, sealing her away from any external comfort. Her spirit faltered, as though from lack of oxygen. She might live through this experience, but just for now, she'd rather not.

## EIGHT

### FUN HOUSE CHRONICLE
# The Visitor

*W*hen her father was no longer sane enough to live alone, Caroline delivered him to a nursing home. Its social worker gave her this advice. "It may be just minutes before your dad forgets you were here, but it could be a lifetime of bad memories for you. Reserve your resources. Come less often or stay less time on particularly bad days." But Caroline could not conquer the guilt that said her father gave her eighty years – surely he deserved a few months back. The good advice simply came at her too soon.

She quickly learned it wasn't just watching the increasing frailty of her own loved one. It was the ruination of dozens more. The worst was just getting down the hall to her father's room. Caroline thought of it as running the gauntlet which, if she remembered her English history, involved being whipped and beaten by savage warriors. Here, the gauntlet was the old, the fragile, the confused who impaled her with their misery. She was angry to be exposed to so many losses just when trying to handle her own.

Caroline solved her quandary by adopting a dog and bringing him along. Like most dogs, he could soak up sorrow when it overflowed. He enjoyed sniffing a good *bit of snot, piss, shit, spit and puke so these oldsters were doggy heaven. He wiggled in skeletal laps and licked clutching hands and waggled his tail when they cackled. The closer he got, the farther away Caroline got to stay.*

*The angry residents grew gentler and the panicky residents grew calmer. The dog was far more help to them than Caroline could ever be. She'd found her own best way to travel down that terrible path.*

JESSICA'S HEART may have been broken by Ed, but now she realized the fractured pieces could be stomped on yet again. The idea of Lily in a nursing home was toe-curling awful. She'd finally stopped talking about suicide and now this.

Jessica could think of nothing to make herself feel better except shopping. She'd heard about a new store called Horse Tales. She always enjoyed looking at things for Latin Lover, new blankets or special treats or silver-buckled hackamores. She didn't leave herself out either and browsed through the show clothes, horsy jewelry, riding boots and western shirts.

*There's no money for this stuff. Especially now without income from caregiving.* She sighed, put back the wooden plaque that said 'My Barn, My Rules' and headed resolutely toward the door. Suddenly she was snapped back as if by an invisible bungee cord. Her eyes had been captured by brass medallions, replicas from the hardware on decorative coach harnesses. *Gorgeous! Expensive!* She absolutely needed a dozen of them to display in the barn.

Her treasure helped soothe the ache all the way home. When she got there, she parked near her house then walked immediately toward the barn to hang the little beauties on posts between stalls. Folly saw her coming and caroused around her in joy.

"I've only been gone an hour, you goofy mutt," she chuckled, pulling a Milk Bone from her pocket and throwing it for him to chase as she crunched down the wide gravel track toward the barn.

Two storage and feed sheds along with a small house trailer flanked one side of the track and on the other was a large covered corral. Jessica used it in good weather or bad to give riding lessons. She owned two mares for students without their own horses, and boarders often requested lessons as well.

She also had her yearling colt, Latin Dancer. The beautiful buckskin was the heir apparent to Latin Lover, a son with the sire's promise as a show stopper. Dancer would one day be a second source of income at stud, but now he was a curious, happy-go-lucky adolescent, too young to ride.

"And a drain on finances in the meantime, just like you," Jessica said to Folly who gave her a tongue-lolling smile in return.

The barn was long, low and looked rich to her eyes. It was painted creamy white, like the far fancier digs at Churchill Downs that she'd seen on TV. Both sides were lined with large box stalls, twelve of them in all. One end of the barn was devoted to a tack room for her barn manager, as well as for people who boarded animals with Jessica.

Grassy paddocks on each side of the barn made it easy to turn the horses out. Beyond them, her acreage included a large seldom-mowed field where boarders could ride. Her land nearly touched the county's extensive system of equestrian trails, so boarders could ride for the day without having to trailer and haul their horses. She knew this was one of her property's best assets, and she charged accordingly.

What with boarding, riding lessons, grooming and stud fees for Latin Lover, her twenty acre ranch provided enough income to hire a barn manager and to have a little profit left over for her. If she really worked at it. For the months when there was a shortfall, she still had a little of Ed's insurance money, but without Lily…

*Stop it. She'll be back home. She will. It will all be okay again.*

Her barn manager, Sam Hart, was using a manure fork to separate road apples from cedar shavings in one of the stalls while the horses were out in a paddock. Jessica helloed him, then went to the tack room to find a hammer in her old toolbox. When she looked up, Sam had silently sidled up next to her.

"What's up, Sam?"

"Ma'am," he said, touching the brim of the ancient straw cowboy hat that was welded to his head as far as she knew. She'd never seen him without it. He was nearly as thin as the handle of the manure fork he held, with a scarred face and a missing front tooth. Broken veins in his nose and a slightly loose screw suggested to her that he had lost a bar fight too many. Sam would win no beauty contests but he was dependable, happy to live in the trailer in order to be on hand day or night, and the horses liked him. So did she, for that matter, even though he could hardly carry on a conversation.

"I keep telling you, Sam. Call me Jessica."

"Yes ma'am. Couple stopped by."

"Oh? Who?" *Maybe new customers!*

"Don't know. Didn't ask."

*Shit.* "Well, what did they want, Sam?"

"Said they had a pony they wanted to board for their kid, and did we have room, and do you give riding lessons, and how much." He took a deep breath after such a lengthy soliloquy. He'd rather talk to horses than people any day. "Told them they'd have to talk with you," he finished, turning to go back to work.

"Did they leave a number?"

"Not with me."

*Jeez. Do you think they left it with Latin Lover?* "All right. If they're interested, I guess they'll be back."

Sam returned to the manure cart, and Jessica walked over to one row of stalls to hammer in a hook for the first medallion.

"It was Amanda Marin and her husband."

Jessica looked up, startled. Only Gina Lola, a Percheron workhorse, was looking back at her from across the barn. She walked to the horse's stall and saw Ben Stassen currying his old mare. The dapples on her enormous rump were sleek and the feathers around her feet were as white as her mane.

"I recognized Amanda Marin because she was one of the few teachers my daughter didn't tell to go screw herself." He gave Jessica a crooked grin. Ben had a wild teenager who had disappeared into the Seattle street culture.

"How you doing, Ben? I haven't seen you for a while," Jessica said, stroking Gina Lola's satiny nose. Ben had been Ed's friend, and he had needed a place to board his big pet. That's how she'd met him a couple years back.

Ben and Ed were as different as white collar is from blue. Ben was fairer skinned with darker hair, neater and actually styled. He had a stockier build than Ed's lanky cowboy frame, and the planes and angles of his face were not so gaunt. Jessica figured Ben's muscles came from the gym, not from ranch work. And even though his hairline was getting a touch higher than it used to be, and the waist button on his shirt pulled just a little, he was a fine looking specimen. Especially the way he always looked ready to laugh, one corner of his mouth curved up a fraction higher than the other.

Jessica liked to watch him with the old mare. In her experience, the people with little fear of horses were often the gentle ones. "Might have been easier to get a tractor years ago, Ben."

"Yes, but it's hard to love a tractor," he said, starting to work on Gina Lola's shoulders.

"How old is she, do you think?"

He stopped grooming for a moment, considering. "Almost exactly a quarter century. My granddad got her as a foal the year I started high school."

As he continued working with the curry comb, Jessica did the math and figured he must be just around forty.

Ben interrupted her thoughts, saying, "Sam tells me you got another job."

"I've been working for a woman who needs a care-giver afternoons and evenings," she said while she propped one foot up on the gate to the stall. Thinking about Lily reactivated the ache. *Oh, Lily.*

"Long hours, Jess." Ben shortened her name the way Ed had. It felt personal, intimate. She realized she'd missed hearing it.

"Helps pass the time. I don't think so much about Ed, you know? If I keep busy, I mean." *I'll come visit tonight, Lily. Promise.*

"I miss him, too, Jess." For a moment the crooked smile was gone altogether as he gave her a candid glance. "But you need to take care of yourself."

"Well, I've lost the job now anyway. Mrs. Gilbert is in a nursing home. Guess I wasn't much of a caregiver."

"I doubt that. Not the way you look after everything around here."

Even through her melancholy, Ben's comment pleased her. *Someone noticed!* The business was a lot of work for a woman with a staff of one. She smiled and bent down to scratch her dog's ear. "Anyway, I guess it's back to the late night *Creature Features* for Folly and me."

"Maybe I could come by one night so I can scare the crap out of myself, too. I might even have some DVDs that will fill the bill."

Jessica chuckled. "Sure, Ben. A fright night. It's a date."

"Okay. How about next week, say, Thursday?"

That's how Jessica found herself with plans to entertain for the first time since Ed the Evil hit the highway to heaven.

\* \* \*

Alvin Jacobs looked distinctly like an old silvertip grizzly, round faced, hunch shouldered, dark beard streaked with gray. From the day that Gladys had pointed at him and called him Bear, the nickname stuck. In fact, after his first couple weeks at Soundside, nobody remembered his real name without a hunt through the records. Which was fine with him. He didn't really want anyone from his past finding him here. He'd been a serious tough guy as a private investigator, capable of defending his turf.

He hadn't realized that his turf would go downhill right along with his health.

He didn't mind the move as it turned out. Madrona Park had been more refined. Fewer residents peed in the halls. Maybe that was the biggest difference between assisted care and a nursing home. But prettier art and fancier drapes didn't mean better care. Refined or not, Madrona Park had dumped him. Soundside caught him before he landed in the gutter. For that reason alone, he gave them the benefit of the doubt.

Madrona Park had kicked him out when he hit Medicaid. Oh, they said there was another reason, that he was too big for them to handle easily. And he had to admit it was getting harder for him to transfer from the bed to the wheelchair to the toilet without help. A big man's muscles running to fat. Plus he'd packed on weight by ordering out for pizza or fried chicken or burgers instead of joining the dining room crowd. He'd paid the aides to bring other stuff including any candy Rite-Aid had on sale that week. There wasn't money for that crap any more.

Once they'd busted him, his options had been to wheel himself off a pier into Puget Sound or see if one of the guys from his past could bring him a gun. *Kind of a lot to ask of an old buddy.*

He was damned relieved when Soundside had said they could handle a bariatric patient. Bariatric. That meant fat. Too big for standard wheelchairs and commodes. Big as a bear. The more he considered it, the more he liked the nickname.

And he really liked the Hoyer lift they had here. It was fucking weird at first, this web of straps attached to a machine that could scoop him out of the bed, dangle him in the air, then deposit him into his wheelchair. Two of the aides, Rick and Chrissie, could use it with the finesse of crane operators. Once they got him up in the morning, he was set for the day. No stress, no hassle. Too bad the lift scared the shit out of so many of the wrinklies up and down the hall. The aides couldn't use it with everybody.

His biggest gripe so far was a roommate. This one buzzed logs like a saw mill. But an interesting thing about this Charlie guy? He got a nurse to touch his balls nearly every day. *Maybe I can get me some of those wheelchair sores, too.*

All in all, he was giving Soundside a good try before giving them too much hell. But it was in his nature to be a trouble maker. Slowly he wheeled himself from his room to go steal the sports section out of the parlor. And maybe nobody had dribbled all over the crossword yet.

He'd heard a new patient had arrived. Maybe he'd check that out, too.

\* \* \*

Clarice was running late. But Kit Kat and Hershey had cat tracked a roll of red ribbon all over her living room. The two Burmese looked like highborn sophisticates, but they were veteran troublemakers. They actually belonged to her son Cole who was away now at Western Washington University, so she had inherited them.

If she had any hope of saving the ribbon, she needed to rescue it before leaving for work. It circled her floor lamp, looped over the sofa and took a hairpin turn back to the glass top coffee table. Kit Kat was under the table happily killing the spool. Clarice hunkered down to extract the ribbon from his flailing paws, ignoring his dramatic hissing.

A sudden burst of joy brightened the rainy morning. She went to her computer, called up her weight loss list and added:

– *I can hunker again.*

Clarice got to work with enough time to go to the break room for her cup of swill to begin the day. The morning staff was there bitching about all the crap the night staff hadn't finished.

"...and he didn't get the bedpan to Robert in time once again..."

"...left the goddamn dinner tray in there all night..."

"...didn't change the sheets so I had to do all the rooms on East..."

They talked about residents, too, but rarely the short timers who were mostly there for rehab or recovering from surgery. They'd be gone soon enough. The staffers were more concerned with the degree of difficulty of the lifers.

"What's this Bear guy like?"

"And the new lady? The one in with Gladys?"

"Son of a bitch is huge."

"She's pretty weak, I think."

"She looks like a sweet old thing."

"He's one of Madrona Park's rejects."

Clarice ignored their chatter, got her coffee and went to her office. As long as the bills were paid so she didn't have to go collect from the poor old geezers, they mostly went their way, and she went hers.

\* \* \*

Lily's first days in the nursing home were the darkest

of her life, even worse than when Harmon died all those years ago. Back then, she'd worked double shifts and raised a child on her own. Simple exhaustion kept grief from leveling her.

Now, she faced a future of uselessness. As she recovered physically, she plummeted spiritually. She acknowledged little and communicated less. Just one thing was unequivocally clear. She'd lost access to her store of insulin at home or she would have used it without question.

What brought Lily back to the reality of the day to day was the presence of a roommate. She'd lived alone for twenty years, other than brief stints with interesting men. Now she shared space with Gladys. It was an assault on her senses.

"Who the hell are you?" Gladys had said, peering around the curtain the first morning. She slumped so low in her wheelchair that Lily could see nothing but her face.

*Looks like one of those shrunken heads made from a carved apple.*

Suddenly, a good looking guy pulled back the curtain, drenching Lily's portion of the room with florescent light from the other side. If she'd had a gun, she'd have shot him.

"Gladys, Lily is your new roommate," the big kid said. "She's tired now and needs to rest. Maybe you can talk later."

As he started to wheel Gladys away, he flashed Lily a radiant smile, revealing his dimples. "I'm one of the aides, Lily. My name is Rick. We'll leave you alone for now, but if you need anything at all, just push that button."

*Go to hell. I'm no sucker, not even for a dimple.*

"Let's eat!" Gladys commanded, and Rick hustled her out of the room.

The second assault was living on public display. Lily had lost all privacy. She could not get up in the morning until a nurse unwrapped her leg and searched for infection, so morning toileting was done by bedpan. The color and consistency of her feces became a matter of public record on a chart. She no longer took a shower; she was given a shower. She'd administered her own meds for years, but no longer. There was no way to build up a stash now.

Following advice from the intake specialist, Sylvia had removed anything of value from Lily's room lest other residents or staff steal it. Lily had no money, no ID, not even her watch.

The loss of control in all things felt like another amputation.

Lily knew she was trapped. She needed a plan. Maybe she should handle this experience as if she were a prisoner of war. By keeping low and following orders, she might live long enough to plot an escape.

But her plan was foiled the first night she was well enough to be wheeled down to the dining room. All the sorrows of broken bodies attacked her there. True, the tables had silk flowers, and the chairs all matched, and the dishes were so pretty some residents might forget they were unbreakable plastic. But Lily wasn't fooled.

Residents wore striped terry cloth bibs like ancient babies who were expected to mess. "Get away from me with that," Lily hissed at an aide who tried to Velcro one around her neck.

Her dinner companions had holes in their throats, or bodies vibrating with palsy, or mouths so paralyzed from strokes that the food fell out. Aides fed those who couldn't remember how to use flatware, and the cooks pureed all meats and vegetables for those with no teeth or swallowing disorders.

*Who could eat here? Whose appetite wouldn't fail?* "I can't do this," she announced to herself and the room at large.

"You'll get used to it, love," Nurse Happy Face chirped. "You'll find that lots of these folks are dear old souls."

"No doubt they are. But I'll never get used to it. I don't want to eat here. Not now. Not ever." Tears streamed down Lily's face.

"Well, we could provide a tray in your room if you prefer." A slight wrinkle appeared on Nurse Happy Face's brow.

"Is that an option?"

"Some of our residents choose it," the Nurse confessed. *The ones in their right fucking minds.* "That's what I would like."

"But we feel that social interaction is good for you." The happy face looked dangerously close to pouty.

"Okay. I promise to talk with someone every day."

Nurse Happy Face missed the sarcasm altogether. "Well then, all right. It'll be our little pact," she said with a wink.

So Lily learned her first lesson about living in a nursing home. By speaking up, she created an oasis for herself when the others were feeding at the trough. Three times a day, Gladys buggered off, as she liked to say, with the rest of the crowd in wheelchairs, pushing walkers or hobbling along on their own fragile feet. Lily's room and the halls became quiet. No screams or blaring televisions or warning buzzers or chattering aides. *The sound of silence.*

Maybe there would be other ways she could improve her situation, other lessons to learn. She'd always been good at games, regardless of the board, field or rules. Was this just another one she had to learn how to play?

**NINE**

**FUN HOUSE CHRONICLE**
## Time of Death

*The old bastard is close to death. He no longer snarls at his wife, and aides don't fear he will hit them anymore. Real people have slipped from his perception. What remain are shadow visitations from his past. He calls to them. Maybe they answer, maybe not.*

*Death used to mean the cessation of heartbeat or breathing. Now either can be prolonged. So science has turned to 'brain death' as the time of death. Now even that has become more specific. The cerebral cortex must die in order to be considered dead as a door nail.*

*You may believe in death as an instant in time. But spend a while in a nursing home, and you learn the line between life and death gets hazy toward the end. It is a process more than an event. The brain shuts down until it no longer knows who is in the room or in the shadows. It stops telling the body it needs to hydrate or nourish itself or take its medicine. The body suffers malnutrition which slows the brain all the more.*

*And so the old bastard approaches the end. The nurse applies a calming touch and cool cloth just as if he were one of her kinder charges. She has participated in this drama again and again, and sometimes the actors are better than others.*

*Each death touches those at a nursing home.
Residents are mostly relieved it isn't their turn. Nobody
will shed many tears for this old bastard. But everyone
will shudder when death passes through.*

VISITING SOUNDSIDE depressed Sylvia even before her mother was installed there, but now it gave her the heebie-jeebies every day. She parked out front and sat in the car, listening to a motivational CD or some airy classical tune, maybe Chopin. Sometimes she allowed herself a square of dark chocolate or a short vanilla latte. Finally, she'd exit the Volvo, smooth her skirt, lock the car and approach the nursing home as stiff legged as a Halloween cat. As she walked, she compelled herself to uncurl her toes and release the tension that had her every orifice clamped shut. By the time the sliding glass doors whooshed open, she'd arranged a grin on her face. She marched through the artificial cheer of the lobby, striding purposefully on down the hall.

Sylvia could force herself to do it if she pretended to be in some dreadful play, hitting her marks and reciting her hackneyed lines which invariably involved the weather.

"Wow. It really is coming down," she might say to Lia at reception.

"Be sure to grab your umbrellas," she'd chirp to nurses on their way to lunch.

Once she got to know some of the fossils by name, she branched out to "Hello, Charlie," or "How's it going, Judge?" But she studiously avoided the worst of the crippled old bodies parked along the hall in conveyances so outlandish they looked more like medieval torture devices than medical equipment.

*Don't look too close, don't stop too long. Make the turn to the left and left again and you've done it; scoot into her room. Now to get past Gladys. "Damn you, too," with a smile and finally home base.* Sometimes when she drew back the curtain that separated the room in two, Lily's space was empty. On those days, Sylvia found her in the sunny courtyard if an aide had taken the time to push her there since Lily was still too weak to do it for herself. But in weather like this, Lily was in her room.

The walls were a biscuit brown meant to soothe, but mostly it looked bleak to Sylvia. *I have to get some artwork in here, maybe something bright from the house.* The curtain was a tone-on-tone beige, and the battered nightstand, dresser and wardrobe were an indeterminate blonde wood from a decade long past. Lily's bed was hospital issue, with all white bedding. A white sink and counter were mounted on the wall low enough to be reached from a wheelchair. The actual bathroom was on Gladys's side of the room.

A guest chair was upholstered with tough green vinyl, but it was usually covered by a stack of linens left behind by forgetful aides as they scrambled room to room. *At least it's the clean stuff.*

Sylvia often sat in the window seat. It was the one nice feature of the room. A bay window faced the courtyard and the employee parking lot beyond. From her bed, Lily could observe the landscapers at work, as well as the comings and goings of the staff. She could see who was a smoker and which aides carpooled and who seemed to be friends. While Sylvia would have chosen a different roommate for her mother, she knew that the view from this room gave

Lily a certain amount of comfort. It was the best Soundside could offer.

Her conversations were now too brittle, too bright with her determination to spare Lily from seeing her tears. "Hi, Mom, ugly day, huh?" Sylvia exclaimed, shaking rain from her coat and draping it over the battered dresser to dry. "I knew you wouldn't be outside in this weather." *Well, duh.*

Sylvia flashed back to a night long before they moved to Washington. A Midwest storm had broken an insufferable heat wave. Her mother had scooped her up and run out to the backyard, waltzing with her until they were both drenched. "They call this kind of rain a real toad strangler," Lily had laughed in her ear. The next day, little Harmony Sylvia had looked high and low for dead toads.

"I believe there'll be dead toads out there soon," she said, smiling as she placed her Coach tote on the pile of clean laundry then pumped a blob of Purell into her hands.

"Dead toads? If there's anything dead around this joint it isn't a toad."

They'd shared the story for years, a family tradition for a twosome that had few of them. Now it had irritated Lily. Was there no room for happy memories when her mother was battling just to get by? That sadness slapped Sylvia in the face. She barely kept the gloom from her voice. "I've brought you a few more things from home."

Sylvia reached into her tote and pulled out two of Lily's favorite old shirts plus a cherished sweater. Lily slipped into the chenille cardigan immediately, cuddling into its familiar warmth with a noise not unlike a purr.

"I hadn't realized how big that was on you," Sylvia frowned, looking critically at her mother. "Are you losing weight?"

"A leg at a time."

Sylvia turned her face away and reached back into the tote. "I bought some new things, too. Pull-on slacks will be easier than your jeans, so I thought you might like to try fleece." She shook out a light blue pair of pants with a yellow stripe down the side, and held them up for Lily's review. "They'll look okay without getting wrinkled."

"Sweat pants! I'll look like a one-legged track star."

"I guess they aren't much of a fashion statement."

"Perfect for the Hop n' Hurdle event. Or the one-legged race."

"Give it a rest, Mom." Sylvia finally snapped. Then sighed. And reminded herself her mother would need time to adjust to her new circumstances. *Like maybe a century or two.*

Sylvia handed Lily a laundry marker. "Here, put your name on the labels."

Lily chuckled. "I haven't marked clothes since you went to camp."

"I never went to camp."

"Whatever."

While Lily wrote, Sylvia unpacked two more blouses and a sweatshirt. "I got you a cotton nightie, too. I know you prefer nylon, but this one isn't so see-thru. It's in the bottom of the bag." Sylvia began to hang the blouses in the narrow wardrobe unit assigned to this half of the room.

Lily had enough strength to roll her wheelchair next to the tote. She reached down to pull out a brushed cotton nightgown printed with tiny butterflies. "An old lady nightie! Wouldn't want anyone to see through to these deflated old boobs."

Sylvia began her new mantra. *Patience, patience, patience.*

As the days passed, Sylvia established a pattern of visits timed to suit her mother best. The morning meal, meds, washing, and cleaning all took time and created commotion in the room. Lily told her that mornings were the easiest part of the day, because time didn't linger. But afternoons spread out endlessly.

"Babs tries to fill the time with entertainment, but it's geared to the worst of us," Lily explained to Sylvia. The clear thinking residents felt patronized. "We've been elected officials and teachers and business people, for Christ's sake. We don't choose to join every sing along of *My Bonnie Lies Over the Ocean.*"

Sylvia was glad that afternoons worked for Lily, because they were best for her, too. She could handle her clients early in the day, then take a couple hours for her mother before returning to work. Besides, she was simply stronger herself as the day progressed.

\* \* \*

The noise got Lily down. On top of the symphony of clattering med carts, bickering staff, endless alarms, and televangelists – not to mention Gladys – there was always a layer of mournful cries or furious roars. *Old people do not go quietly anywhere.*

A couple of days earlier Sylvia had brought her a CD player with several disks, including one of meadow sounds. She didn't like ear phones, but she'd never lived where the decibel level approximated jet engines. *A stench in the ear. That's what Ambrose Bierce called such a racket.*

Lily wedged the tiny buds into her ears, and was immediately serenaded by a variety of chirps and whistles, even beezers which she remembered from the Midwest. *Sylvia really does try. I'll have to remember to tell her that sometime.*

She liked to play the nature disk on mornings when this particular nurse washed and rewrapped her leg. Nurse Baby Talk had a patronizing way of speaking at the residents as if they were children. "Now we haven't got that too tight for your tootsies, have we, Sweetie?" she boomed loud enough to be heard over the recording.

*Jesus.* "Our tootsies are topsy," Lily boomed back, entirely louder than necessary.

When she was still in her own house, nurses only came three times a week which, as it turned out, might not have been enough. Here, the wrapping ceremony was a daily occurrence. Infection hovered in the wings like a vampire bat. She wondered if it ever really left her body completely.

As Nurse Baby Talk left, pushing the curtain wide open, another woman strutted into the room, her sensible shoes clopping across the tile floor. Lily removed the ear buds at her approach.

"Up your blow hole," Gladys screeched, lost in some seadog reverie. The woman ignored her and passed to Lily's part of the room where she helped herself to the Purell.

"How do you do, Mrs. Gilbert, I'm Patricia Bergeron, the Soundside Social Services Director. May I have a moment of your time?"

"It would appear I'm going nowhere at the moment," Lily said with a chill, never fond of authority figures. The Bergeron woman was tall and thin as a stiletto, with about the same amount of curves. Her face was so narrow it didn't appear to have enough room for two eyeballs. Maybe that's why she looked bug-eyed behind the wire framed glasses. Her suit was that nameless shade between brown and gray and so was her hair. Even her compressed lips bespoke a tightly controlled officialdom. Lily had met these people before, the ones with a molehill of authority making it into a mountain.

*This may be amusing.* Lily said, "Have a chair. Director of the SS, huh?"

"Well, yes, although I don't like to call it that for obvious reasons." She opened a weighty notebook and stared at a page for a moment. "I thought it might be time to meet with you and your daughter – Sylvia Henderson, isn't it? – about your case."

"My case?"

"Yes, it is normal for the family and the resident to meet with Social Services on an ongoing basis to cover your options, financial, mental and physical, now and in the future." She peered at Lily over the rim of her glasses.

"In this case, my case is just me."

"It is wise to have a family decision-maker involved in all planning."

"Director SS. I'm seventy-six years old and have made all my own decisions for well over half a century. I really don't need a family member doing any planning for me. Please do remember that, unlike many of your residents here in the Fun House, I am within my right mind even though my body has taken the wrong exit."

"Very well then, Mrs. Gilbert. I will direct all my attention to you." Patricia Bergeron issued this pronouncement with a stage-worthy sigh.

"Thank you for that."

"The first thing we need to cover is your immediate financial situation. You understand that Medicare will cover ninety days of nursing home care, is that correct?"

"Yes, they will."

"No, I know they will. I mean, is it correct that you understand that they will?"

"Director SS, are you having some sort of communication difficulty? Should I call someone? A family member, perhaps?"

"Really, Mrs. Gilbert, sarcasm never helped anything." She compressed those lips all the more.

"It seems to be doing me a world of good." Lily was feeling quite a bit perkier.

"Please let me go on. After the ninety day period, you will become a private pay resident, should you choose to stay here at Soundside. During that period you could request a private room if you like." She glanced in the direction of Gladys. "You might find it less stressful."

"And more costly?"

"Well, of course. Should your stay here outlast your financial abilities as a private pay, Soundside also accepts Medicaid residents."

"Bet I'd lose that private room pretty damn quick, huh?"

"Yes, there are limitations to what Medicaid will cover. You will be assigned a State case worker at the proper time. I can help you through those transitions. I'll need to oversee a great deal of paperwork at that time."

"Okay, you just keep me posted."

"That's all we need cover for now. We can discuss future housing options at a later date." Mrs. Bergeron snapped the notebook shut, clearly eager to be on her way.

"I look forward to it. And, by the way, the next time Gladys gives you or your blow hole a greeting, you might speak back to her. Seems to me it's the social service thing to do."

As Mrs. Bergeron stood, spun on her heel and strutted out past the curtain, an orange tiger paw shot out with lightning speed, slashing at her sensible shoe.

"It's that cat again," Mrs. Bergeron howled to nobody in particular. But Furball was long gone.

Lily snickered. She'd have to ask someone how the nursing home happened to have a cat. "You da man, Furball."

Once she was alone again, her bleak mood returned. She would live out her days ensnared by officialdom like Bergeron. She replaced her ear buds to listen to the lovely meadow sounds once more. But the CD could only do so much. It couldn't soothe the defeat she felt over everything she'd saved throughout her life, every nickel she'd hoped to pass on to Sylvia, disappearing down the Fun House drain.

\* \* \*

"This is what happens when you get all mushy about an old woman," Jessica said to the great outdoors, stopping to push a headstrong curl behind her ear and wipe forehead sweat onto her sleeve. "You inherit a garden." She'd promised she'd keep the garden in shape, at least while the summer flowers bloomed. It was the thing she could do that would please Lily the most.

"Of course you will," Lily had said the last time Jessica had visited. "I never imagined anything else."

As Jessica finished transplanting sprigs of mint, thyme and rosemary into a small pot, she smiled at the old woman's knack for making her do her bidding. "They don't season the food around here," Lily had said. "Everything's bland as Styrofoam. Bring me herbs to set in my windowsill."

Jessica would have tended the garden free of charge, but Lily wouldn't hear of it. They agreed on an hourly rate for errands and chores. It was Lily's way of lending her a hand, now that she'd lost the full time job of caregiver. Jessica didn't want charity, and Lily wouldn't offer it; they both would expect her to work hard for the money.

Along with the garden, Jessica had taken over washing Lily's clothes after the second blouse was stolen from the laundry room. The head laundress basically said that if a resident really cared about her personal items, it would be better for the family to do them. Lily and Jessica shared a bitter laugh and called it the DIYOWSI policy. Do-It-Yourself-Or-We-Steal-It.

Errands and chores didn't make up for a full time paycheck. And yesterday Jessica had received notice of the increase in her property taxes. *How the hell will I make up for that? Find an entire elementary school that wants riding lessons? Turn Latin Lover loose on more ladies?* There just weren't enough quality Paso Fino mares around to increase income from stud fees all that much. She could fire Sam, but she couldn't handle all the work without him. *Besides, I could never fire Sam.*

In addition to the vacancy in her checkbook, she still needed to fill the one in her evenings. So she began visiting Soundside after dinner. It didn't conflict with Sylvia's afternoon visits, and Lily always seemed pleased to see her. Their friendship kept expanding.

Jessica liked to have things to tell Lily about, so she decided to mention that she'd spent an evening with Ben

Stassen. Ben had brought along two nail biting classics, *Psycho* and *The Exorcist*. Jessica enjoyed a good 'Boo!' but she vetoed both of these as too scary back when they were made and too scary now. They settled on the actual Creature Feature for the evening, another rerun of *Tremors*. "Gigantic people-eating earthworms are scary enough for me," Jessica said while corn popped in the microwave.

"Besides, there are at least two sequels, so we're set for hours of superior entertainment in the future."

"Nothing I like more than night after night of enraged slime."

Jessica was surprised to be a little nervous. She'd used a perfumed soap and even done a little extra crowd control on her curls. She looked at Ben while she opened beers for them both. She noticed a faint scar above his left eyebrow that kept his looks from being too boardroom perfect. *He's not on a date, right? Just a movie with a friend.*

Ben asked if she'd heard from Amanda Marin, the woman who had tried to leave a message with Sam.

"Yes I did. They've purchased a big Hackney pony for their daughter. Between the boarding and riding lessons, it's a nice little piece of business." It was the one bright spot in her finances this month.

Ben plunked down in Ed the Evil's old recliner, while Jessica and Folly shared the sofa. The movie began, and it wasn't long before the dog was snoring softly.

"He loves a good flick, I see," said Ben.

"He prefers *Lady and the Tramp*. Worms on the attack are a real horror story for a dog."

They watched in companionable silence until all cast members were up on the roofs shaking in their boots.

"Another beer?" Jessica asked.

"I'll get it," Ben said, starting to rise.

"Naw, stay put. It's nice to see someone using that chair." As she said it, she realized how much she meant it. She was enjoying the company.

"You mean this was Ed's chair?" Ben asked, slapping the scuffed leather arms of the old recliner.

"A decade of Monday Night Football was quarter-backed from that very location."

"He was a good friend, Jess. But you know what I don't get? Why he put that Ed the Evil decal on the truck."

Jessica explained it the way she had told the same story to Lily. She added, "He never had time to get the tattoo on his arm or ass or whatever piece of real estate he had in mind."

Ben glanced at her as Kevin Bacon and Fred Ward ran from the slippery monster.

"But did he have a tattoo on you?"

"On me?"

"You know, like *Property Of*. Or might you consider a guy such as me?"

"Consider him for what?" Jessica knew what he meant. *I guess he's on a date, after all.*

"Continued friendship. Movies, dinners sometimes, nature walks, maybe some bowling. Help me out here, Jess, before I sound like a personals ad."

"Piña coladas? Caught in the rain?"

"Hell, I've always been attracted to you. Ed stood between us when he was alive, of course. But is he still standing there?"

She sat quietly considering his question while the worm crashed to its demise. "I don't know, Ben. Maybe. I just don't know. Is that an okay answer for now?"

"Anything but no is a fine answer for now." He tilted the recliner upright and stood as the movie ended. "I guess that's a good exit line."

"It's been fun."

"Next time I'll provide Raisenettes."

"Now you're talking my language." But as she shut the door, Jessica had no idea whether she'd always be haunted by a man dead too soon on a lonely highway, the scary movie that played daily inside her head.

TEN

FUN HOUSE CHRONICLE
# HEAR

*W*hen *Human Resources doesn't have enough to do, it tinkers. This month the aides are sporting HEAR ribbons beneath their name tags. H = Heed; E = Empathize; A = Apologize; R = Resolve*

*This is how a conversation is supposed to go, now that the aides have learned to HEAR:*

*Resident: Miss, my feet are cold.*

*Aide: Oh my goodness, I hear you (HEED)! Don't you hate when that happens? I surely do (EMPATHIZE). I am so sorry you suffered this calamity (APOLOGIZE), but I know just what I'll do. I will place a fuzzy blanket directly over your feet to make them toasty warm (RESOLVE)!*

*Resident: You are a godsend, an angel to take note of my plight and identify with it; you recognized your negligence, then handled the problem with creativity and alacrity. Truly I am blessed to be here, basking in your compassionate glow.*

*Now. This is an actual conversation from Day One of HEAR:*

*Resident: Get that fucking spoon away from me.*

*Aide: But you have to eat (HEED).*

*Resident: Shovel it in your own pie hole.*

> Aide: *Maybe a sip of juice would help it go down* (EMPATHIZE).
> Resident: *And maybe you should just sit here and crap in your pants.*
> Aide: *I'm sorry that you don't like the pureed peas* (APOLOGIZE).
> Resident: *Here. You try them.*
> Aide: *Okay, then. I'll be back as soon as I change* (RESOLVE).

"I'M HOPING to profit at least $40 on each gift basket if we can display them in the lobby," Babs reported at Jeff Parkinson's meeting with his department heads.

"Of course you can. And if you do that well, Southside will throw in another $20 for each basket sold," Jeff said.

"Why...why that's enough money for a proper party! Not just pizza in the break room!" Her huge grin made Babs look like a Walmart smiley face to Jeff. None of the former administrators had ever made such an offer, and the corporate drones might frown on it. But Jeff was trying to soothe hurt feelings over the lack of bonuses for the hourly workers again this year. He wanted them to know Soundside valued them so they would want to stay.

He'd explain it that way at the next meeting with the big cheeses. They were sure to see the wisdom of his ways.

\* \* \*

The days passed. Lily developed the habit of pushing herself down the hall toward the vending machines in a small alcove just short of the Soundside lobby. It was a long journey, but it was daily exercise she needed to recoup what strength she could. Sylvia had brought her a stash of quarters that she kept hidden in her Kleenex box. Lily rewarded herself for the journey with a Diet Coke each afternoon.

Today, a mountain of a man was trying to maneuver his wheelchair through the small archway. She'd noticed him before on the opposite side of the activities room and wondered if he was one of the sane ones.

She waited. He angled one front wheel into the narrow entrance. Then he backed out and tried the other. He tried it head on. No luck. The chair was simply too wide to fit.

"Like the camel through a needle's eye," Lily observed.

Bear swung his massive head to look at her. "I guess this joint doesn't think bariatric residents need bags of Cheetos."

Lily liked the gravelly baritone. "They get wound pretty tight if their diabetics gobble up the Milky Ways, too."

Bear rumbled what might have been a chuckle. "Maybe you could get me a diet pop?" He handed her his quarters and backed out of the way.

Lily slickly whisked into the vending room. Her chair, several inches narrower, easily fit through the entrance. And she wasn't above showing off. She bought two cans of soda, placed them in her lap, executed a spin worthy of a figure skater, and left the alcove.

She and Bear positioned themselves side by side, just where the hallway opened onto the front lobby. She handed him one of the cans. He took it in a huge paw and extended the other for her to shake. "Name's Bear."

"That fits. I'm Lily Gilbert."

"I know who you are, Mrs. Gilbert."

"Lily, please. How do you know me?" She stared at his

round face, trying to determine the features behind all the facial hair. Like many men, the wrinkles, ridges and scars that would have been ruination to a woman made him look weathered and wise.

"I make it my business to investigate all the newcomers. In case some of them still have their wits about them. Seems like you qualify."

"Not the best compliment I've ever received, but I take what I can get these days. Speaking of wits, what's going on here?"

They turned their attention to the lobby. It was usually serene to appeal to visitors, but today it was a jumble.

"Ah, entertainment," Bear said with satisfaction as he popped the top and slurped his drink. "They're getting ready for the great charity auction."

"You mean we're a charity now?"

"Nope. They are. For the staff holiday party. They have to get donations to have one at all."

Together, they settled in to watch and comment. Lily was reminded of those Muppets in the balcony, Statler and Waldorf.

None of the staff appeared to notice that they had an audience. Babs was giving orders like a pint-sized Patton. Dominic and Rick muscled furniture back toward the walls and set up folding tables. Alita covered each with a white cloth, followed by a red one.

"Not like that," Babs directed. "This way." She demonstrated to the housekeeper how the red, at an angle, allowed both colors to show.

Alita placed the last red tablecloth as Rick began carrying baskets out of Babs's office. When she stretched to smooth out the cloth, her scrub top and bottom parted enough to reveal a ring of smooth naked skin. Lily noticed. She also noticed Rick and Dominic notice.

"Say, Alita, could you place this next basket on that other far corner?" Rick asked.

But Alita simply took the basket, walked around the table and put it down. "Okay here?"

"Yea, sure," Rick said, his disappointment audible.

Dominic approached carrying three more baskets. "If you really want buns, Rick, I'll put some in the break room."

"Score for the kitchen staff," Bear whispered to Lily.

"That's okay, dude. Maybe I'll get me some later tonight," Rick said to Dominic.

"Seems to me it's Rick who's going to score," Lily answered Bear.

"And all we get is another performance by the Fiddle Dee Dees," Bear said.

"Would you rather meet in the parlor for a game of Scrabble?" Lily asked.

"You any good?"

"Oh no, just a rookie. I'm sure you'll win." If her eyelashes hadn't thinned out years ago, she would have batted them at him. *Sucker.*

Lily was feeling pretty good by the time she wheeled herself back to her room. She'd noticed that Clarice was delivering the dinner trays, so she hurried. Lily planned to plant a seed in the bookkeeper's brain.

When Clarice entered her room, Lily was looking at several small brown birds on the feeder outside her window. She sighed deeply, possibly even theatrically.

"It's dinner, Lily," said Clarice, setting the tray on Lily's bed table.

"Shit bird."

"No, actually, I think it's beef stew."

Lily turned in her wheelchair, stifling a giggle. This Clarice had a bit of cheek once you got to know her.

"Shit birds are what I always call the sparrows. They eat the cheap stuff. If you want better birds, you need better seed."

"They're that choosy?"

"Oh, my, yes. Some birds like millet. But to get nuthatches and chickadees and goldfinches, you need sunflower seeds. If they don't like it they won't eat it."

"Yeah, I know how they feel," Clarice said, leaving Lily's room.

* * *

"Yeah, I know how they feel," Clarice said, thinking about her dinner of celery sticks and fat free yogurt as she pushed the food cart on down the hall. *That was kind of interesting though, that bit about the birds.* She considered the residents a bunch of old heartbreaks, so sad they were hard to get to know. But this Lily was okay. She could hold up her end of a conversation. Even start one, for that matter.

Stopping short, Clarice was struck with an astounding thought. *Maybe I'm the one that's hard to get to know.* Feeling something snake around her ankles, she looked down at Furball, the fat orange tabby. "Is that true, Furball? Am I hard to get to know?"

Furball answered with a delicate meow completely inappropriate for a cat of his magnificent proportions.

"I didn't think so either," Clarice answered. Lily had asked her about Furball the last time she had delivered trays to the rooms. Come to think of it, Clarice sort of looked forward to their little chats.

"Nobody knows how Furball got in here or when he first showed up," she'd told Lily. "I think he must be the oldest resident."

"I'm surprised he's allowed in."

"He's not. But nobody pursues it too hard except Patricia Bergeron from Social Services. They despise each other. Furball doesn't much like anyone except for the sickest residents."

"What do you mean?"

"He seems to have a soft spot for people who need his warmth most. The nurses often find him dozing with a terminal patient."

"But who takes care of him?"

"He gets by on staff hand-outs."

"Where's his litter?"

"He must have a place he can get outside. At least I've never heard complaints from Jimbo."

"Jimbo?"

"Mr. Personality. The maintenance guy. No complaints from housekeeping, either."

"To people who clean up after people, a cat turd would hardly matter."

Clarice laughed, imagining Alita scooping up a turd the size of a mini-Tootsie Roll and wondering which resident had done it. She watched Furball stroll on down the hall, belly swinging side to side, tail straight in the air. She made a mental note to add to her list:

– *Now the only thing that wiggles is my ass.*

The next day Clarice was in the break room when Jimbo came in, and she asked him about seed. He'd put up the feeders at Jeff's request, but made it abundantly clear that filling them shouldn't be any effing responsibility of his.

"Most of the old farts could care less," he mumbled waiting for his burrito to heat in the microwave. He looked around furtively. Jeff didn't approve of that kind of talk. But Clarice was the only other staffer there, spoon poised above her container of sugar-free apple sauce.

"They may not be capable of telling you they're interested," Clarice said, not liking his attitude. "But that doesn't mean they're not."

"Well if they don't ask, their feeders stay empty, is all I'm saying." He swallowed about half the burrito in one bite.

"Lily Gilbert says it's the wrong kind of feed." *Who died and made me the Good Samaritan?*

"Then Lily Gilbert can get it herself," he said, shoving the last of the burrito into his mouth and stalking out of the room.

Clarice chose not to tell him he had a bean stuck to his chin.

* * *

A few days later, Lily showed up at Clarice's office door with a well-thumbed field guide to Puget Sound birds. "I thought you might like to borrow this. I've bookmarked pages with some of the common birds that come to feeders."

*Well, sure.* Clarice had nothing better to do than to bone up on birds. But she did have to admit that the little guy on the cover was kind of cute. She looked up the black-capped chickadee and read: highly sociable, joins small flocks. The song is a hoarse, insistent call. *Not unlike Lily Gilbert.*

Following the afternoon sittercise class, Lily told Clarice to look up the Washington state bird to see something really pretty.

"What is it?"

"Nope. You have to find it yourself."

Clarice realized that Lily was not going to give up on her campaign to get better seed for better birds. She suspected that Lily had chosen her to wage the war because the bookkeeper might know how to fund it.

*Is the old lady that cunning? Is chocolate better than sex?*

So here she was, tapping on Jeff's door. She saw the flash of panic cross his eyes when he looked up. A visit from the bookkeeper could be a very bad thing for the head administrator of any business. She smiled shyly to indicate she came in peace. "Hey, Jeff. Got a minute?"

"Sure, Clarice. Come on in."

She moved inside the door frame but didn't sit. "You know the garden center that donated those birdfeeders a while back?"

"Yep. Nice gesture. Gives folks a touch of the outdoors."

"According to Lily Gilbert, there's a problem. The seed we have is the wrong kind to attract songbirds. She seems to know her business."

"Well, she's right if it's mostly corn."

Clarice was surprised by his answer. "I must have missed the bird food lecture in school," she said. "Anyway, the right seed is a lot more money. I've checked. Is there any chance I could try to work it into the budget?"

"Why, Clarice, it's a pleasure to see you take so much interest in the residents." Jeff beamed.

She shuddered. *There goes my reputation.*

"But I'm sorry, no can do. The birds would need to benefit all residents to be a line item."

"Oh. All right, then." Clarice was disappointed, but what more could she do?

"But maybe you can solve it another way. What are you doing next month on the tenth? That's a Tuesday evening."

Clarice's mind executed a total eclipse. She couldn't think of one single plan she might have in order to avoid whatever the hell Jeff had in mind. *Zip line through the rain forest? Salsa lessons? Nothing.* Finally she mumbled, "Well, I guess I don't have plans."

"My wife and I are members of the Olympic Birders Club. The club meets each month on the second Tuesday. Come with us, and you can ask the chapter to donate toward better seed."

"Oh, no. I couldn't. You do it." *Public speaking? I'd rather be drafted.*

"It wouldn't be appropriate since I'm a club member. This sounds perfect for you. And my wife always enjoys meeting the staff."

"But I–"

"There, that's settled. We meet in the library conference room at seven. I'll introduce you to the gang."

Clarice had heard that no good deed goes unpunished. That's why she so rarely did one. *Shit, shit, shit.*

\* \* \*

"Shit, shit, shit," said Gladys, giving Lily a toothless grin. She was so bent she peered over the handrails of her walker as if it were a Harley.

"Gladys, where did you get that mouth?" Lily asked.

Rick overheard when he came in to bring them clean towels. "I've been told that her father worked the fishing boats in Alaska, going to sea for long periods of time."

"She seems to have inherited his vocabulary," Lily observed.

"She's a gentle enough soul, though. Sweet. We all like her, don't we Gladys?"

"Damn straight," Gladys placed a warm towel fresh from the dryer against her face.

Lily had to admit it. She was getting to like the old girl, too.

## ELEVEN

## FUN HOUSE CHRONICLE
# The Creature

*The Creature entered the nursing home fourteen years ago and never found the exit. He is the young victim of a head injury that robbed him of everything but life. He no longer walks, nor does he talk. He can only screech. This happens whenever aides interact with him. Wheel him to dinner, he cries. Shower him, he shrieks. He is even traumatized by his own bowel movements. Whatever is going on inside his damaged brain, he is in constant fear or rage or pain. His earsplitting desperation stresses the rest of the residents, all of whom are fighting their own battles.*

*For fourteen years caregivers have fed and clothed and diapered him. He recognizes none of them, takes no comfort in their touch, never has a visitor. The State pays thousands each month for his upkeep. Whoever he was before he became the Creature is locked up in a resident file that has never been seen by this staff. His identity was lost long ago, even to himself.*

*Inevitably this leads to thoughts of euthanasia. Should the Creature be kept alive in misery when he could peacefully drift away? Is the money better spent on patients who can recover from strokes or falls? Doesn't everyone else deserve a little silence? Who should make these decisions?*

*For now, there is only misgiving when the Creature's shrieks rattle the walls.*

"HENDERSON INTERIORS," Sylvia answered the phone. "Bring clippers and scissors with you today." After a beat Sylvia said, "Mother?"

"Of course it's me. Who else would ask you to cut her hair?"

"I just thought my mother would start a conversation with hello, or how are you, my dear?"

"Sylvia, I'm in a nursing home. I have no time to waste." Lily hung up.

*She is such a brat. Is a little consideration too much to ask?* Sylvia stuffed the styling kit into her tote. She had cut her mother's hair since she was a kid. But she also wanted Lily to join in the social life, such as it was, at the nursing home. So when she arrived, Sylvia said, "I thought the local beauty college sent trainees here for the residents to try."

"I don't have that much courage. From what I've seen, those rookies would make better lawnmowers. But if you don't want to help me –"

"Of course I'll help. Why would you say that?" Sylvia was exasperated. Her mother should be adjusting to life here by now. Couldn't she try to be pleasant?

"You didn't sound exactly eager. But I don't want to start looking like crap just because I'm caught here."

It was a subject they could agree on. Neither understood why people who had so little left had to lose personal dignity, too. They both hated to see residents with tangled hair and in mismatched clothes, stockings puddled around their ankles. Didn't they have family?

Were the aides really too busy? Most residents couldn't do the personal niceties for themselves anymore, not with fading eyesight or palsied hands. Even if they could, things like tweezers or nail clippers were easy targets for theft. *And yet my mother had to ask me for a haircut.* Sylvia felt ashamed of herself as she began. She sat behind Lily's wheelchair on the hospital bed which she could raise and lower depending on where she was cutting. "We may have our differences, Mother, but personal standards is not one of them. You've always looked nice. And you will always look cared for. I won't ever question it again."

"Sylvia, I know you're willing, but I still hate to ask. Jessica is paid to do most things, but she just doesn't cut hair."

Sylvia wanted to defend herself. *I have my job, my husband. I am a dreadful caregiver. You and I fight. But mostly, Mom, it breaks my heart every fucking time I have to see you in this awful prison.* Instead, she swallowed her misery and revealed just a little of her envy. "Maybe I should be more like Jessica."

Lily must have heard the pain and the guilt anyway. She reached for one of her daughter's hands, brought it to her lips and kissed the palm. "No you shouldn't. I was out of line. Jessica is a wonderful caregiver. But she'll never share my history and my heart like you do. I hope you know how much I love you."

Sylvia felt nearly breathless. Maybe, just maybe, they were getting to know what they expected from each other in this new phase of life. "Do you think you could say it a little more often?"

"It's a deal. Truce?"

"Truce." For a time just the snipping of the scissors fought the din from the hallway. Lily broke their silence. "Do you remember the first time you cut my hair?"

"No. But I'll bet it looked God awful."

"You had a doll you named Lucy, after Lucille Ball. It had short curly red hair."

"I remember Lucy!" Sylvia's smile broadened. "I took her everywhere. And you made lots of clothes for her."

"Right. You got it in mind that if you cut my hair short, it would curl like Lucy's. For weeks I had spikes, long before they were popular. I looked like a hedgehog."

"That's what you get for giving me scissors. The bad fairies dropped off the points right onto your head."

Lily laughed. "I'd forgotten about bad fairies dropping off if you carry scissors with the blades down."

"I still believe it," Sylvia said. "My mother told me, so it must be true."

"Speaking of heads, do you remember what happened to Lucy's?"

Sylvia stopped cutting, and tried to dredge up a memory. "Something about her body falling apart, right?"

"Lucy's body was made of a different plastic than her head, so it started splitting. Her stuffing was coming out. You were distraught."

"How terrifying."

"But you didn't want another doll. You always hated change. You only wanted Lucy. So one day when you were at school, I bought another doll and decapitated it. Then I removed Lucy's head and attached it to the neck of the new body."

"That's right! Now I remember. I came in the house and there she sat on the sofa good as new. I thought a miracle had happened." Sylvia had to give her mother her due. Lily had always been there for her, even if *there* kept changing.

Maybe Sylvia hadn't always been happy, but everyone is damaged by their past somehow. It was time to get over it. Her mother and she were different, and that was simply that. She leaned forward, brushed snippets of hair off the back of her mother's neck and kissed it gently. "I wonder where Lucy went," she said.

"I wonder where that little girl went," said Lily.

\* \* \*

Lily had once read that the more helpless people get, the more self-centered they become. *Revert to big babies.* And she was about to throw a toddler-type tantrum over the TV remote.

Televisions were hung from the ceiling, making them easier to see from bed. Lily figured it was also the Fun House way to keep the wrinklies in their rooms and out of the halls. The television speaker was actually in the remote control. It was weird, looking one place and hearing from another, sort of like going to a drive-in movie. It irritated Lily no end. If she set the remote on one side of the bed, she couldn't hear with the other ear.

"I'll have to explain the concept of stereo to the house guard," she was muttering when a male voice answered, "I think we have the concept. But most of our residents don't have one good ear, much less two."

"Well, I do," Lily whined then looked at her visitor. *Ye gods, he's a homely man.* He was so big and stretched the top of his scrubs so much that ironing would never be necessary. His speech and his mannerisms were slow and deliberate.

"Good hearing, huh? That's because, by nursing home standards, you're still a youngster." He stuck out his hand. "My name's Ernie. I'm your physical therapist."

She shook his hand. "I'm Lily, the new young hottie on the West Wing."

His laugh was full and sincere, even though his smile didn't really improve his looks. "I'm here to begin your torture program." Ernie explained that Medicare would cover some physical therapy, more than if she were still at home. His plan was to have her work on upper body strength so she could more easily transfer from bed to wheelchair and back. He gave her a pair of three pound weights and sat with her while she did a round of arm lifts.

"Nice job," he said. "You're in pretty good shape already. Just do these lifts adding a couple each day, and I think you'll soon be ready to try standing."

*To try standing?* Was it really possible? The thought thrilled her, but she was nobody's fool. It wouldn't be easy. Still, if she was going to live here, it was better to live here strong.

Maybe the day would come that she could even get to the toilet on her own. That might be the day she'd stop thinking about suicide.

\* \* \*

Jessica and Lily were in the activities room having an evening cup of chamomile tea along with sugar-free cookies that Jessica had slightly overbaked. "I checked out a library book on cooking for diabetics. What do you think?"

"Sort of like non-alcohol beer," Lily assessed. "A hint of the flavor but none of the kick."

"If you don't like them, why are you on your third?"

"It's the closest thing to a real cookie I'm likely to get around here."

"Now that you mention it, you really don't complain much about the food."

"Too cheap a shot. Bland grub from cheap ingredients will never meet the standards of Bobby Flay."

A round little dynamo bustled up to their table. "Is this your daughter, Lily?" Babs asked.

"Nope. Jessica is my…my BFF. She visits in the evenings after things quiet down around here."

"How nice! Did you hear the Olde Tyme Tunesters last night? I just love barber shop quartets, don't you?"

"Gosh, I'm sure sorry to have missed them."

"Can't be helped, can't be helped. Lily, you must give your friend a heads up next time." Babs waved a cheery "Toodles!" and bounced away.

Jessica and Lily had both managed to keep straight faces. Now Lily said, "Must have had really important plans to keep you away from that."

"Ben Stassen came over to watch a creepy movie with Folly and me."

"That's right! You had a date!" Lily burst out, coming to attention faster than a soldier.

"No, not a date. TV with a friend." Jessica couldn't control the blush creeping into her cheeks.

"Well it's a start. You have to stop socializing exclusively with a dead man's ghost and a soon-to-be ghostly old woman."

Jessica's blush deepened. "Well, if you don't want me to visit…"

"Of course, you ninny. Of course, I love seeing you. But you need more. I know who Bennett Stassen is. I've seen him. He's a fine looking man. A good one, too, discounting that wretched daughter of his."

Small towns have no secrets. "Lily, he's a customer. He was Ed's friend, and now he's mine. And that's all there is to it."

"Oh, piffle. Of course that's not all. He's looking for more than friendship."

Jessica sighed. Lily was right, of course. So why not tell her the truth? She wanted to confide in somebody other than Folly and Latin Lover. "No, you're right. Ben wants to know if Ed is standing between us. And I don't know what to say."

"Do you want him coming around?"

"Well, I'm glad Gina Lola is in my barn. He has to keep stopping by." *And I like the way the skin around his eyes crinkles when he smiles.*

"Ben's a courageous guy to even take a shot at it."

"I feel like I'm playing around on Ed. I know that's foolish, but it's how I feel."

"Nobody's going to replace Ed. But you can accept someone else. Like with kids. Having a second one doesn't mean you love the first one less. At least so I'm told."

Jessica felt a chill, and God knows it was never cold in the nursing home. It was too damn hard, feeling guilty on the one hand and scared to take a second chance on the other. She'd had enough for now. "I'm just too uncomfortable to talk about this anymore, Lily. I need to think for a while. But you've given me stuff to consider. Let's talk about you instead. Did you find another man after Harmon?"

Well, roll me on down to my room, and I'll tell you all about it." Jessica cleared their clutter from the table, then unlocked Lily's wheelchair brakes. This late the halls were mostly unpopulated and quiet. It was almost pleasant.

"Men. Of course I've had my share. My face didn't always look like a topographical map, you know. My arms weren't always bat wings." She flapped to demonstrate the wobbly skin on her upper arms. But Jessica knew she was actually proud of the arm strength she was developing using the physical therapist's weights.

In fact, Lily seemed more settled lately. Not happy, but …resigned maybe? Maybe she was coming to grips with her situation or something. *Wonder if that's a good or bad thing?* "I'm sure you've broken plenty of hearts in your time. But I meant a permanent partner."

"Not since coming to Washington twenty-five years ago. No permanent partners. Although you know what they say about Northwest loggers."

"No, what?"

"They have the best wood."

Sometimes Lily actually shocked her. "Lily. Have you been spending too much time with Gladys and her vocabulary?"

"Hey, in here, things get pretty basic. Or base if you prefer. I'll have to introduce you to my new friend, Bear." A small knot of walkers and wheelchairs was assembled around the evening snack cart. As Jessica weaved the wheelchair through the obstacle course, Lily continued her story. "I started my garden when I first bought the house, and it's been my closest companion. It's more entertaining than most men. More reliable, too."

Jessica pushed the chair into Lily's room, crossing in

front of Gladys's empty bed. The old girl must be out on the high seas.

"Sex was different when I was young," Lily continued, grabbing the room dividing curtain and pushing it out of their way. "In the sixties and seventies it didn't seem like the dangerous game that it does today. There could be consequences, of course, but they didn't seem so fearsome."

Lily parked next to her bed as Jessica closed the curtain again. "Things weren't the same for us as they were for you and Ed. It wasn't a time for settling down. Harmon and I never owned a house, didn't have roots, and were disowned on both sides. After Harmon died, I just couldn't get comfy in any one spot."

Jessica removed a blue cotton nightie from the dresser and placed it on Lily's bed.

"I nearly provided a new Daddy for Sylvia when I worked for a garden center in Charlotte, North Carolina." Lily stopped talking to pull her sweater and camisole over her head, then slip into the nightie. "I met Paul there. A really nice, even tempered man, a gem in every way. Just too steady for me, I guess, since I was such a free spirit. But Sylvia loved him. We were together for nearly three years. When I left him, it devastated her. I think she'd have chosen to stay with him instead of move on with me. But it's hard to get your own way when you are only nine."

Lily prepared to transfer from the chair to the bed. She set her brakes, removed a wheelchair arm, and handed it to Jessica to set aside. Using the bed's remote control, she lowered its surface to be level with the wheelchair. Jessica helped Lily position the transfer board, a three foot long piece of tough polyethelene. One end went on the chair under her hip and the other end on the bed. Lily inched her way across the board, lifting and balancing with her one foot.

"That's terrific. Better than you did at home." Jessica was delighted with Lily's arm strength.

"Don't tell anybody I did it now. Management doesn't want us transferring without an aide. But I feel safe with you." As she settled onto the bed, she continued her story. "Sylvia never forgave me for dumping Paul. She stayed in touch with him, wrote him letters. He even answered for a while. I went to work as a picture framer in Phoenix and made a collage with photos of the two of them together. Best gift I ever gave her. It was the first thing she'd unpack to hang in each new bedroom. But eventually he stopped writing, and I kept moving. By the time Sylvia and I arrived out here, she was no longer hanging the collage."

"She's lucky to have even one loving parent. She went more places and saw more things than most kids." Jessica gave a tug to the fleece pants as Lily lifted her butt and shimmied out of them.

"About the time she'd find a new friend, I pulled up stakes. She eventually quit trying. She never learned to fit in. It's all she ever wanted, and all she wants now. A stable, perfect lifestyle. Kyle fuels that in her."

"Fuels it? I don't follow."

"He's the same way. She chose him because he's so terribly tasteful in every way."

"He seems okay to me," Jessica said, wondering what Lily found so objectionable about the tall, pleasant man she'd met at the hospital. She spread a fresh sheet and light blanket over Lily.

"Maybe. But that's another story. I'm not bursting that bubble for her." After a brief pause for a dab of night cream, Lily seemed to deflate. She turned sad eyes to Jessica. "You should see her pain when she visits me."

Jessica sat on the side of the bed. "You're her mother, Lily. Of course she's pained to see you here."

"And now I have to make it worse."

*Oh-oh.* "What do you mean?"

"I'm going to tell her to clear out my house and sell it all."

\* \* \*

Personnel issues were the bane of Jeff's administrative existence. He liked everything else about his job, but when the he-said-she-saids started, he pretty much wanted to throttle all his employees.

Nurse Ernestine stood across the desk from him, fury having made her face an unfortunate shade of scarlet. Jeff knew this was the woman that Lily Gilbert called Nurse Happy Face. The nickname had spread like wildfire until Ernestine was the only one who didn't know it. He clenched his teeth in order not to chuckle.

"It's no laughing matter, Jeffrey. It was right there on the floor! It could have been a resident with a heart attack. *I* could have had a heart attack. THIS IS A SERIOUS INFRACTION OF THE RULES!"

Jeff bit the insides of his cheeks. Then he realized she was waiting for him to say something. *Breathe deep.* "Certainly it is, Nurse Hap…Ernestine. I will look into it immediately."

The problem was the life sized dummy that trainees used to practice bathing a bedridden patient or placing one on a bedpan correctly. Somebody had put the dummy on the floor, with its nude legs sticking out the doorway of the activities room. Nurse Happy Face had been steaming down the hall with an armload of medical supplies when she saw the legs, shrieked, and hit the alarm. Every staff member knew the clanging bell meant "Help, come running."

The nurse dropped the load she was carrying. Bandages unrolled everywhere. By the time she discovered that the legs belonged to a dummy, staff from all departments had gathered around and were having a good laugh. At her.

She was not amused.

"See that you do get to the bottom of this, see that you do," she huffed, pulling down on her scrub top, straightening her spine, and marching out.

Jeff could see Lia at the reception desk outside his office. He called to her. "You know who's behind this, don't you?"

"Well, yes."

"You're not going to tell me, right?"

"No, sir."

"What if I threaten you with your job?"

"What if I threaten to never make another coffee run?"

"Glad we had this discussion," Jeff said.

He moved on with his second personnel issue of the day. Alita and Rick. The whole staff was aware they'd become an item. Relationships developed between coworkers here as often as in any business. But not all businesses have beds in every room.

One private room was currently empty, awaiting a high paying guest. But Patricia Bergeron, the Social Services Director and a true blue company gal if ever there was one, had overheard the younger staff gossiping about Alita and

Rick. They were grabbing quickies in the otherwise empty room.

Jeff was in a fix. The buttinsky had told him about it so now he had to do something. Rick and Alita were both good workers. Jeff liked them, although Rick probably had something to do with that dummy incident. People who did these jobs with minimal complaints were hard to find. Especially male aides. In the old days, of course, Jeff would have just fired the woman. But not anymore, HR issues being what they were.

He thought for a while, tapping a rhythm with his fingers on his desk. He picked up the phone and placed a call to the maintenance supervisor. "Hey, Jimbo," he said when the supervisor answered. "You know the empty room on East? Until we admit a resident, please remove the bed from that room."

Having finished with personnel at last, Jeff could now get to his phone messages. One was from the corporate drones. That was never a good sign.

## TWELVE

FUN HOUSE CHRONICLE

## Cremains of the Day

*H*er Uncle Leroy died late one afternoon in a nursing home that she'd never seen. She hadn't even seen Uncle Leroy for a decade, what with living in Chicago while he logged the Washington forest. The nursing home had her listed as next of kin. Hers had never been a prolific family. The social services person wanted to know what she'd like done with the body.

*Eventually, the nursing home recommended a local funeral parlor. She called, paperwork was exchanged, and they settled on cremation. There would be no memorial service since Uncle Leroy had specified he wanted none.*

*"Now, what shall we do with the cremains?" the funeral director asked.*

*Cremains? Well every industry has its own trade speak.*

*She decided she would fly out to Seattle and rent a car. She picked up the cremains in a plain gray wooden box, the most basic container she could buy. She'd discovered by then that, jokes about coffee cans and oatmeal boxes notwithstanding, the crematorium demands a sturdier structure.*

*She knew Uncle Leroy had liked the woods even though he cut it down for a living. She borrowed a*

*Phillip's screwdriver and some scissors from the funeral parlor, then drove away with Uncle Leroy on the seat next to her. He used to be a better conversationalist, she thought.*

*She drove to a riverbank in the national forest, and there she broke the law. She used the screwdriver to release a sliding door on the box. Then she used the scissors to clip open a corner of the bag inside. Sprinkling Uncle Leroy into the rushing river was not a difficult task.*

*The only music was the serenade of river rapids and song birds. Plus lyrics about a famous final scene that ran through her head.*

"TODAY'S THE day," announced Ernie having found Lily in the sunny courtyard.

"What?" Lily looked up from her Stephanie Plum book. "You're learning to fly? Swimming to Canada?"

"No, but you are getting your butt out of that chair," he said, grabbing the wheelchair and pushing Lily back inside, down the hall and into the physical therapy room. "You've built up enough arm strength to give it a try."

Ernie pushed her chair onto a wooden ramp, between two parallel bars. He lowered the bars until they were just above elbow height to her seated position.

Lily began to feel edgy. *Am I up to whatever the hell he expects of me?*

Ernie asked her to scoot forward on the seat of her wheelchair.

She didn't move. "You know what you're doing?"

"More or less."

"Oh, that makes me feel secure." Still, Lily complied. She steadied herself with her foot and pushed forward with her arms.

"Good. Now, I want you to put on this belt." He helped her fasten a wide black fabric strap in place. "I can hold on to it in the back while we try this together."

He squatted down beside her with one of the parallel bars between them. "Put your hands on the bars and grab hold. Center your foot under you, and try to lift yourself up. Pull with your arms and push with your foot."

Lily sat stone still.

"Are you ready to try?" Ernie prompted.

"Well, of course not. I can hardly feel my foot. How do I know if it's holding me?" She no longer held sway over her body, and the loss of control scared her.

"That's why I want you to center it under your body. With only one leg, it can't be to the side."

"What if I execute a half gainer right out of this chair?" Lily's tummy fluttered and her nerves jangled.

"Not a chance unless you think your little chicken bones could pull over a big ol' tub like me," Ernie gave her belt a tug. "I'd never let you fall. I'll be standing up right along with you."

She nodded. She had no choice but to trust him. She could not do this by herself. She gathered her courage. Slowly, she raised her arms and took hold of the bars, tightening her hands until she could see her knuckles turn white.

"Ok, now, on three," Ernie commanded. "One…Two …Three!" Lily pulled with her arms and pushed with her foot. No motion, just a great constriction in her muscles. *This is not going to work. How could I possibly think that it would?*

"Don't quit now. You can do this," Ernie coached.

Then slowly, so slowly she began to rise. From the pressure on the belt around her waist, she knew that Ernie was keeping her balanced. She leaned slightly forward, but up she went. As her bottom cleared the chair, she looked down and could see her knee tremble as it began to straighten. Then the tremble reached her thigh. Soon after that, she realized she wasn't using her hands for strength any more, only for balance. Instead, she was pushing up with her leg. Ernie was close, but she was lifting her own weight.

So hard, so frightening, and at last, so exhilarating. Lily was upright. She wobbled, but she was up. Her clenched teeth gave way to a huge grin. Ernie whooped and yelled, "Yes!"

For a delicious moment, she stood and looked around the room. "I may need oxygen this high."

"Then I think that's enough for one day," Ernie said and began to lower her back down. She didn't have the strength to do it all for herself without collapsing.

"That was wonderful, doll," he beamed at her. "Better than I ever thought for your maiden voyage."

As she settled she heard applause. Bear, three other residents and two aides were cheering her victory. She was numb, she was exhausted, but she was bursting with joy. "Like Gladys says, Ernie, Goddamn."

\* \* \*

Deep down Lily knew that the Grim Jokester punished pleasure with pain. She should have anticipated the next day.

"It looks too puffy to me," said the Physician's Assistant.

"And red," said Nurse Baby Talk, nodding agreement.

"See how the skin is weeping here?" The PA poked at Lily's leg. "Let's send her to see Kim."

"Hello…hello," snapped Lily. "I'm up here at the other end of the leg. What's going on down there?"

"Ah, yes, Mrs., um, Gilbert," said the PA, consulting the papers on his clipboard. "It appears that your lymphedema may be acting up."

"Oh, God. Is my leg infected?" *It can't be. It can't be.*

"I would like a lymphedema therapist to take a look at it. Just to be on the safe side. And to tell the nurses here how to treat it."

Nurse Baby Talk stared arrows at him. "I'm quite sure we will know how to treat it when someone gives us a proper diagnosis." She switched to the patronizing tone she used with residents. "We do our very, very best for our favorites, don't we, Lily?"

"Yes, you always, always do."

A short while after the PA left, Nurse Baby Talk bustled back into the room to tell Lily that she had an appointment with the specialist for the next day.

"How do I get there?" Lily asked.

"Paratransit will take you." The nurse explained that this was the transportation service for the disabled. Vans arrived at scheduled times to take residents to medical appointments around the community. In theory, the nursing home had the appointee ready to go on time, and the van arrived on time.

The morning of her appointment, Lily waited in the Soundside lobby for forty-five minutes. Lia called Puget Paratransit after half an hour, but the dispatcher could not find the reservation. She ordered a van sent, and it eventually picked Lily up, but of course, Lily had missed the appointment once she arrived at the busy clinic. She was given another appointment for the very end of the day, and a van was called to take her back to Soundside in the meantime. She waited another hour for it.

Lily was exhausted. More than that, she was livid. By the time she was finally back in her room, she'd wet her pants in front of other residents in the hall. *The humiliation!* "I'm not incontinent. I'm just surrounded by incompetents," she raved while the aide, Chrissie, quickly cleaned her and put her to bed.

"Yes, ma'am," Chrissie said. "There now. Maybe you could get a little rest."

Lily wouldn't be mollified. "Not fucking likely. Get me one of those complaint forms."

"Yes, ma'am."

"Get me a stack of them." She shivered in rage.

Lily refused to do the whole thing again at the end of the day, still furiously filling out forms as new gripes came to mind. *And another thing,* she wrote. *I want one of the blue curtains instead of this ugly shit brindle one.*

Chrissie hovered close by, peeking around the curtain now and again like a prairie dog checking the whereabouts of a coyote. Chrissie was not a pretty girl to begin with, what with the straight stringy hair, weak chin and defeated posture. The spooked expression in her eyes did nothing to improve her looks.

As the day progressed, Lily was done with yelling. She spoke to no one and refused her evening meal. She sulked and seethed, cooling as slowly as a post-eruptive volcano. In the early evening, a stranger appeared in her room. "Hello, Mrs. Gilbert. I understand you have had a difficult day."

"Not as difficult as the day everyone around me has had."

"I'll watch my step. My name is Kim Richards. I'm the lymphedema therapist."

"Ah. So the mountain has come to Muhammad."

"Yes. Soundside is on my way home. I thought it might be easier for me to come here than the other way around."

She was short with a slightly crooked back that made Lily think of scoliosis. She had sun damaged skin, short shaggy hair, and calloused hands, whether from work or sports Lily could not tell. Like so many caregivers, she appeared to take very little care of herself. But she had bright intelligent eyes and no difficulty meeting Lily's gaze.

"All right. I'm going to give you the benefit of the doubt. I am grateful you are here. And I'm not Mrs. Gilbert. I'm Lily."

Kim raised the hospital bed to a convenient height, then unwrapped Lily's leg. She nudged and massaged the skin to help fluid in the lymph system move out of the leg, taking dead proteins with it. She showed Nurse Baby Talk how it should be cleansed and wrapped, but the nurse seemed almost hostile. *Does she resent Kim's intrusion?* Lily wouldn't put it past her.

Finally, Kim said, "I think they caught it before much damage was done."

"But how did it happen? Am I doing too much?" Lily loved the therapy sessions with Ernie and hated to think she might have to give them up. Not when she was so close to real progress.

"No, not at all. Activity is good for you. But crazy infections are around all the time. New viral strains materialize overnight and bacteria run rampant.

Unfortunately, you're just more susceptible than most." Then Kim addressed the nurse. "Be sure they keep the room as clean as possible."

"Well, of course." The nurse turned sharply enough to squeak on her rubbery soles and exited the room, muttering to herself.

"I believe Nurse Baby Talk is thinking some very big girl words," Lily whispered to Kim. They exchanged a grin. And before she left, Kim showed Lily how to waggle her toes and foot, then bend the leg upward. "Doing that can help keep fluids from building up. It lowers your risk."

At long last, someone had given Lily some no nonsense guidance on how she could help fight her own battle against infections.

"I will see you again in a week," Kim said.

"But next time, Muhammad will come to you," Lily said, sure she could conquer paratransit. She was nearly limp with relief that this wretched day was ending with good news after all.

When Kim was gone, Lily pushed her call light. Chrissie approached with the caution due to a she-wolf. "Yes, ma'am? What can I do for you?"

"You can accept my apology."

Chrissie stared and moved slightly closer. "For what, Miss Lily?"

"I got mad, and you got in the way. You were just trying to help me. I'm sorry if I made you feel bad." She felt like a horse's patoot for frightening this youngster.

The apology flustered Chrissie. "Why, I, well, that's okay, Miss Lily. Everybody has a bad day now and then."

"Especially in here."

"But not everybody apologizes. At least not to me."

The next week, Soundside sent Chrissie with Lily to her appointment, to help avoid screw ups between the nursing home and paratransit. The aide sat on a bus seat, next to Lily's wheelchair.

Lily was overjoyed to be outside the nursing home, if only in a medical van. She would have liked to hang her head out the window and sniff the air like a spaniel, letting the wind blow back her ears. Late summer had touched the town while she had been in stir. The maples and chestnuts were still voluptuous in deep green attire, but dahlias were also appearing, some blossoms as big as dinner plates.

A quiet ride would have been fine with her, but Chrissie kept up a running commentary. Lily had been adopted by the girl as her personal patient ever since the apology. The van lift lowered Lily's chair to the ground, and Chrissie pushed her into the clinic, still chattering about her family. Her boyfriend Mark was her baby Jacob's dad, and he might just let Chrissie and Jacob move in with him, but he didn't want her little girl Hannah because she wasn't his, but of course Chrissie couldn't leave her, could she, so she had to stay with Mom until she could save enough for a place of her own, but then she'd have to get daycare and who could afford that, so she might as well go on living with Mom because Mom looked after her kids, and it didn't cost anything other than groceries and utilities. Lily's ears were ringing by the time she was ushered into the therapist's office.

Kim unwrapped her leg and frowned. "Wrinkles."

"Well, yes, I am in my late seventies, you know."

"I mean in the bandages." Kim examined the leg thoroughly, shaking her head. "You like that girl who brought you here?"

"Actually, yes. Quite a chatterbox."

"A good aide?"

"Very."

Kim went to get Chrissie from the waiting room. "Now, Chrissie, I'm going to show you how to take care of this leg."

"Oh, no, ma'am. I'm just an aide. Nurses do that." Chrissie looked ready to bolt for the door.

"Nonsense. Now watch carefully."

Kim first debrised the leg with soap and water, scrubbing gently with her palm. "If you ever see lots of flaky skin, or hard particles of plaque, don't try to remove them. Call me. If you see redness or breaks in the skin, call me." Then she covered the leg with safflower oil, and pulled a soft, thin stockinet over it.

"Be sure each layer is absolutely smooth. A wrinkle in the material can cause a lesion in Lily's skin because it's so fragile. That increases the chance of infection." She began wrapping long strips of fleece from Lily's toes up to the knee. Over the fleece she wrapped a compression bandage, also from the toes up.

"Never start at the top, because you want to move the fluids upward out of the leg. Now, you got it?"

"Oh gosh. Well, I think so," Chrissie replied.

"Good." Kim undid all the layers again. "Now you do it."

Chrissie might be incompetent at life, but she was a natural as a caregiver. She went through the whole process under Kim's eagle eye, repeating each step aloud to herself.

"Acceptable," Kim pronounced. "You do this every day you work. Nobody else should touch this leg."

"But what about my days off? Should I come in?" Lily and the therapist exchanged a flabbergasted look at the girl's eagerness to serve.

"It won't need to be done on those days. Eventually, every other day will suffice as long as you see no problem areas."

From that day forward, Lily called Chrissie her wrapper chick. Nurse Baby Talk was displeased that a mere aide would be so trusted, and Soundside had to give special dispensation, at the recommendation of the lymphedema specialist and the written consent of Lily.

"Now you have another big baby to care for, Chrissie," said Lily.

"The pleasure is all mine, Miss Lily," answered the girl, beaming. "I'm not used to grown-ups counting on me."

*With a smile like that, she's not such a homely girl after all.*

\* \* \*

That evening Lily was feeling downright chipper. She decided to take a spin around the halls. She rolled into the activities room, and there was Bear at a table staring into a tiny computer.

Lily pulled up beside him. "Looking at porn?"

"No. Not a bad idea, though."

"I myself saw a lymphemaniac today."

"Oh? I thought that kind of entertainment was more for the men around here."

"Not a nympho, a lympho. A specialist in lymphedema. She's helping me manage infection. Maybe I can keep leg number two."

"That's fabulous, Lily." If a bear could look happy, he did.

"Thought you might help me celebrate." She reached for the tote on the handle of her wheelchair and extracted a jar of lightly salted dry roasted peanuts that Jessica had given her. They each took a handful and chewed companionably.

Then Lily turned her attention back to the computer. "Isn't that awful tiny for big paws like yours?"

"Well, yeah. It's called a netbook. I can hide it under my pillow where the thieves can't get at it."

"What do you do with it?"

"Same stuff everyone does with computers. Read, play games, surf. I did most everything online back when I still had stuff to do."

"Could I buy things on a computer?"

"Of course."

"Could I write letters and such?"

"Sure."

"Think you could teach me to use one?"

"Absolutely. You interested in getting one?"

"Maybe so." She left the peanuts for him and rolled out of the room on down the hall, wheels turning in her head as well.

## THIRTEEN

FUN HOUSE CHRONICLE
## Homecoming

*G*randpa Harry lived quietly in a room in his son
Evan's house. It had been the youngest boy's room,
but he was moved in with his brother, much to the disgust
of both, when Grandpa Harry came to stay. The room
remained decorated with Power Rangers and wrestling
stars against the day the child reclaimed his turf.

The boys didn't think Grandpa Harry was as much
fun as he used to be, and they grew cruel about how he
told the same jokes over and over. His son was gone all
day, and his daughter-in-law had all she could do to keep
up with the house and the boys. Nobody had time for the
old man. It was a story as common as dirt.

A stroke hospitalized Grandpa Harry for several
days then he was sent to a nursing home to recover. He
was given physical and speech therapy for motor and
communications skills. Both would take a fair amount
of time, but there was hope he would improve. The
therapists were rooting for him, and he didn't want to let
them down.

As he began to reconnect, he noticed that the other
residents were often unhappy. He let them talk for hours,
and as his own language improved, he joined in. The
men would tell dirty jokes in a huddle and cheer for their

*favorite baseball team and stare at the nurses' breasts. With the lady residents, they would play bingo.*

*Grandpa Harry hated chicken so the kitchen would serve him a minute steak; at his son's house he was too embarrassed to tell his daughter-in-law how he disliked the food she served most often. Here if he pissed on the toilet by mistake, nobody tsk-tsked him. And he came to love Paratransit. He would take a van to the hospital, along with any other resident who required the trip. From there he could wheel himself to a Walmart or watch skateboarders whiz through the half pipe in the city park. Only once did he get too exhausted to return to the nursing home, and then the cops brought him back, tickled that he was such a tough-spirited codger. He had trouble imagining why the other residents weren't happy here.*

*The day came when the social worker said, "Good news, Grandpa Harry, you are well enough to go home. Your son is coming to get you."*

*At the home someone occasionally remembers how ol' Harry short sheeted a bed or pinched a nurse or what a funny joke he told that time. They wonder how he's doing now that he's back home.*

*All things considered, it's better if they never know.*

SYLVIA NEVER visited the nursing home on Sundays. She couldn't take the agony. It was the day most families chose to come do their duty, so it was the hardest day for residents who never had guests and for those who cried inconsolably after their sons and daughters escaped. Besides, Lily had told Sylvia that she preferred to avoid all that misery, too. She stayed in her room listening to her CDs while she read, maybe something juicy by Nora Roberts.

So Sylvia was surprised when Lily asked her to come by this Sunday afternoon. And to bring Kyle along.

"What do you suppose she wants? I can't remember a time she actually asked to see me," Kyle said. On the short trip to Soundside he was driving the Lexus that he used to squire around real estate clients.

"Don't be silly, Kyle. I'm sure she loves to see you," Sylvia said as she freshened her lipstick in the visor mirror.

"Well, thanks, hon. But, no, she doesn't."

"No, she doesn't," she admitted after a pause to smack her lips like a guppy. She patted his knee as he parked, and he kissed her temple before they got out of the car.

The lobby was filled with colorful baskets on display. Kyle asked Sylvia what was going on, and she explained the staff auction.

"Let's bid on this one from the Village Fudgery," he said, staring with open longing at the tower of rich, gooey goodies. As slender as he was, Kyle had a hyperactive sweet tooth.

"Not a chance. But how about this one from the Book Nook? We could donate the paperbacks to Soundside, and keep the coupon for ourselves. There's a new guide to feng shui kitchens I'd like. And a tour of the wineries in Southern France that might interest you."

Kyle entered a bid on the Book Nook clipboard. Then he said, "I guess we've put this off as long as we can. Lead the way, Pilgrim."

They made progress until the hall was virtually blocked by two women in wheelchairs, one turned on a diagonal so their wheels had locked together. They pushed against each other, using decrepit feet for propulsion like battling dung beetles. A circle of fragile onlookers gathered around to watch the show. The aroma of fresh urine permeated the air.

One of the women was a skeleton with skin, a stringy topknot of hair pulled back to reveal her high cheekbones. Her rictus mouth wailed non-stop. "I have to get out of here, oh please, I'm so late, I have to get home. The baby! Where's the baby?" The other was enraged, accusing the first of something in an indecipherable barrage of croaks and squeals. Her transport encircled her so that she could not fall out. It also limited her reach so her flailing fists missed the mark.

The skeleton tried to pull free, turned to Sylvia and cried out her grief. "The baby! Where's the baby?"

"I don't know where it is, Ma'am. I can't help you. I'm so sorry." Sylvia had no idea what to do.

"Now, now Josephine," said an aide rushing up to help. "And you, too, Helen. Let's call it a tie." She separated their wheels and aimed them in opposite directions. They crept away, one still crying for the baby and the other muttering about the unknown.

The aide gave Sylvia and Kyle a shy glance through stringy bangs. "Guess you can move now, too. Sorry for the confusion."

The competence of this youngster shamed Sylvia. *This ...this girl handled a situation that stymied me.* "I didn't know what to do."

"You learn fast around here, ma'am. Do you need directions?"

"No, we're here to see my mother...Mrs. Gilbert."

The girl lit up. "Oh, Lily! She's my fave. Such a sweetie! Okay, 'bye." And off she went, following Helen down the hall. "Helen? Let's go get you cleaned up."

*Fave? Sweetie? Lily?*

On cue, Lily appeared in her doorway. "That was Chrissie. She's my fave, too. Sorry about the traffic jam. They roam all the time, the unhinged ones. Most of them are looking for a way out. We call them the travelers."

\* \* \*

Lily wheeled passed her roommate's empty bed to her own side of the room, explaining, "Gladys was running a fever so they took her to a single room this morning. Just in case she might have something contagious."

"I'm sure the aides got an earful," Sylvia said. "I can't imagine why you get such a kick out of her."

"I've learned a few colorful sea shanties, that's for sure. Like one about a mermaid who couldn't get laid, but she could go down on Davy's jones."

"Oh, for heaven sake, Mother. That's just vulgar." Sylvia shot a glare at Kyle, who stopped snickering.

"I imagine she'll be gone for the night, so we have privacy here," Lily said. "That's why I asked you to come even though it's Sunday. Or we could talk in the parlor if you prefer."

"This is fine," Sylvia and Kyle said simultaneously.

Sylvia added, "I'm not sure we're ready to navigate that hall again at the moment." She sat on the bed. After using the Purell, she passed it to Kyle.

"You're looking well, Lily," he said, settling into the guest chair with the elegance of a large water bird coming in for a landing.

Lily smiled at him, which was not her custom. But just now, she was grateful to her son-in-law for giving her an opening. "I have a mirror, Kyle. I'm not looking better. Just more resigned."

"What do you mean, resigned? What's going on?" Sylvia began to pick bits of lint off the blanket on the bed. Lily knew she couldn't sit still when she was nervous, not even as a kid.

"You'd like me to believe I'll get out of here soon. But if I said I was coming home, I'd be as out of touch with reality as those travelers out there."

"But…but…of course you will. You're getting better. Even Kyle noticed." Sylvia's alarm seemed real.

"True, I'm getting stronger. But I'll never be able to live without intense medical care. I've tried. I've failed. And I'm a realist."

"But the next time we could be more vigilant. I'll get better caregivers."

"Sylvia, stop. My caregivers were fine. You've done everything you can. No one could expect you to do more. But I'm a danger to myself at home. I realize that now. Toileting is hard and bathing is nearly impossible. Too much chance of injury. How graphic do I need to get?"

Sylvia capitulated. "I guess I knew you'd never be able to be home again. I just didn't know you knew."

"You two do have trouble speaking clearly to each other," Kyle observed.

Both women shot stares at him.

"Not that it's any of my business," he added.

Sylvia turned back to her mother. "But I didn't want you to give up hope. It scares me that…what you might do."

"If I go home, I die. If I stay here, infection may be controlled for a long time. I can live with that."

"You really mean it? You'd be content?"

146

Lily kept her face from revealing the lie. A poker face. "Yes, I really mean it. So it's time to sell the house. Kyle, will you list it for me?"

"Sell your house? So soon? I mean eventually, but..." Sylvia came to a halt.

"No time to waste, my dear. If I'm not coming home, I'll need the money here. My Medicare days are ending soon."

"Of course, Lily. If that's what you really want," Kyle said.

"Bring me the necessary papers tomorrow, and I'll sign them. Thank you, Kyle. And Sylvia. I need you to supervise staging it. You're so good at that."

"I wouldn't do it the way you..." Sylvia choked on her sentence.

"Nonsense. You'll make it look ten times better than I ever did. Hire Jessica to help and Aurora, too. They both need the work. Keep the things you would like. There's not much of value except my silver. Sell the rest."

"But, are you sure you're ready for this? This is so sudden."

"After Medicare runs out I'll have to pay thousands every month. So it has to be done soon. And you're the only ones who can do it for me."

"Well. As long as you're sure," Sylvia blew her nose and straightened her back. "We'll start tomorrow, won't we, Kyle?"

*Mission accomplished.* Lily had sentenced herself to the Fun House so Sylvia wouldn't be burdened with guilt. She watched her daughter assume a look of resolve, already beginning to plan. But when Lily glanced at Kyle, she was not so sure he'd bought her act.

Nothing was mentioned until the next day when Kyle brought the comparable listings. Lily and he arrived at a price for her house that seemed reasonable for a quick sale. "It's a shaky market but that's an attractive number," he said. He had her sign a contract naming him as her realtor. He would list it as soon as Sylvia said it was ready. "Thank you, Lily, for depending on me."

"Oh, I've always found you dependable, Kyle."

From the very beginning, Lily had recognized Kyle as a serious young man, one who seemed to respect and love her daughter. He'd been Sylvia's first and only real rebellion against her mother. She'd met him at design school, and they had married very quickly after that. Lily knew he'd won Sylvia all those years ago because he was in no way as flamboyant as the men she herself had attracted or been attracted to.

"He's so refined and cultured. So self-contained. He thinks my sense of design is quite sophisticated. Refreshingly so, he says," the twenty year old Sylvia had enthused to her mother.

Lily felt attributes like refined and self-contained could easily be euphemisms for boring and inhibited. She made it clear she would have chosen a more adventurous spirit for her daughter. Someone who could expand her universe, instead of reinforcing the boundaries Sylvia had already constructed.

"I've had adventure enough, thank you very much. Now I want to settle in," Sylvia had insisted, and Lily had finally said no more.

Now she looked at her son-in-law sitting across from her in a nursing home parlor, all these years later, using a briefcase as his desk. She felt warmth for him that was long overdue. "I know we've never been close, Kyle, but you have been good to my daughter. Thank you for that."

If Kyle was surprised by her statement, he was too refined to express it. "I'm sorry we haven't known each other better, Lily. It's been my loss."

"I'm too old to mince words any longer, Kyle. You've never been honest with me about who you are. I've always felt you didn't think I'd accept you. And I've resented your lack of trust."

"Would you have accepted me, Lily? Would you have allowed your daughter to marry a gay man?" Kyle looked her in the eye.

"I thought she needed a stronger man, straight or gay. More courageous."

"You mean one more willing to tackle opposition than to hide from it?"

"Well, yes. But I've come to realize your strength is your self-control. You've helped her create the orderly life she always wanted for herself."

"I'm gratified you see that. She's created it for me, too. And I love her for it."

"Does she know the truth?"

"We don't discuss it. At this point, I think we'll just leave it that way. Complete honesty can be too much honesty." Then he changed the subject. "And speaking of honesty, I don't believe you're being completely truthful with Sylvia either. About staying here."

"Of course not. I would so much rather go home to die. I'm tired of losing ground inches at a time, and I'm ready for it to end."

"That could be your choice."

"But it would grieve her if I give up. I'm not willing to do that."

Kyle was quiet for a while. "So we both hold the power to damage her by telling the truth."

"Sometimes keeping your mouth shut is the greatest expression of love."

\* \* \*

When Kyle left, Lily needed to restore herself by visiting the plants in the courtyard. She wanted some time to quietly celebrate her victory. She had done right by her daughter, no matter the cost to herself.

Soundside was U-shaped around the small landscaped center. Residents and their families could sit outside and visit. On late summer days, the afternoon sun was still warm enough for old bones. A landscaping service maintained the courtyard although Lily had been critical of their work when she first arrived. *I could tell them how to do a thing or three.*

She'd made it clear that she would be happy to demonstrate a few superior techniques. She'd done this by simply refusing to get out of their way. Eventually, they let her deadhead the potted roses, the ones that she could reach. Today, one of the yardmen loaned her clippers the moment she arrived. Lily was sure the Soundside management would have a fit if they knew. "None of their bee's wax," she muttered to herself. "I'm not about to plunge them into my heart."

"Or anybody else's, I hope. But if you do, I have a couple candidates for you." The old voice startled Lily. She turned and saw a wisp of a woman leaning on a fluorescent blue cane, smiling at her. She was dressed in grass green capris with a flouncy silk blouse, and sported a hair cut spiked up with mousse. Rhinestones twinkled in eyeglass frames that were far too big for her raisin of a face, and a charm bracelet created its own music on her wrist.

"I'm Eunice Taylor, the thousand year old woman," the stranger said. "May I join you?" Without awaiting an invitation, Eunice plopped herself down on a decorative iron bench near the pots that Lily was tending. "I love the floribunda roses. They bloom so late into the season with a little care." Eunice inhaled deeply and sighed.

"With a little care," Lily nodded, giving the older woman the once over. *Talk about late in the season...she's close to ninety?* "I'm Lily Gilbert. You a resident here, too?"

"You mean here among the ruins? Absotootinlutely. I prefer it to being home alone." Eunice nattered on about her husband who had died at Soundside a while back. "I visited him everyday until the end, and just kept on visiting. I'd made friends with a lot of the residents and most of the staff by then."

"You just kept coming for the hell of it?"

"Well, lots of these old farts need someone to chat them up now and again, don't you know. I just kept visiting and yapping until I up and broke my hip. I moved in to recuperate, and I've been here ever since. Now I guess I'm too rickety for a clean bill of health, although Ernie's doing what he can to fix me up." She shrugged. "I like it here. Where else you going to hear the Happy Trails Yodelers take on *The Old Rugged Cross*?"

While they talked, Lily noticed an unfolding drama. She pointed it out to Eunice. At one end of the courtyard, a landscaper was looking for his missing glove, accusing another of taking it. At the other end, the huge bulk of

Furball was in the process of killing it. Both old women snickered.

"Well, if it isn't the Giggle Sisters," said Ernie, startling them both. "Come on, Eunice, I said walk around the courtyard, not sit on your butt in the courtyard."

"Damn slave driver," Eunice muttered, but she staggered up, leaning heavily on the cane. Lily could see her hands turn white with the effort. And she saw pain shoot through Eunice's face. But like so many old combatants, Eunice suffered in silence. She pointed out the athletic shoes that looked like enormous marshmallows on her toothpick legs. "He made me trade in my stilettos for moon boots."

"He's a mean piece of work, Eunice," Lily said with a nod.

"Your turn is coming next," Ernie said.

As Eunice crippled away with Ernie at her side, Lily watched her go. Eunice seemed to be in her right mind. Did she really like living here?

* * *

Sylvia entered Lily's house through the kitchen door. She brought along a cardboard box, and placed it on the faded laminate counter. *We need new countertops. A neutral granite, I think.* The home stager was on the job. She would make it a triumph. Lily had owned the house for years, but Sylvia had not lived there long before she married Kyle. *Leave it to Lily to finally settle down after I move out.*

In the absence of all other noise, the ticking of a wall clock was as insistent as a metronome. Intermittently, the refrigerator rumbled to life to accompany it. Sylvia clicked on the old kitchen radio, then jumped when the joyful beats of a Spanish station burst free. *Aurora.* Sylvia listened for a few seconds and decided she liked the raucous music. Sylvia would ask her to clean out the fridge and cabinets. Aurora could keep the non-perishables or take them to the local food bank. Sylvia wouldn't want them since she and Lily didn't like the same brand of hardly anything. She dug out her *Suggestions from Sylvia* pad and jotted a note.

There were a few items that Sylvia knew she would keep. She'd already taken home her mother's silver tea set. It had always been displayed on the marble top table that was visible through the living room window. She hadn't wanted it there in plain sight in an invalid's house. Too vulnerable, both the silver and the invalid. Come to think of it, she might just take the marble top table home, too. Both had belonged to her great-grandmother, the one she was named for. They were among Lily's few possessions when her parents kicked her out. Even though Sylvia had never met her ancestor, she thought the old marble and silver gleamed with family and tradition.

Lily had let her play with the tea set, serving her doll Lucy as her guest. She herself would never allow a child to touch that old silver for fear of dents. Any household with kids is hard to design. *To make it both beautiful and indestructible is a challenge.* It had been important to her that Kyle never wanted children any more than she did. His own childhood hadn't been such a picnic that he wanted to sire a new generation. Besides, neither of them was fond of mess and sticky fingers and unpredictability.

She imagined Lily as a teenager, stubbornly convinced her views were the correct views, leaving home with her duffel full of clothes, an LP record player, a bit of furniture and very little cash, all stuffed in an old Nash Rambler. Sylvia suspected her mother had lived in that station wagon for a time. She knew little about this part of Lily's life because Lily never talked about it. "Not happy memories, so why bring them up?" she'd said long ago.

*Or maybe I just never really listened. Was I too involved with my own life to think about hers?* How hard things must have been for Lily, trying to make it on her own with a kid to raise. Maybe all the moving had been more about looking for work than looking for adventure.

She wandered room to room, accompanied by the salsa music and the faint aroma of natural lavender, rose and cedar potpourri that Lily made and distributed throughout the house. The earthy, rich scent was as much a part of her mother as her refusal to balance a check book, or her belief that socks looked fine with sandals, or her work hardened hands with the short utilitarian nails. "Who wants talons like a parrot?" she'd said when young Sylvia first minced home with acrylic nails.

*The rose glass hurricane lamp. Yes, I'd like that, too.*

Lily had framed a photo of her husband, Harmon, in his uniform. She'd also framed a photo of herself and an eight-year-old Sylvia running along a beach, trying to launch a kite. They were sprinting full tilt, mouths caught wide open in a wild laugh, arms extended as the kite bobbed along behind, not quite flying but at least off the ground.

It was Lily's lover Paul who had taken the photo, back when he was part of the family. He had done many of the Dad things that Sylvia had missed out on earlier in life. Without him she wouldn't know how to throw over handed or how to foxtrot or how to deliver the final smashing blow in a ping pong game. As she cradled the photo and looked at her mother's beaming face, another thought stopped her short.

Maybe her mother put down roots in Washington because she needed to stay close to Sylvia after all. *When I would no longer move on, she chose not to, either.* If that was true, she'd shaped her mother's life more than she had ever realized.

But there was work to be done now. She wanted to fill the cardboard box with things to take to her mother at Soundside, so she placed both photos in it, then filled an empty jelly jar with the potpourri. She walked back to Lily's bedroom, and picked up a tapestry jewelry box. Regardless what her mother said about selling everything, Sylvia knew she would want to go through this old treasure chest. She placed it in the box, then tucked a light weight shawl over the contents.

One box of memories for the nursing home. One box. This is what it all comes down to.

FOURTEEN

**FUN HOUSE CHRONICLE**
## Cognitive Corner

*T*hey call themselves Cognitive Corner. This is a not altogether pleasant group of residents who can still think. They are aware life has dropped them at the wrong station, and their reactions can be wicked.

Two commandeer chairs at the end of the hall and comment throughout the day on the size of the nurses' butts or whose roots need touched up. Another opens the exit door allowing one of those annoying travelers out to get lost in the courtyard.

They've tried the civilized approach of filling out complaint forms, but they've found direct action achieves results. One tips over her dinner tray to protest exceptionally nasty food. Another urinates on the floor if the aides haven't provided protection in a timely fashion.

Life is as basic as when they were babies.

Irritating though they may be, Cognitive Corner residents serve a valuable function. Because they can still communicate, they are the unwilling spokespeople for the less capable. They demand a standard for food and care that the others can't express for themselves, so they all benefit. They are the last line of defense, and like cornered animals anywhere, they must be approached with care.

"WHAT THE hell do you wear to a meeting with a bunch of bird brains?" Clarice asked Kit Kat who was rolling in the pile of clothes she'd tossed on her bed. "Especially when two of them are the boss and Mrs. Boss. What is her name again? Tammy? Tweetie?"

Clarice was getting ready to attend the evening meeting of the Olympic Birders in order to request a donation toward bird seed. She envisioned everyone sitting around in khaki walking shorts and pith helmets, binoculars hanging from their necks.

When she'd put on her dress slacks, they'd slid right back down her hips. She was thrilled until she realized she had nothing to wear but her work clothes. And no time for a complex tailoring job. So she'd explored the depths of her closet, excavated an A-line skirt from the back of beyond and run simple seams up the sides to take it in. Her new bittersweet-toned sweater went rather well with it, as did the amber beads that had been a gift from Dickhead before he pulled up stakes.

Since Kit Kat had shredded her only pair of panty hose, she would have to go bare legged. That meant shaving them, damn it. But she noticed that the job had grown a great deal easier now that reaching the backsides of her calves wasn't an aerobic exercise.

– *I can shave my legs all the way around.*

Clarice arrived at the library a half hour before the meeting. She didn't want to enter the conference room before Jeff and whatever the hell her name was, so she spent the time skulking in the stacks. She felt all conversation stop when she finally entered the conference room, but of course this wasn't true. It was just her reluctance to mingle.

"Clarice!" Jeff said in some surprise. "How diff... nice you look. Have you met my wife, Terri?"

The round faced woman launched herself to grab Clarice's hand as eagerly as a pup learning shake-a-paw. "I'm so pleased to meet you, Clarice. Jeff told me how interested you are in birds, and what a wonderful idea you have for Soundside. I think it is brilliant."

"Oh, well, sure," she stammered. *Me? Interested in birds? My idea?* "Nothing's too good for Soundside."

"Come sit next to me. We'll get to know each other better after the meeting."

There were eighteen people in the room, none of them in safari-type gear, Clarice noticed with a slight sense of disappointment. In fact, they were quite normal looking people.

The chairwoman called for order, and everyone took seats around the conference table. It was a tight fit. They discussed the SOB project which, Clarice soon gathered, meant Save Our Beaches. The group had volunteered to join other environmental organizations on a weekend in September to clean summer refuse off Washington's public waterfronts. They also set dates for hikes during fall migratory periods on the Olympic Peninsula.

"And don't forget to sign up if you want to go to Skagit to see the snow geese and swans again this Christmas," said the chairwoman. "Next, we have a guest with a special request. Jeff?"

Jeff stood and cleared his throat. "As most of you know, I'm the administrator at Soundside Rehabilitation and Healthcare Center. Our bookkeeper, Clarice Hagadorn, came to me with a request. I thought it might be something you would like to hear. Clarice?"

"Um, thank you, Jeff. I –"

"Oh no, no, Clarice," said the chairwoman. "Come up here to the head of the table where we all can see and hear you better."

"Oh, sure. Great idea." *Where you can all see I'm fat. Fatty, fatty two by four.* It took three years to worm her way between the wall and the membership to the front of the room. She was pretty certain her face was the color of a tomato, which would be a lovely clash with the bittersweet sweater.

"Well, I think I should start by leading a sing along of *Feed the Birds,*" Clarice began with a tremble in her voice, hoping for a laugh. It never came. Some of the audience looked openly sour.

"Don't worry, dear," said the chairwoman. "Not all of us believe in feeding the birds, thinking they need to learn to survive on their own. But the rest of us think it is fine."

*Great. I stepped in a cow pie on my very first sentence.* "Then I guess I am here to speak to the rest of you who think it's fine." Clarice opened a file folder, took out three photos, and handed them to the handsome man seated just to her right. "Could you pass these along for me?" she asked. He took a look at each then handed them on.

"These are pictures of members of the Soundside family, about whom we care very much," she said, sending a glance Jeff's way. He beamed, no doubt tickled by her use of the company line.

"The first one is Eunice. Her husband died in the nursing home last year, and now she is one of our residents. She's in her late eighties and strolls the halls, handing out cheer to anyone who wants it. She appears to thrive on this stewardship. The other residents love her. And she loves birds."

She paused as the pictures made their way down the line. "The second is Charlie. Some of you might remember him. He was the manager of Collins appliance shop on Main for ages." Some members of the group confirmed that they had, indeed, known ol' Charlie, what a good guy, always up for a joke, and how's he been, anyway?

Clarice went on. "He's been a resident at Soundside for over a year and misses being busy. He's prone to sores that keep him bed-ridden, but when he's up and about, he's very eager to help with projects like the one we have in mind.

"And the third one is Lily. She's a tough old bird herself. She told me that many song birds won't come to feeders that have low grade seed. I guess I can't tell you what she called the birds that do." This time, a couple of the birders chuckled, including the handsome man who helped her pass out the photos.

"This project is for Eunice and Charlie and Lily and all the other people at Soundside who can benefit from the comfort of wild things, still out in the world living free lives with a little help from their friends." As she said it, Clarice suddenly realized she meant it. She was beginning to care about the birds that could so easily give the residents a little bit of joy. And the residents that could give joy to anyone who got to know them. *Good God, don't let me start to bellar.*

"Northland Garden Center donated birdfeeders to us. But we need better seed. If Olympic Birders would consider donating toward seed for Soundside, Charlie has volunteered to fill the feeders. Eunice and Lily have volunteered to teach the other residents about birds. And I will ask my coworkers to help me keep the feeders clean and filled." Clarice figured she could convince the Staff Benefit Committee to help. *Hell, Babs can be talked into anything.*

"As the Soundside bookkeeper, I have tried to estimate the amount of seed we might need, but you know more about birds than I do, so I am sure you'd be better at approximating the rate at which they eat. I figured on filling fifty feeders once a week with cracked sunflower seeds. Lily told me that there would be less mess on the ground without seed casings."

"And less chance of rats," said a youngish man, no doubt one of the anti-feed faction.

"Well, that would be a good thing, too, wouldn't it? Northland has offered to provide it at half price. That would mean a donation of $312.50 every quarter. That's what it would take to put smiles on a lot of faces like Eunice and Lily and Charlie. And, I guess, me. Thank you for listening."

Clarice lunged back for her seat, eager to be out of the spotlight. A round of polite applause accompanied her to her place.

"Well, thank you so much, Clarice," said Madam Chairwoman, reclaiming the head of the table. "I'm sure you have given us a great deal to think about. If you wouldn't mind leaving now, the membership will evaluate your proposal, and we will get back to you very soon."

Clarice, surprised to be asked to get out, gathered up her folder and purse, then clambered behind the members one more time to leave the room. As she left, the handsome man handed her his business card, and whispered, "Could you give me a call tomorrow? I'd like to ask you a question."

*Did I just get a bum's rush?* Clarice wondered as she left the library and walked to her car. It hurt. She was surprised how much it mattered to her. She unlocked the car and slouched in behind the wheel. That's when she noticed the business card she still had in her hand. It said Ben Stassen, Marketing Consultant. *What the hell does he want?*

The phone was ringing when Clarice came through her kitchen door from the garage. She dropped her tote bag, leaped over Hershey and made it on the fourth ring before voice mail cut in. "Hello?" she puffed, slightly out of breath.

"Hi, Clarice. This is Terri, Jeff's wife? I am so excited! Jeff and I thought you were brilliant, with the photos and everything. Wonderful appeal. You had all us birders eating out of your hand. Well, you know what I mean." She giggled.

Clarice was too tickled to think scathing thoughts about the dreadful joke. *The birders are impressed!* "Well, thanks, Terri. That's nice to hear. I thought I offended the anti-feeding faction."

"Oh, poo. We're talking about bird feeders, not a welfare state, for heaven's sake. Anyway, you'll get an official letter and all, but I wanted to give you a hint that a thumbs up is coming your way."

Clarice couldn't believe how thrilled she felt.

*– The taste of success is not fattening at all.*

"I didn't know they'd ask you to leave so they could discuss it tonight. I was hoping to chat after the meeting. Call me when you get the letter, and we'll plan the next steps." Terri gave Clarice her number and they said good-bye.

"Hey boys," Clarice called happily to the cats. "High paws all around." But Kit Kat and Hershey were far too self-absorbed to share in Clarice's fifteen minutes of fame.

\* \* \*

Jessica was thinking about Lily and Sylvia as she drove home from Soundside that evening. It seemed to her that parents never got free of parenthood. *Maybe having a child to live for would have made it easier for me to go on without Ed.*

The thought dispersed as she turned in her drive and saw lights that didn't belong in one of the pastures. They glowed like camping lanterns. *What the...?*

She drove up the gravel track toward the barn, seeing a van parked ahead of her. As she got close the hairs on the back on her neck began to stand. The Econoline belonged to her vet, Doc McGrath. She braked hard next to it, jumped from the Toyota and yelled for Sam.

"Here, Jessica!" She heard his shout from the pasture. She scrambled over the fence then ran toward the lantern light. The dark forms of horses moved away from her like spirits in the night. Why aren't they in the barn? Why hasn't Sam...?

In a patch of light created by three lanterns she saw two humans on opposite sides of a large flat rock...no, a rolling tree trunk...no, a fallen horse. *Oh God.* She ran faster, then skidded to her knees, slipping on liquid so dark it looked black in the night. *Oil? No...the metallic scent of blood...Sam and Doc...and Latin Dancer.*

The yearling lay on his side, his light buckskin coat soaked with his own blood. Jessica tried to speak, but a knot formed in her throat. Doc McGrath never looked up, just kept cleaning and sewing and crooning an Irish lullaby to the colt. Sam cradled Dancer's head, holding his ears and the flat cheek of his head. Jessica could see the terrified whites of the yearling's eyes. And worse, strips of bloody skin hanging from its muzzle.

It was Sam who looked at her and spoke in a voice choked with anguish or fury, she couldn't tell which. "I heard him scream. Scream just like a human. I grabbed the rifle and came running." Jessica saw him shudder as if with cold. It was never easy for Sam to talk but now the story tumbled out. "The other horses were running but Dancer was standing his ground, head down and teeth bared. Like a boy soldier, protecting the herd." He grunted, struggling with the frightened horse as it tried to fling its head away from the pain.

Finally, Jessica found her voice, just a small sound squeezing past the knot. "What did this, Sam? Was it a cougar? A bear?"

"No, dogs. A pack of feral dogs. They attacked him from both sides. Smart as hyenas. I shot in the air. Most of them took off. But one clamped on. It hung from Dancer's head when he tried to shake it off. I finally shot it…over there." He indicated the direction with his head, and Jessica saw the carcass. "Jesus, I hated to shoot a dog, but it could have killed the colt."

Jessica glanced at the body again then locked her eyes on Dancer. He struggled, but Sam held him down as the vet worked on a jagged tear on the cannon, below the knee. "Easy for dogs to reach him down here," Doc McGrath spoke before returning to the lullaby in a surprisingly haunting tenor.

"Let me help you, Sam," Jessica said, adding her strength at the crest of Dancer's neck far above the withers. The yearling could not rise if he couldn't get his head up first.

"Is he…is he?" Jessica said but couldn't finish.

"Is he going to die?" Doc said looking up at her. His open face had never saved her with well intentioned lies before, and Jessica didn't require it now. Anyone who worked with livestock knew the countless ways animals could damage themselves. Of all the risks in the business, it was the scariest.

McGrath was a crafty doctor when he wasn't riding a barstool at the town taverns, and Jessica was very grateful to have him here now. "Not from the wounds themselves, but infection could set into any of this mess. And he's lost a lot of blood." He went on with his work while he talked. "I've given him antibiotics and Sam helped me get him down so I could work out here to stop some of the bleeding. I've sutured what I can see, and I don't feel any broken bones. But the first tranq is wearing off."

Doc leaned back into a squat then stood, his knee joints popping. "Let's get him up and into the barn to start on the other side." Sam and Jessica released their grip. "Okay, son, let's see what you're made of," McGrath entreated.

Dancer tossed his head, using the momentum to help rise off his side. Next, he lifted his weight on his forelegs and stood. He trembled from the effort. Blood oozed from the sutures on his left, and the wounds still open on his right ran freely. Jessica spoke low encouragement to him as she took his halter and slowly began the trek to his stall. The shredded skin on his muzzle terrified her.

"If we can get him to heal," Doc warned, "he's going to carry some scars."

Jessica walked, talking to Dancer calmly. It was a massive effort since she mainly wanted to shriek and shake her fist at the sky. She was aware Doc was now frowning at the limping horse's right foreleg. Then he nodded at the dog carcass as they passed it. "I'll have animal control come tomorrow and look for the rest of the pack. We'll check that one for rabies…and any others we can catch."

She could hear Latin Lover whinnying from inside the barn, and she fancied she heard dogs howling far in the distance. Other horses, calmer now, began to close in around them, curious about the injured member of their herd. When Latin Lover whinnied again, Sam explained. "I hadn't let the others in, or him out for the night when all this happened. So he was in the barn."

"That's one good thing at least." Jessica didn't think she could survive an attack on Latin Lover. He was her first Paso Fino, the one that started her business, a present from Ed. It was bad enough that the victim was his son.

Once they got to Dancer's stall, Jessica said to Sam, "You need to get the rest inside in case the dogs come back." The herd was eager to comply so it didn't take Sam long. After he offered them food and comfort, he soothed Latin Lover, settling him down by his presence alone.

"He's magic with horses," Doc McGrath said as he completed a visual examination on Dancer, now in the lighted barn. He had Jessica help lay the colt down again, this time with the right side up. Another tranquilizer was administered. Jessica worked ahead of the vet, cleaning wounds with gauze and sterile saline. None of the bites in the abdomen were deep, but a tearing gash down the right shoulder was ugly. A bite into the forearm was the deepest. The vet worked steadily, stitching and bandaging. Jessica couldn't watch as he clipped the hanging skin from Dancer's muzzle.

During the long night, Sam went to his trailer and came back with a thermos of coffee. He repeated the trip and repeated it once again. Finally, in the hours before dawn, the job was done. The colt was quiet, and the makeshift medical team was exhausted.

"It'll be a bitch to heal," Doc said staring at the wrap around Dancer's foreleg. "Hard to keep a youngster quiet. Let him up when he's ready, but keep him in here. No pasture yet. I'll be back this afternoon to change some of the wraps and give him more antibiotics."

He turned to go, then spun back with an expression on his face that looked dangerously like defeat. "And be prepared, Jessica. He might not be doing much dancing from now on. We'll have to see."

Jessica sat in the cedar shavings holding the youngster's head. *Not doing much dancing from now on.* It was a bleak diagnosis for a Paso Fino who was all about the sophisticated steps of the corto or the largo unique to their breed.

Sam materialized with a blanket and wrapped it around her. Then he sat next to her in the cedar shavings in the stall. They started a vigil that would last until the horse stirred.

"My gut says he'll live, Jessica."

"Maybe. But he'll never be a show horse now." Without a show record of his own, he'd never command the same high stud fees as his sire. The loss was as crippling to her business as it was to her colt.

"I'm sorry." Sam said.

"Sorry? Don't be Sam. You saved his life." *Now if you could just save the ranch.*

She raised her arm and made room for the old man under the blanket, too. The two of them sat through the rest of the night. *This is enough child rearing for me.*

## FIFTEEN

## FUN HOUSE CHRONICLE
# Violet

*S*he is delivered by the paramedics late one night and holes up in her room for a time. But at last, Violet is steered out in a reclining wheelchair and parked in the hall, moving little, talking not at all. She is the victim of a vicious stroke.

*For days, this broken woman is a true Shrinking Violet. But then she starts to moan. The moan becomes the growl of a cornered badger. It is low and long and mean. With a hand that has been heretofore immobile, Violet flips up her nightgown, grabs her catheter and begins to yank. Visitors passing in the hall gather around, flapping their hands and screaming EEEEAHHHH! One woman tries to pull Violet's gown down to cover her wide open spaces, only to be soundly kicked in the chest.*

*A nurse, two aides and the Activities Director arrive to calm Violet, all the while preaching the importance of leaving the catheter alone. At last, Violet feigns sleep. Everyone goes about their business.*

*Within seconds, the gown is up and Violet is hauling on the catheter again, wanting free of this leash. She is whisked back to her room and not seen again for several days by which time the catheter has been removed, presumably by some process gentler than popping a*

> *recalcitrant cork from a bottle. In the weeks that follow, Violet regains some speech and mobility. She is as untrustworthy as a komodo dragon. Other residents steer clear. Nurses learn to duck and weave when giving her meds.*
>
> *An herbalist might tell you that a violet symbolizes confidence in new opportunities. But this Violet, who is completely dependent on her caregivers, trusts nothing. Obstinate, noncompliant, disobedient, this wild Violet soldiers on.*

BEAR'S PAST as a Private Investigator fascinated Eunice. He told her story after story of his youthful exploits, and she seemed to adore each one more than the last. She'd gasp and duck and yell "Pow!" at all the appropriate points, her face resembling an exhilarated prune.

Lily was pretty sure some of these exploits were old episodes of *Magnum, P.I.* and *The Rockford Files.* Besides, if Bear had as many flesh wounds as he claimed, he'd look like Belgium lace. And if that weren't proof enough of perfidy, he winked at Lily when he told Eunice a real whopper. But what the hell did it matter? It was a more spirited way to spend the evening than watching Soundside's 128th showing of *Mary Poppins.*

*Tonight he's going to outdo himself.* Lily watched the big man wheel into the parlor, his shirt collar pulled up like a makeshift trench coat. He slunk low in his chair, shifting his small eyes warily side to side. A hanger hooked on the chair handle was festooned with a tiny print blouse so colorful it could put Peter Max to shame.

Eunice inhaled like a child at Christmas, her mouth and eyes round as ping pong balls. "My blouse! You found my blouse!" It had been missing for several weeks, another victim of the laundry's black hole. Eunice had fussed about its loss without much interest from Bear, until his own best pair of sweatpants disappeared.

"Goddamn it to hell," Bear had roared. "Pants that fit a guy my size shouldn't be all that easy to misplace. The only replacements they have around here belonged to the last fat man they found face down. Probably died in them. Ugh."

"Where did you find the blouse?" Lily asked, playing Watson to Bear's amazing find.

He served up the story with a dash of hard-boiled grit. He'd interviewed all members of what he called the Lost In the Laundry Gang. "They claimed I'm all wet. Said they'd never come clean. Stuck together like iron-on patches –"

Lily couldn't take any more. "Okay, okay, we got it. Then what happened?"

Next Bear had enlisted the help of Alita. "I sent her in undercover as a housekeeper."

"She is a housekeeper, isn't she?" Eunice asked.

"Alluring Alita, the men call her. The doll with the long, long legs that go from here to heaven." His really bad Sam Spade was getting worse. "I spun her a tale of loss among the inmates. Carcasses without clothes. Bare butts and balls and boobs. Told her we're all feeling lower than a rolled-over dime. Only a sharp sighted, sharp looking vixen like her could pick us off the Fun House floor. I warned her to keep her eyes open and her mouth closed. To watch out for the dirt bags from the Lost In the Laundry

Gang. Especially Big Mama Iron Hand who'd gladly put her through the wringer."

"I'm warning you Bear," Lily mustered a growl herself. "Not one more wash day word play."

He ignored her. "I stood guard, ready to sound the alarm as she slipped in and out of each room just as cool as slipping between the sheets. Her only weapons were a bucket and mop. She swished to every wardrobe door then peeked inside. At last she found the hide-away."

"Where, Bear?" Eunice gasped.

"A dozen different garments were stashed away in an empty room. Big Mama claims they were misdelivered to a resident who exited long ago." Bear pointed to his oversized chest. "I claim we saved them from the slave trade between here and Goodwill. Case closed, ladies."

"You are so full of shit," Lily said.

"You are my hero," Eunice said.

And from another grouping of chairs in the parlor, Charlie said, "You think you could find my missing wife? I haven't seen her around here for weeks."

*  *  *

"I hired a bookkeeper today," Ben called down the length of the barn from the stall where he was removing a tangle from Gina Lola's mane. "I just never get around to doing the paperwork. Hate it."

Jessica was in an end stall, with Latin Dancer. A large part of each day was spent medicating the colt and keeping him quiet. "I could use some help in that department, too," Jessica said quietly, not wanting to startle the youngster. She envisioned the explosion of aging bills in her office.

Plus some new budget busters from Doc McGrath. *What a mess. I have to start looking for work. But I can't leave the horse. But I can't afford the horse if I can't leave the horse. Shit.*

Ben appeared at the stall's door. Jessica was sitting in the cedar curls, smoothing an antibiotic cream onto Dancer's pasterns. The colt was a mass of stitches and wounds but seemed to be healing. He snorted and pricked his ears when he saw Ben. "How you doing, youngster?" Ben said putting out a hand and scratching the skin under the yearling's chin, carefully avoiding the injured muzzle. Dancer slowly relaxed and even leaned into the gesture with pleasure.

"Oh, that's good!" Jessica exclaimed, feeling a burst of pleasure in this lousy day. "I've been worried he's displaying a new shyness around strangers. That the attack made him leery of the world at large."

"I'm no stranger, am I bud? We're old friends." Ben turned from Dancer to Jessica. She saw the sadness in his eyes. "A damn shame, Jess. He's such a fine animal. What's his prognosis?"

She shrugged. "Well, he has the heart to recover. And the rabies test was negative. Doc's mostly worried about the right front leg and whether the limp will be permanent. Even if it isn't, Dancer will never be the top earner that I had in mind for him."

"I can give you the bookkeeper's number. Let her help with the worrying. Her name's Clarice Hagadorn."

"Clarice? I know her," Jessica said in surprise, pausing in mid stroke of cream on ankle. "She works at the nursing home where Lily is, right? She's not leaving, is she?"

"No. That's her day job. I just need a few hours, and she says she can do it in the evening."

"That's okay then. I'd hate to see her leave. Lily likes her. And there's not much to like in a nursing home." Jessica stood and wiped the cedar shavings off her butt. She gave the yearling a pat on the neck and left the stall. "I hated visiting there at first. But I'm getting to know the residents as individuals now. I like a lot of them. Staff, too."

Ben looked impressed. "You're a damn sight better at this compassion stuff than I ever was. I never got that far when I visited Rachel in rehab. She was a big enough problem that I didn't want to think about all the others."

Ed had once told Jessica how Ben's girl fought addiction with little success. "I'm sorry about your daughter, Ben."

"Yeah, well, I'll tell you all about it one day when we both would like to feel like crap. But for now, I have a proposition for you."

"*Proposition?*" She raised one eyebrow. "Then come into my field office, and have a seat." They walked to the tack area and sat, Ben on a sawhorse between saddles and Jessica on an empty paint pail that she flipped upside down. "What do you have in mind?"

"I've been looking for a saddle horse."

"Instead of Gina Lola?" Jessica was so taken aback she nearly lost her balance on the bucket.

"No, of course not." Ben reached over and grabbed her shoulders helping her right herself. "In addition to Gina Lola."

"Oh. Okay then."

"I'd like a good trail horse, and you've about convinced me that a Paso Fino is the only way to go."

"Absolutely! Why, not only Latin Lover but my mares are –"

"Will you button it so I can make my pitch? I've been looking but not finding just what I want. So here's my thought. If he recovers sound, I'd like to buy Latin Dancer, and hire you to train him. Then I'd know the job's done right."

"Buy Dancer? Ben, he's a mess. He'll always have scars, and I think he might have some problems with fear now."

"Jess, I don't care about a show horse. I want a first rate pleasure horse. If anyone can work through his issues, you can. You're a great trainer."

Thoughts and emotions tumbled and shoved their way across her brain. *Sell Dancer? I wanted him for myself. But the money...if Ben owned him, and I trained him, it would sort of be like Dancer was still mine. Or is Ben offering just because I complained about business? Who cares?* She felt a world of worry lift from her shoulders. The sale wouldn't see her out of the woods, but it would keep the stable in oats while she figured out what to do next.

*But wait.* She had to ask. "If I agree, it won't change things, right? I mean, no obligations..."

Ben rolled his eyes. "Other than as a horse trainer? No. If you ever feel obligated to me, it'll be because you want to be."

*Maybe I do want to be. Maybe I do.* But she stayed focused on the deal, and their negotiations continued. By the end, they had decided that Ben would pay the purchase price, get a cut rate for boarding, and ride one of Jessica's mares until Latin Dancer proved his worth as a saddle horse.

"I'll also provide dinner and a creepy movie each Wednesday. I like to cook as long as you don't mind another chef in your kitchen," Ben said.

"Fine by me. I feel about cooking like you feel about paperwork."

"I know."

"You do? How did you know that?"

Ben looked sheepish. And appeared speechless.

She quickly went from a question to a glare. "Okay, Bennett Stassen, what did Ed the Evil tell you?"

From a nearby stall, they heard Sam or one of the horses begin to chuckle. It was a low heh heh heh that really could have been either. Jessica jumped up from the bucket and stood arms akimbo in front of Ben.

"I'm not telling," said Ben. "I'm just a customer here."

"Sam?" she yelled sternly.

"Just a worker here, ma'am."

"Yeah, but I can threaten you."

Pause. "He said it was hard to tell the difference between your cinnamon buns and the horse buns –"

"He never!"

"– but that it didn't matter much because your coffee killed the taste of pretty much anything."

Jessica turned a spectacular shade of pink as the two men burst into laughter. Finally, Ben put an arm around her, bent down and whispered, "Who cares, Jess? Your buns are just fine with me."

*Did he just wipe the last of the cedar shavings off my ass or was that a caress?*

\* \* \*

True to their bargain, Ben came to ride one of her mares, and he made dinner on Wednesday, even delivering a tray to Sam in his motor home. He took Dancer for his first slow walk around the pasture, side by side with Gina Lola. The steady presence of the old girl seemed to calm the colt.

Ben's cooking was far better than her own, and Jessica enjoyed learning kitchen tricks from him. However, she was miffed when he had the grit to start rearranging her equipment. "The salad bowl goes there," she said pointing to the top of fridge.

"Not anymore," he said, putting it in a lower cabinet where he had nested all serving dishes inside her huge popcorn bowl.

"I won't think to look for it there." *Dammit, it's my bowl.*

"Then you'll have to keep me around," Ben answered with a smile. "But if you insist…"

"Oh, no. Have it your way."

If there was one thing she had learned about men, it was the wisdom of choosing your arguments. Ed the Evil hadn't listened to her when she asked him not to drive at night or in shitty weather. And if she were honest, it wasn't the only time her wishes took a back seat to his. Would there be more give and take with someone like Ben? He really did seem to be pretty easy going. And he really did have the most intriguing hollow just below his jaw line.

After dinner, they drove to the waterfront and parked, then slowly ambled along the beach. It was Folly's favorite walk. The cocker/dachshund mix loved rooting under driftwood for dead crabs or zigzagging behind sandpipers.

As they ambled, Ben slowly and painfully told Jessica the story of his daughter, which started with his ex-wife. "She called me at work to tell me she'd bought some new shoes, and that she was going to take a walk to break them in. She never came back. You can't say the woman didn't have a sense of humor."

"How could anybody be so cold?" Jessica wished the ex hellfire and damnation.

"Neither one of us was much interested in the marriage by then, so it wasn't too hard on me. But Rachel surely felt abandoned."

"Well she was," Jessica said, upset for Ben's daughter now, too. "What an awful thing to do to your child."

Ben nodded as they walked along, dodging the small waves lapping up the beach. "Her mother made it perfectly clear she didn't want any more to do with either one of us. Rachel was, what, maybe twelve then and a bundle of preteen angst. I didn't help her with abandonment issues either. I worked long hours making my business a success. Never had enough time for my daughter. So she filled in with drugs and boys. Oldest story in the book."

He sat down on a large log that had possibly floated all the way from British Columbia before beaching decades ago. Jessica sat in the sand in front of him, and listened to his story while she picked burrs out of Folly's coat.

"Drugs eventually won out, and she disappeared into the streets. I found her and brought her home three times. Rehab failed each time. When she turned eighteen there was no way I could make her come home anymore."

Jessica looked around and up at him. "Do you ever see her?"

"Not much. She calls sometimes. She's still somewhere in Seattle as far as I know. I want her home but only if she's clean."

Jessica leaned back against his legs and watched the passenger ferry cross over from the Olympic Peninsula. *What damage we do.* "She's not all I want in my life, Jess. You know that." He bent forward and kissed her softly on the top of her head. "I am considered quite a catch in some circles."

Jessica leaned against him a bit more.

"I have fallen for a younger woman who is still mourning a lost love. I don't want to deny you the good memories, just to add more to your life. My only baggage is a screwed up daughter, and it's up to you whether you want to let her take a shot at your heart like she has at mine." He kissed her earlobe. "I don't demand marriage, but I would like that as a goal if you would consider it." He moved down to kiss her neck, his breath warm on her ear.

She sat as still as if she were meditating. She thought again about Lily's advice. And then, her decision was made. It wasn't love at first sight. But it might well grow into something with deeper roots and greater promise. It was worth a try.

She lifted herself onto her knees, turned toward him and looked him in the eyes. "You know, Ben, I think we'll be kissing a lot from now on. So I think I'd like to practice right now."

## SIXTEEN

**FUN HOUSE CHRONICLE**
# CNAs

*There are people who choose to help others dress, bathe, eat, toilet, turn over, and move. If unpaid and working with babies, these people are called parents. If paid and working with the elderly, they are called Certified Nursing Assistants.*

*Arnie was the perfect CNA, pleasant, attractive, a good worker. He wooed another aide, Sherri, so she and her children made room for him in their home and hearts. One night he picked her up and threw her across the room, while her children watched. He threw her again. And again, this time slamming her into a wall. She was hospitalized with torn muscles; he was arrested. The police found multiple complaints of assault and three open warrants against him from other counties at the time of his arrest. And yet, this man was employed to work with the fragile population at a nursing home.*

*Many care facilities are desperate for quality personnel. As Baby Boomers age and take to their beds, there may be no one to empty the bedpans. A Certified Nursing Assistant needs no prior medical experience, and training to receive a certificate takes as little as three weeks. In theory, CNAs have submitted to drug testing and criminal background checks and display loving, nurturing natures.*

*But ask Sherri, and she would disagree.*

FOR JEFF, that night was a special delivery straight from hell. Damn near the worst thing possible had happened well after midnight. He wanted nothing more than to commit murder.

A new resident had been moved into Eunice Taylor's room. Olivia Carlton was hazy and confused, recovering from a stroke. During the small hours, Eunice was awakened by strange noises on the other side of the curtain. She heard Mrs. Carlton moan and say something about pain. Then she heard a rustling of clothing and sheets. A body moving on a bed and more whimpering. Then a voice said, "This is how we give pain relief around here."

As the crying increased, Eunice sat up, reached out as far as she could and pulled back the curtain. "What's going on…" she said. Then she screamed. And screamed. The man, an aide she'd never seen before, rushed past her and out of the room.

The night nurse could not calm her. Following Jeff's standing orders, she called him at home. "I don't know what happened. But Mrs. Carlton can't speak clear enough for me to understand, and Eunice won't stop crying. Maybe she was dreaming, but she seems terrified. What should I do?"

Jeff knew he must get to Eunice. He pulled on his pants and left the house. The night traffic was light. A car careened out of the lot as he turned in. It took him just seconds to run down the hall to her room.

The nurse backed away and he replaced her, cringing at the fear in Eunice's face. "I've known you for a long, long time, Eunice," he said, stroking her hair. He put his arms around the fragile old body, and she allowed it to happen. He whispered, "Tell me."

And so she did. When she had thrown back the curtain, she had seen Olivia Carlton in bed. The sheets were pulled down and her nightgown pulled up. A man dressed in scrubs stood beside her, with one hand pressing down on her naked stomach, his other arm between her legs, holding her knees apart with his elbow. Eunice believed he had his fingers inserted in her vagina.

"But that can't be, can it? Nobody would do that," she sobbed. "Nobody."

Jeff was nearly speechless, but far from stunned. Resident abuse was the living nightmare of every administrator. Somehow, he managed to convince Eunice she was safe, and that Mrs. Carlton was safe. He would take care of everything. Finally, Eunice began to calm. She was still sitting up in bed, clutching a pillow to her chest. But her trembling was getting back under control. Jeff's gentle voice finally relaxed her enough to lie back down.

Jeff asked the night nurse to examine Mrs. Carlton while he went to hunt down the aide. *I'll murder the bastard.* But the man, a temp provided by an agency, was gone. *The car leaving when I pulled in...that was him.*

"I believe he violated a sick old woman," he told the police officer who responded to his call. "But I can't prove it. Mrs. Carlton is not, um, coherent enough to talk or maybe even to remember. The only witness can't believe what she thinks she saw could possibly have happened.

She is distraught."

He stayed in the room while the officer spoke with Eunice. The night nurse joined them. But Eunice could not be sure of anything.

*No proof. No fucking proof.* The cop told him they would look for the guy, maybe scare him some. But with no witness, what more could they do?

"For Mrs. Carlton's sake, let's try to keep this as private as we can," Jeff said to the night nurse, who agreed.

The special delivery from hell went through the rest of the night well into the following morning. Jeff sat in his office, unshaven, in a rumpled pajama top, feeling beaten. He was so upset the desk was actually cluttered. Lia quietly brought him cup after cup of coffee and warned people away from his office.

He felt awful. Trapped. Emasculated by corporate intervention.

He had called the medical employment agency at first light. CompreCare used the organization to fill temporary staff vacancies. It had provided the son of a bitch. Jeff was outraged to the point of tears, even after the service said they would fire the monster. He wanted full disclosure of how the bastard ever slipped through their safety net. They told him that criminal background checks were so flawed. A check, they maintained, could only catch someone convicted, not charged or even excused with a plea bargain. Worse yet, the agency intended to do no more than fire the man, claiming there was nothing more they could do.

Jeff didn't buy it. He was pushing the agency to improve its hiring requirements so that such an ogre would never darken his door again. At least he had pushed until a call from the corporate office came in on another line.

When he took the call, they gagged him. Cut him off at the knees. Both the agency and CompreCare wanted the matter resolved without public scrutiny if at all possible. He had been indiscreet in his comments to the police. Soundside might suffer. And that was the end of that. Oh, and one more thing. The CompreCare management requested his presence in the home office in Portland, Oregon in two week's time to discuss that matter further.

He had other things he must do. He looked down at a pile of resumes. That butthead Jimbo had resigned so Jeff was elbow deep in candidates for the maintenance role. Next to the resumes was an evaluation form for the cheese strata – whatever the hell that was – that the kitchen had introduced to the residents.

The only good thing was the message from his wife saying Clarice had joined the Olympic Birders. Clarice's new role as Terri's protégé took pressure off him to attend all events. Without knowing it, Clarice became his only solace in the night from hell.

\* \* \*

Lily had less and less to offer in conversations with visitors from the outside, feeling distanced from the active lives her guests lived. She hated the stress of searching for anything relevant to say. Even more, she hated their discomfort when the chitchat ran out. Jessica was her one exception. The girl had never known Lily as a healthy woman. Their visits weren't savaged by memories of what had been.

Relationships formed inside the Fun House were Lily's new reality. She hadn't expected any such thing, but

Eunice had told her it wasn't uncommon. "When I visited my husband for so long, I watched it happen again and again. It dismays family members when their loved one appears more interested in goings-on here than at home. But, all in all, I think it's a good thing."

Chrissie brought her kids and her boyfriend to meet her fave. Clarice was so droll she could make Lily laugh out loud. Ernie was a godsend. Rick entertained with outrageous tales of his success with girls. When Nurse Mary Beth found out that Lily actually understood Gladys, she enlisted her help as a translator.

Most residents were too sick, depressed or nuts to befriend. But Bear and Eunice and Lily sought each other out, with Charlie sometimes joining in if he was having a good day. Their bodies might be wrecks, but their wits were as lively as ever. Bear started referring to them as Cognitive Corner.

Charlie was in the parlor looking through a *Newsweek*, while Bear and Lily were playing paper scissors rock over possession of the crossword. It was peaceful. But then Eunice tottered in and whispered to them all, "I need to talk."

"Eunice!" Lily said, alarmed by the pallor of the normally sunny face. "What's wrong?"

Eunice told them what she had seen the night before, in a voice as sad as a mourning dove. "I think I saw it. But I can't imagine something like that. Could I have dreamed it? Am I as crazy as a traveler?"

"Of course not…no way… can't be," Cognitive Corner responded. Bear's deep rumble rose to the top. "There's plenty of evil in the world, Eunice. Some of the slimiest visited your room last night."

"What happened afterwards?" Lily asked.

"Jeff was wonderful." She told them how he'd helped her, called the cops, and told her that he and the night nurse agreed to keep it private for Mrs. Carlton's sake.

"So we should, too," Lily said, looking around quickly to confirm they were not overheard.

"We can do better than that," Bear said. He outlined a plan. From then on, Cognitive Corner would be on the alert on nights when an unknown male came from the agency. Each of them could handle two hours a night on watch. Hell, only Charlie slept all that well anyway.

"Like our own Neighborhood Watch!" Eunice exclaimed.

"Exactly," Bear said then patted her bird-like hand with his huge paw.

"You think it's dangerous?" Charlie asked.

"Could be, but who cares? We're the only ones who can do it." Lily knew the nurses were too busy to roam the halls, dogging strangers.

"You're right. We're not just helpless old fossils," Charlie said, shooting both thumbs up. "But when it happens, I have to take the first shift. None of you could wake me up once I go asleep."

Nobody would be violated again. Not on their watch. Lily saw the color come back to Eunice's face and the determination on Bear's and the pride on Charlie's. She felt the strength in their bond. *An action plan!*

She was still thinking about it when she rolled back to her own room. Gladys was peering at the tapestry jewelry box Sylvia had brought her. The old salt smiled at Lily, patted the box, and cooed, "Treasure chest."

"It's pretty, isn't it?" said Lily parking next to the crone. Lily ran her own hand across the case. "It's an antique, like us. A wedding present from my husband. And look at this." She opened the hinged top. "I keep his medals in this top part. And these pictures he sent from Nam. See?"

Slowly, Lily lowered the lid. "I don't have much jewelry and it's not worth a thing. But I keep it in these drawers." Gladys gasped when Lily slid opened the first little compartment.

That evening, Gladys buggered off for dinner dripping in jet beads. Lily sat alone in their room with her tray. It had been a day of drama, sorrow, friendship, solidarity. *Ah, family life.*

\* \* \*

Sylvia wasted no time staging Lily's house so Kyle could put it up for sale as soon as possible. She and Jessica began by tackling the garage. They surveyed the two-car space, now used for storage. Sylvia remembered selling the car when her mother had scared her to death with it. *Did she do that driveway wheelie on purpose?*

There was really not a lot to go through, Sylvia decided as she surveyed the project. "Mother moved us across the country every twenty minutes. We didn't build up a lot of clutter," Sylvia said to Jessica. "We'll need room to bring things from the house out here for a garage sale. So let's stack the keepers along that wall, and put anything for the dump out in the driveway."

The sale pile included old luggage, a small gas grill, a fat-tired three speed bike, LP albums and a plastic bin of curling ribbon, raffia, sheets of organdy, a grafting knife and other florist equipment. "Did you know that crock pots are the single most common garage sale item?" Jessica said to Sylvia as she pulled one from a large box of cookware. "Lily must have stayed in one place at least long enough to make slow-cooked meals."

Sylvia wondered if Jessica was making fun of her. *So what if she is? It was kind of funny.* "Minute steaks were our safest menu choice."

Jessica laughed as she replaced the pot and dragged the cookware box to the designated sale wall. Sylvia decided it was pleasant to work alongside a...a what? The barrier between employee and friend was getting pretty damn permeable. Her twinge of jealousy toward Jessica had evaporated since her mother had gone on record about her own worth.

"What's all this for?" Jessica asked staring at a joiner, heat press and glass cutter that were stacked in one corner.

"Lily was a picture framer, after she was a florist, after she worked in a dental lab."

"I hope we don't come across a box full of dentures." Jessica opened another bedraggled carton. She picked a handful of paperback books off the top layer. On the covers long haired beauties writhed in front of men who had lost their shirts. "Old romance novels. Steamy stuff."

"I wonder who owned them?" Sylvia asked. *Aurora, maybe?*

"Uh...Lily?"

"Oh, no. I don't think she ever read romances. She just had romances."

They continued lifting and opening and sorting. *Now let's see. What has mother told me about her? Oh yes.* "You raise horses, isn't that right?"

"Oh yes," Jessica said. "In fact, one of my mares just foaled. A filly. I spend a lot of time petting her, getting her used to people. Imprinting, it's called. Suppose to make them easier to raise and train. I imagine I'll have to sell her before I find out."

Sylvia heard the sorrow, but didn't understand. *Isn't that what the horses were for? To raise them and sell them?* She turned back to deciding what to sell, and she proved ruthless, setting aside almost nothing to keep for herself. As a designer she disliked clutter and the things that had been relegated from her mother's house to garage would only add disorder to her own home.

But one old cardboard box stopped her in her tracks when she opened it. Yellowing tissue paper was wrapped snuggly around a bundle that looked like a miniature mummy. Sylvia carefully opened it, the tissue shredding easily when she tugged at it. "Lucy!" she exclaimed. She picked the doll up and its eyes opened, revealing periwinkle blue irises. "Momma," it cried as Sylvia held it upright, then cradled it in her arms. She sat on an old bar stool that was awaiting its turn to be hauled to the keeper pile.

"Lucy?" Jessica asked, abandoning the sewing machine she had just unearthed.

Sylvia patted down the doll's curly mop of red hair. "She was my best friend when I was growing up." Sylvia told Jessica the story of the head transfer from one doll body to another. "I just can't believe Mother kept her all these years."

"She knew you'd like it one day."

"I suppose she must have." Sylvia couldn't have been more surprised. She propped Lucy on her lap, dug further into the box, and found the doll's wardrobe, handcrafted by Lily. There was the little cowgirl outfit, in black polished cotton, with white fringe. A hand embroidered pony galloped across the vest.

"Look at that tiny stitching," said Jessica.

"Mother was good at this stuff. Look at this." Sylvia held up a beautiful little ruby red velveteen dress with a dropped waist. "I remember her making these puffed sleeves, with the material held around two fingers." Her mother made this party dress while she and Lucy watched in awe that something so beautiful was for them. The memory clutched her heart and squeezed until she had to turn away from Jessica. "I guess we better keep moving if we're ever going to finish," she said, her voice grown husky.

Jessica went back to work, but Sylvia lingered over the box of memories. On the bottom, she found her childhood notebooks, school projects, and scrapbooks. There was a pad of her drawings of impossibly endowed ladies in outlandish fashions. A stack of report cards from half a dozen different schools. Ticket stubs to movies and concerts and museums that her mother and she had attended together. The gardenia from a prom corsage, pressed and dried. Class photos of the pretty, winsome girl she had been. Letters to her from her mother's one time lover, Paul.

She was stunned by this collection. She believed her childhood had passed virtually unnoticed by her mother in the shuffle from state to state. Instead, bits and pieces of it had been preserved wherever they went.

"I never really understood my mother," she said quietly, not expecting an answer and not getting one.

The memory box wasn't the only surprise Sylvia uncovered that day. Once they created enough room in the garage, Jessica carried out things from the hall, guest room and linen closets for the sale. Sylvia took on her mother's bedroom. She had already delivered the jewelry case to the nursing home, but it was time to go through the rest of Lily's personal items.

The closet was a jumble of sweaters, blouses and pants hanging willy-nilly. Sylvia's own closets were organized by season, purpose and color. She started the excavation by packing a tote to take to Soundside. Then she selected clothes for the garage sale and bagged the rest for Goodwill. When she got to the bottom of the closet, she realized that Lily had thrown out all shoes for a left foot. *I don't know…hilarious or heartrending?*

In the very back of the closet, she found the only item hung with any particular care. She unzipped the heavy garment bag to reveal her father's uniform. She had last seen it when they moved here twenty-five years ago. Sylvia set it aside to take home with her, handling it with the respect it deserved. When finished with the closet, she called Lily. "We've done the garage, Mom, and I'm going through clothes. I'll take a couple of your winter coats home with me to store, but do you want any jackets there?"

"No, no I have plenty here. But there is one thing I'd like you to bring."

"Just name it." Sylvia was feeling particularly warm toward her mother for keeping Lucy safe all these years.

"Take a look in my nightstand, the bottom drawer. You'll find some letters with a rubber band around them."

"Okay, I'm looking." She opened the drawer and shuffled aside the heating pad, book of crossword puzzles, sunglasses, a half package of soda crackers, and travel size packs of tissues. Underneath, Sylvia found the bundle.

*Love letters from Dad?* But as she lifted them closer she saw they came from Nguyen Duc Trai of Ho Chi Minh City.

*Nguyen Duc who?* "I found some letters from someone in Vietnam. Is that what you mean?"

"Yes, yes bring them next time you visit."

"Who is he?"

"I'll explain then."

Another secret. Her mother was becoming a regular Mata Hari.

\* \* \*

*Hot damn!* Clarice leaped off the Soundside scale and did a happy dance. *Another four pounds!* She'd lost enough already that her granny panties had bagged in the butt. For the first time in years, she'd purchased some lacy little numbers called high cut. She couldn't really feel them clinging to her skin as she strutted down the hall to her office, but she loved that they were there.

– *Today high cuts, tomorrow thongs.*

It was a busy month for somebody who used to have no more involvement in Soundside than doing its books. The auction ended, and Clarice handled the money. Babs announced the results to the Staff Benefits Committee. "All of the gift baskets sold, averaging a $42 profit each. Add in the $20 match from Soundside, and we have enough funds for a real buffet with dancing and a deejay." The only committee member who didn't seem stoked was Dominic from the kitchen staff. He was more excited about his own announcement. He'd finally learned how to cut an enormous sheet cake into fifty-six identical pieces.

Clarice made blow-ups of photos so Lily and Eunice could deliver a speech to the residents about birds. The lucid guests were pleased to have peers speak to them as though their minds were still intact. Others had no idea what the two were talking about but enjoyed pretending to fly. They circled and swooped their arms in their wheelchairs.

"Not a bad way to keep old limbs limber," Ernie whispered to Clarice as they watched the presentation.

Olympic Birders opened an account for Soundside at the garden center. When seed was needed, Clarice purchased it. Each week, a staffer lowered the feeders so Charlie could fill them. Lily told Clarice, "It gives him something to think about other than why his wife won't come see him anymore."

Clarice was sitting at her desk when Jeff plunked a cage of canaries down in front of her. "Violet's family is so thrilled to see her take an interest in something non-violent that they donated these to us." Clarice put them in the activities room for all to enjoy and took responsibility for keeping them fed and the cage clean.

Babs told her that she had tried to incorporate a bird theme into the activities for the month by letting trivia participants choose names for their teams. It got out of hand when Bear suggested Bushtits for the women and Woodcocks for the men.

Much to her surprise, birding became an actual interest for Clarice. On her first hike with Terri and other Olympic Birders – *Ben Stassen was there along with Lily's friend Jessica and aren't they just too gorgeous for words?* – Clarice huffed and ached with the physical effort. But, still, she accomplished it. She even saw a Steller's jay although her co-birders thought that wasn't much of a prize.

"They shriek," they said.

"They eat other birds' eggs," they said.

But the large swash of cobalt blue flashing in the sun pleased her, and she began to keep a life list of the birds she saw. She suspected that, as her stamina grew, so would her enjoyment. "Maybe I'll lose even more weight by birding," she confided to Terri even though it was a lot to expect from a few ounces of feathers.

The only problem Clarice encountered with her new interest involved Hershey, Kit Kat, and the house finch they placed on her doorstep one morning. It was so dead it might as well have cartoon Xs drawn over its eyes. Neither cat cared much about her screeching, but they did wonder why they now had to wear these damn bells.

\* \* \*

The Grim Jokester waited until the very last day of the month to pull the rug out from under everyone. When Clarice arrived at work, Lia was in tears. Other staffers looked as stunned as zombies.

"What's happened?" Clarice asked, hearing the apprehension in her own voice.

Lia hiccupped and sniffed, then told her Jeff had driven down to visit the corporate drones the day before. "They fired him!" she gasped between sobs. "They sent a crew this morning to clean out his office."

"But why, for the love of God? Why fire the best boss we've ever had?" Clarice raged. Lia shrugged. Clarice tried calling the drones. "I'm the bookkeeper. I need information now," she demanded.

The assistant to the HR director only told her that Jeff would not be allowed back into Soundside. A temporary replacement would be named within the next few days. Until then they should all do their jobs, business as usual.

One thing Clarice knew for sure: for the staff and the residents, business would never be usual again.

SEVENTEEN

FUN HOUSE CHRONICLE
## Good-Byes

*After a weary, painful time, Harold's grasp on life loosens, and his family assembles to say their last good-byes.*

*The nursing home doesn't want to disturb them, but a shortage of space requires them to move a post-surgical patient into the room. At least post-surgical patients can be counted on to sleep a great deal, so they won't disturb each other much.*

*When his exhausted family leaves deep in the night, Harold is still clinging by a wisp. The night shift is a lonely time to die, so the aides look in on him often. At six in the morning, Rick comes on duty, and his first mission is to check on Harold.*

*The old man has not only made it through the night, he is sleeping comfortably. But the post-surgical patient has died.*

*Is that the Grim Jokester laughing?*

SYLVIA WAS uneasy about the change. She admired Jeff. She would have to keep an even closer eye on Soundside's standards now. She tried to cheer Lily by telling her all about the garage sale. Kyle, Jessica and Ben Stassen had all turned up to help her, and wasn't that Ben a nice man? Looked to her like Jessica had made quite a find.

Sylvia had deposited the proceeds into Lily's account. Now Jessica would help her paint the kitchen and bathroom and arrange the remaining furniture. Following a thorough cleaning by Aurora, the house would go on the market.

"Next week is our goal," she enthused, removing a fan of paint colors from her tote. "I'm thinking this Warm Toast for the master bath, and Sugar Cookie for the kitchen."

"Oh, dear. They look a little bland, don't they?" Lily puckered her brows.

"People are intimidated by bright colors. Besides, we had a granite counter top put into the kitchen that really peps up the Sugar Cookie. And we're painting the cabinets a latte to pull everything together. It'll be lovely."

"Granite, huh? Spendy stuff. And anything you drop on it breaks."

*Sigh.* "I know, Mother, but it's what people want today."

"Dull and inconvenient?"

"Warm and durable."

"Okay, okay, you're the expert."

"As a matter of fact, I am," Sylvia replied with a smile. She was getting better at understanding Lily's moods. Like now. It wasn't just the changes at Soundside that had Lily on edge. Sylvia had been so enthused about the upgrades to the house that she'd forgotten the emotional impact for Lily. Selling her home meant the Fun House was forever.

"Look, Mom, I know this isn't easy," she said. "Is this still what you want?"

"Yes, yes, of course it is," Lily answered quickly. "And I know you're working hard at it. I guess I'm just having an off day. Now, what else do you have in that bag?"

Sylvia took out the stack of letters. "Who on earth is

Nguyen Duc Trai?" she asked, handing the little bundle to Lily.

"Ah, the letters," Lily said, taking the stack and gently patting it the way she might a small dog. "Thanks for bringing them."

"I'm dying to know." Sylvia had wanted to open and read them for herself but she still half believed her mother had eyes in the back of her head.

"I've kept them private for so long. Secret from everybody. But now I think you should, we could talk about them…" Lily stopped a moment, then said, "It's time you know."

"Know what?" Sylvia asked, beginning to pluck lint from her mother's blanket. "Who is he, Mom?"

Lily drew a deep breath. "He's your brother. Well, half brother. He's your father's son."

"He's…what?" Sylvia felt instantly lightheaded.

Chrissie chose this moment to stroll in, delivering the day's mail. "Just a Wayside Gardens catalog and a card from…" She looked up and stopped. "Oh, I'm so sorry. I didn't realize you had company." Chrissie started backing out of the room.

"That's fine, Chrissie. Just give us a few moments."

"Sure…I'll just come back later."

A very loud silence echoed off the walls of the room. At last, Sylvia managed, "Well?"

"I've never told you this story before, Sylvia, but I think it was for your own good." Lily clutched the letters tighter. "And because it was so personal."

"So personal? I have a brother, but it was too personal to let me in on it?" *Am I hearing this right?*

"That's right. It's personal," Lily snapped. "It couldn't be more personal. Your brother is living proof that my husband was a cheat. He deceived me. I didn't know it. And then he died. God, how I grieved for that man. Only to find out he was not even faithful to me."

Sylvia was speechless watching her mother's dammed up outrage burst free. *My father, the cheat. I have a brother?*

"You should know the story now, but when you were young, I wanted you to be proud of the war hero your father was. To keep him special. All the while I was furious with him. Rejected by him." Lily's tears forged crooked little pathways through the wrinkles on her face. She looked up from the letters to Sylvia. "As years went by, it never seemed the right time to tell you. Until now. I don't have that much time left. Don't hate your dad, Sylvia."

Lily gave the letters back to her, and this time she looked at them with more than curiosity. *Read them or reject them?* She noticed her hands were as pale as that Sugar Cookie paint sample.

Sylvia grappled with how she actually felt. She was wounded that her mother had kept a secret of this magnitude from her. But she was far more wounded on her mother's behalf. *She's the injured party here. Not me.*

"After a time, I tried to forgive him," Lily continued, her voice a little steadier. "War changes people. Maybe having a hot little lover helped him through those awful days."

Sylvia could not have been that forgiving. But then again, considering her own fears about Kyle, maybe she could. "How did you find out?" she asked, finally finding her voice.

"Trai's grandmother wrote to me. Her daughter had an envelope with my return address, one from a letter I'd sent to Harmon. It took a while to find me after the war. We'd moved to a smaller place. But the letter finally caught up.

"His lover died in the war, so the grandmother took care of her little boy. But as a mixed race child, he wasn't safe on the streets. She took him to an orphanage. They asked her for money. And they helped her write a letter to me to get it."

"What proof did she have?" Sylvia looked for a loophole.

"She had a picture of me that I had given to Harmon, and one of him with her daughter. Besides that, the orphanage sent a picture of the boy, and he looks something like Harmon. Half Caucasian, anyway. It might not be proof, but it was good enough for me."

"What became of him?" Sylvia was fascinated with the idea that she had family after all, even if he was a world away.

"For ten years, I sent $50 to the orphanage every month. That covered expenses while Trai was in school. As he learned English, he began sending me letters. At first, I didn't answer. But finally, I came to terms with the fact that he was part of Harmon, and that made him part of my life. Harmon may have cheated on me, but he would never have cheated his child out of an education.

"So I started writing back to him. I told him about his father and about you, his big sister. He knew very little about his own family, only having a vague memory of his grandmother. I hear from Trai still every now and then. He's a shopkeeper in Ho Chi Minh City, with a family of his own. You have two nieces and a nephew. I'm sure that he would be pleased to hear from you. I guess it will be your decision now whether to keep up the connection.

"That's about all there is to the story. Except I never really trusted another man after that. It doesn't take a shrink to figure that's why I kept moving on. I couldn't commit again, not even when I met Paul. Heaven knows he promised to love us both. But in my experience, a promise isn't worth very much."

Sylvia's brain was on overload. Things about her mother were beginning to make sense. A massive hurt lurked behind the constant moving, the independence, the need to question everything. "I don't know what to say. I never guessed at any of this. You never said a word against Dad." Sylvia squeezed her mother's hand and felt Lily return the pressure.

"Still don't. I loved him. And that war wounded everyone. Best forgotten," she said. As if to end the subject, Lily pushed her call button.

But Sylvia was still in Vietnam. "I've always wanted family but never imagined it this way."

Chrissie peeked around the curtain. "Yes, Miss Lily?"

"It's nearly tea time, isn't it?"

"Would you both like a cup?" Shyly she added a hello to Sylvia.

"You know my daughter?"

"We met in the hallway the other night. But I'd know her anyway. She looks just like you."

* * *

Jessica was as surprised by the disappearance of Jeff Parkinson as everyone else. He was somebody that Lily liked. She'd have to ask Clarice what had happened. She hoped his replacement would have his civility.

But today she was just too excited to worry. Other than trips on the paratransit bus, Lily had not been away from Soundside for weeks. Jessica had checked out her plan with Nurse Mary Beth and with Chrissie and with Ernie.

"Yeah, but have you checked it out with Sylvia?" Lily asked, pulling on her sweater.

"I've not only checked it out, she's meeting us."

"Really? She agreed to this?"

"Well, she's concerned, of course. But Ernie and Nurse Mary Beth convinced her you were ready for an outing." Sylvia had been more overpowered by them than convinced.

Ernie met them in Soundside's portico and supervised the transfer from the wheelchair into Jessica's Toyota. "This will be a little harder than chair to bed, Lily," the therapist said. "The car is higher so you have to work your way uphill. Use the car door to help. And that handhold, there, above the door."

Lily swung her stump into the car and then pulled herself across the transfer board onto the car seat. She'd developed enough strength with Ernie's exercises to do the job with aplomb. "I haven't been out for a real drive since I left the hospital a foot short," Lily cackled.

Ernie and Jessica both groaned.

Jessica might have told herself she didn't want to worry, but that didn't mean she wouldn't. As she opened the car trunk and Ernie folded the chair into it, she said softly, "I hear Jeff is gone."

He shook his head and said, "Not good." He shut the lid.

Jessica drove slowly around the town then meandered to the waterfront. They watched the ferries chug to the Olympic Peninsula and back. Lily commented on the dahlias and the shop windows and the fishy odor. But mostly she expressed her curiosity. "Where are we meeting Sylvia?"

Again Jessica said, "It's a surprise."

They drove east into the Snohomish valley at the foot of the Cascades. Jessica turned off the main route onto a narrow road that hadn't been patched since buckboards were in vogue. After a couple miles, she turned again, this time into a driveway leading to a two storey house. It had been built by a Midwestern farmer blown by tornadoes all the way from Kansas. At least that was the story she'd been told by an imaginative realtor.

"This is where I live," Jessica pointed to the boxy white house with only a porch and one bay window to soften its lines.

"It's big," Lily said, considering the house.

"Well, yes. Ed the Evil and I always figured our family would expand." Then, driving by the house, she added, "And this is where my herd lives." She passed the outbuildings to a barn that looked a great deal newer than the house. Sylvia was there, watching a smallish, compact horse in the paddock. When she saw Jessica's car, she waved. The horse pricked up his ears and arched his neck doing his Spanish ancestors proud.

"There's Sylvia," Lily said. "And…would that be Latin Lover?" When she turned back to Jessica, the delight lit up her lovely old face.

While Jessica removed the wheelchair from the trunk, Sylvia wobbled slightly when one strappy sandal slipped on the gravel drive. She watched Lily transfer out of the car. "You're really good at that," Sylvia said, sounding impressed.

"I'm much stronger than I was," Lily answered with pride.

Together, Jessica pushing the chair, the trio walked up the gravel drive and through the open barn door where they were greeted by a rich aroma of hay and horse and manure. She saw Sylvia's nose twitch, but Lily inhaled deeply before saying, "Such a joy to visit a place that's more about life than death."

"Hey, Sam," Jessica called to a whippet-thin man who was mucking out a stall. "This is my friend Lily and her daughter, Sylvia."

Sam tipped his ancient hat first to one then the other. "Ma'am...ma'am." Then he was done chatting and bent back to his chore.

"Sam is the barn manager, and these are the horses that I board," Jessica explained as the women walked along the row of the stalls. Jessica stopped in front of one stall, where a very large head with a shaggy gray muzzle slowly turned to give the ladies the once over. "Gina Lola here is a workhorse so she's a very big girl. Aren't you, sweetie," Jessica said as she stretched high to scratch the mare behind an ear.

"Big as a moose," said Sylvia.

Lily agreed. "Why does anybody want a horse that size?"

"She's Ben Stassen's horse. His granddad used to take her to fairs for pulling events. Now, Ben just comes to visit her. He takes her for walks around the pasture as if she were a pet dog."

Lily said, "You two visit me like an old family pet, too."

"Don't be silly," Sylvia muttered. "I'm far too tidy to ever have a pet."

Jessica realized how much the other two looked alike when they both laughed at the same time.

They heard another horse enter the barn. They turned and saw Latin Dancer led by Ben. The yearling still limped, but he was clearly content to be with Ben, giving him a push in the back with a nose that had been too damaged to touch in the early days. They all exchanged greetings then Lily said, "So this is the poor baby who was attacked by dogs. How's he getting along?"

Ben said, "I started walking him with Gina Lola a while back. She repaired his spirit while Jessica kept him alive. He's fine walking with just me now, and I'd say he's on the mend."

"And Jessica. Do you have her on the mend?"

"Lily!" Jessica was appalled.

"Mother!" Sylvia looked even more appalled.

"I'm old. Can't wait too long to find out."

Ben laughed, and it sounded to Jessica as cheerful as water over river rocks. "I'm doing my damnedest, Miss Lily. Now if I can just teach her to cook."

He said his good-byes then turned into a stall with Dancer, and Jessica pushed Lily's wheelchair to the final stall in the line. "We didn't just come here so you could embarrass me. This is what I wanted you to see. Be quiet, if you think you can manage it." Jessica opened the half door to the stall, and Lily could see a roan horse through the low light. The mare stopped eating, tensed and stared at Lily. She moved her gaze to Jessica, relaxed and resumed munching.

"She trusts you," Lily said.

"Shhh."

From around the mare's haunches, a small head appeared, eyes wide with interest. Knobby kneed legs allowed the foal to stretch around for a peek at the newcomers. A low, gentle "Oh!" escaped from Lily and gained the baby's complete attention. The filly stretched her head toward Lily, then took a step closer.

"This is Latin Lover's daughter," Jessica said softly. "Latin's Marisol."

Lily didn't answer. She seemed as infatuated as the filly was. Marisol had never seen one of these tall pink animals in a shiny contraption with wheels. She was at the mercy of her own curiosity. Lily slowly extended her hand, and Marisol extended her nose. But after the briefest touch, the mare nickered to bring her foal back. As if to apologize for her rudeness, she offered Lily her own nose to pet.

Lily touched the soft skin. "That's okay, my girl. Keep your baby safe."

* * *

Like nearly half all amputees, Lily was plagued with intermittent phantom pain in her missing limb. She'd complained to Ernie, "I have enough aches in the parts I still have, much less the one I've lost."

The next morning, before Lily was out of bed, Ernie hauled a full length mirror into her room. "You willing to help me with an experiment?" he asked.

"You want to know who's the fairest of them all?"

He propped the mirror on the floor and said, "I already know it's you, Lily."

"You better watch out, Ernie. Your nose is growing like Pinocchio's. And I don't want to get near a full length looking glass."

"Well, you might want to reconsider," said the therapist. "I've been reading about research on vets coming back from Afghanistan with amputations. You put a mirror where you can see the reflection of your existing leg. The theory is that it tricks the brain into thinking the other leg is still there. And the pain goes away."

"Sounds like a load of crap to me."

"It's all about electrical impulses from the brain to the missing leg gone haywire. You and your brain aren't the same thing, Lily. I'd like to give it a try."

"All right, then, Ernie. Be my guest."

He carefully maneuvered the mirror onto her bed, placing it lengthwise on its side between her stump and her right leg. She could see the reflection of the whole leg in the mirror, making it appear that she had two whole limbs.

The result was almost immediate. Lily felt the phantom pain change. It began to prickle and then quiet. The effect was heightened when she moved her leg for more comfort. Her brain was apparently deceived into believing she had moved the missing limb, and it became more comfortable as well.

"Oh! Oh my goodness, Ernie," she cried. "Why haven't the doctors recommended this before?"

"They know it doesn't always work, and they don't want to get your hopes up."

"Bullshit, Ernie. They just think it's hocus-pocus if it's not a pill."

Ernie smiled. "You're a smart lady, Lily."

"And you're a smart, wonderful, glorious man."

He looked bashful. "The article says after you do this a few times, the pain might even go away completely. Your brain stops misfiring. I don't really get it. I'm not sure anyone does."

"I don't care how it works. Just that it does."

"I better put this mirror back on the bathroom wall before the new maintenance guy reports it stolen. But whenever you need it, I'll go get it."

"Before you leave…I heard you tell Jessica that nothing good would happen now that Jeff is gone."

"Your ears are a little too good sometimes."

"Tell me what you meant."

He hesitated, then appeared to choose his words carefully. "A lot of us have worked at a lot of places. We've stayed here because Jeff kept higher standards than most. He knew when to bend a little, too." He patted her hand. "Nothing for you to worry about. You know how employees love to complain."

Lily could tell that the smile on his lips never reached his eyes.

\* \* \*

When Jessica stopped by the nursing home that evening, she found Lily in the activities room with a brightly dressed old woman and a man that looked like a tough guy gone to seed. They were staring at the canaries.

"The bottom of that birdcage is dirty."

"Dirty as the bottom of a birdcage."

"Clarice needs to work on that."

Jessica was tickled by the conversation and a little sorry her arrival interrupted it. She quietly set a grocery bag on a craft table, but Lily heard and turned. "Hi, Jessica. Meet Eunice. And Bear. My BFFs. Other than you."

Jessica hated the image of Lily sitting alone in her room so she was thrilled that she'd found a couple buddies. She was particularly tickled by the looks of Eunice. She must be pushing ninety, but still wore large gold hoops that stretched out her earlobes. Her spiky hair was orange. *The rookie stylists strike again.*

Jessica pulled containers of Greek yogurt and fresh blackberries out of her bag. She'd learned you always brought extra when you visit someone in a nursing home. "Anyone for a parfait?"

Eunice's scrawny arm shot up in the air, bangles jangling, "Me!"

Jessica dipped out four portions in wine goblets she'd brought with her, layering the berries and yogurt with granola. "Whose computer?" she asked, noticing the netbook on the table.

"Bear's," said Lily.

"I'm showing her how to –"

"– how to play games," Lily interrupted. "I'm at Depth Fathom Four in Aqua Monster World."

Jessica rolled her eyes. "Okay, so don't tell me."

While they ate the parfaits, they gossiped about goings-on around town, how Marisol was growing, and life in the Fun House. Jessica learned that a night nurse had been arrested for pilfering drugs, and Lily told her how Ernie had helped with phantom pain.

They laughed about two residents who had taken an extreme dislike to each other. "They're both stroke victims, and they share a room," Bear said. "Neither one can use his left arm. The old fools got into a fist fight the other day with only their rights."

"That nurse, Mary Beth? She put a line of duct tape down the center of the room and told them neither one could cross it. I guess they're more scared of her than each other. At least there's a cease fire in effect," Eunice finished with a snort.

Eunice seemed to have a sense of fun as overdeveloped as her sense of fashion. It was good for Lily to know people even older than herself who were still vital. *Eunice is a shot in the arm for us both.*

Jessica was packing up her containers and goblets when Clarice came in to clean the bird cage and fill the little seed cups. When the canaries sang too loudly to their caregiver, Bear snapped, "Cut the chatter, birdies. We'll do the talking here."

Clarice grinned but it was plain to see that she looked troubled.

"Clarice, what's wrong?" Lily and Eunice said together.

Bear rumbled, "You two sound like the canaries."

The bookkeeper came over to their table. "It's just been a long day. I guess we're all feeling pretty glum without Jeff around."

"Whatever did they bounce him for? Seemed like a decent sort as bosses go," Jessica asked.

"No word yet. But I'll call his wife Terri tonight and maybe find out…" Clarice shut down when Nurse Baby Talk came into the room for a pitcher of water, rubber soles squeaking on the tile. "Well, I'm on my way. See you tomorrow," Clarice waggled her fingers and left.

While the nurse was in the room, Jessica and Cognitive Corner hushed. The silence was as intrusive as a foghorn. Lily finally relieved the situation by asking Jessica about Ben. "So how's the romance?"

"When a girl blushes like that, it's gone way past romance," Eunice pronounced.

"Speaking of romances, I picked these up at the library." Jessica took novels by Jennifer Ashley and Adrianne Lee out of her bag. "I'll leave them in your room for later." She wiggled her eyebrows.

"How did you know I like a bit of slap and tickle now and then?" Lily cocked her head.

*She doesn't remember the books stored in the garage.* "I have my ways. And your secret is anything but safe with me."

As soon as Nurse Happy Talk was gone, Jessica asked, "What could it mean, firing the head guy?"

"Nothing positive," Bear said darkly. "This place seemed too good to be true."

\* \* \*

Some things are super secret. Like making a drug buy. Or fantasies about playing Indian maiden and the settler with Brad Pitt. That's how Clarice felt about her visits to Bodacious Babes, the fitness center for women only. She skulked in at 9 pm that night, wearing pull-on sweats and an oversized sweatshirt. But, of course, there were her coworkers, Alita and Chrissie. Fortunately, they were about to leave, looking rosy pink, at the tip top of health.

"Well, hi, Clarice!" said Chrissie.

"We didn't know you were a member," said Alita. Clarice suspected a slight emphasis on the word *you*.

"Next time we could all come together. Wouldn't that be fun?" Both girls allowed it would be just the ticket before they said good night.

The very idea further depressed the depression Clarice felt since her phone call to Terri. Jeff's wife was desolate. CompreCare had really ripped Jeff a new one.

"What on earth about? We all think he's great."

"I'm not supposed to say. If he makes any public complaints he'll lose what little severance they gave him. So keep it to yourself." She told Clarice what had happened to Mrs. Carlton, and how CompreCare had criticized Jeff's handling of the situation. But mostly, somebody had told them he had taken in Medicaid patients that other places dumped.

"They called it poor judgment, and they told him to change his policy. And to begin outsourcing Soundside's problem people. That was their term for it. Jeff said he would never do that, and they fired him."

"Those bastards." Clarice was outraged for Mrs. Carlton, for her boss, her friend Terri, and for what might happen to long term residents.

Three other women, all strangers, were exercising. Clarice removed her protective outer layer, stripping down to shorts and a Tee, then selected a machine she called the Thigh Thrasher. By the time she was done she would be neither rosy pink nor tip top. She'd be fluorescent red, dripping wet, and heaving like an overworked steam engine. Her legs and arms would wobble like noodles. She tied a band around her head and began her routine. It would keep the sweat out of her eyes.

But nothing stopped her tears for the people she'd learned to care about. *There are harder things to lose than weight.*

## EIGHTEEN

## FUN HOUSE CHRONICLE
## Strangers

*S*he goes this route at the same time every workday. *She knows exactly how long it will take to get from her house to the office, including her drive-thru stop for a sugar-free vanilla latte. There are other ways to go, and if she were the type to suffer from boredom, she would probably alternate week to week. But she chooses this one because, in the stillness before rush hour, it is so predictable.*

*The street gang this early consists of the newspaper carrier, zipping driveway to driveway in his little Jeep. Joggers and dog walkers. Now and then, a suburban deer helping herself to someone's rosebush. And this old man. He is always walking away from the mid-block nursing home and on down the sidewalk.*

*All summer and fall he has walked to points unknown to her. Probably it took her weeks to even become aware of him. But she is aware now. He is old but robust enough to take this walk to somewhere. He has a cane but usually carries it parallel to the ground, like a weapon. Maybe it is to ward off an imagined gang of teenagers with pierced noses and brows. He wears bib overalls. She thinks he may have been a farmer in the valley to the east of this town.*

> One morning she smiles at him as she drives by at the exact 30 mph limit. He smiles back. The next morning, he waves. She waves back. Now she looks for him, like she looks for the latte stand and the turn to her office. She is prone to worry, so he is a new egg in that particular basket. Does he have a family that would miss him if he went walking one morning and never came back? Did he once have a loyal dog, an old Shep who died one night in his sleep under the porch? Like the tree in the forest, if she weren't there to see him, would he really be there?
>
> He is part of the minutia that makes up her day. And she'd be a little more lost without him.

LILY GRABBED the newspaper from the parlor, still not getting to the crossword before Bear. *Shit.* She balanced the main news section on her lap and read the headlines as she rolled back to her room. Looking up, she was surprised to see Ernie on a step ladder, anchoring the top of a pipe to her ceiling.

"Is that for firemen, or do you expect me to pole dance?"

"Around here, too many of our pole dancers end up break dancers," he answered, climbing off the ladder.

The pole was a vertical pipe ceiling to floor, held in place by tension. It was positioned next to Lily's bed. "Now that you've developed your arm strength, you'll find holding this pole an easier way to transfer from the chair to the bed than by using a board. Want to give it a try?"

Lily adored Ernie and had learned to trust him, so she was unafraid. By pulling herself up she could pivot from her wheelchair to the bed. And vice versa. "Pretty slick, Ernie. Are monkey bars next? Maybe swinging on vines?"

"Well, maybe, Lily. But you'll have to swing dance with someone else. Our time together is up." Lily saw that Ernie was not kidding, from the solemn look he gave her.

"What do you mean? You're not leaving are you?" Ice water replaced blood in her veins.

"No, but according to Medicare, you've had all the hours of physical therapy you're qualified for."

"You can't be serious." But he was. He couldn't look her in the eye.

"Keep up your exercises, and I'll be around to say howdy whenever I can." He bowed, took her hand and kissed it. "You're a fine lady, and it's been my pleasure to work with you."

The big man ambled out of her room and her life. She knew he thought he'd visit, probably really meant it. But as his days became filled with newer, needier inmates, she would see him less and less. She was under no delusions about the way things worked in the Fun House.

Chrissie tried to comfort her that night, giving her a long gentle bed bath. "It's just one goddamn thing after another," Lily wept. The aide softly wiped the tears that eroded the laugh lines on Lily's face. Chrissie said she would stay past her shift end, but Lily sent her away. It was best not to get any closer to another staffer. In the end they were paid to be in the nursing home, not required to be. They would move on, and Lily would not.

They are not my friends. They're here for a time but migrating through, like the birds.

\* \* \*

Working for Ben Stassen was an unexpected bonus for Clarice. Keeping his books was simple, requiring no more than a few hours one evening a week. A little extra cash never hurt. Jessica had asked her for a few hours each week, too, and the ranch finances were a more fascinating challenge. Clarice had not intended to develop a freelance business, but it had come knocking on her door. Who could resist, especially when it helped her forget the mess at work. "Jumbo shrimp all around," she said to Kit Kat and Hershey, sharing the bounty of extra income. Kit Kat tortured his treat by batting it across the room where it slapped against the wall, stuck for a moment like the last leaf, then slid down for him to terrorize further.

Most of the extra money went to new clothes in a smaller size. If it fit, but wasn't actually a smaller size, she didn't buy it. That's how she convinced herself she was a size 16 and no bigger. Her goal was a 12 which she had read was the size of the average American woman. Since she was taller than average, she would be like those willowy sirens in the gossip rags.

*- Increased odds of boinking Matt Damon.*

It was nice to look good, of course. When her son Cole was home from college for the weekend, he'd looked at her for the first time in years and said, "Ma, you're a babe." She was pretty sure he hadn't meant the Blue Ox. But it wasn't becoming a looker that was affecting her most. It was confidence, the kind she'd never had before.

Take joining the birders, for instance. It gave her a pastime she liked, required a certain amount of fitness, and provided a group of enthusiasts that admired her. They did not think of her as standoffish or former fatty Clarice. To them, she was fun loving, self assured Clarice.

*Guess that's why I'm getting so mouthy at work.* Her new attitude made her braver. She wasn't making much effort to hide her disapproval of the new management. Corporate had made the worst possible choice. After a couple of weeks, they had announced a temporary Head Administrator for Soundside.

They'd given the job to Patricia Bergeron. That brown-nosing turncoat of a Social Services Director had actually applied for Jeff's job. *She's probably the one who squealed about accepting Medicaid patients like Bear.* The back-stabbing buttinsky no doubt promised to toe whatever line Corporate drew in the dirt. Her new regime would be tyrannical.

In the initial staff meeting, Bergeron's first official edict had been issued to Babs. She was to clear out all animals, taking 'that damned cat' and the canaries to the Humane Society immediately. Babs's lower lip had begun to tremble.

Clarice's evil twin – the one she'd just become aware of, the one that didn't understand she never drew attention to herself – straightened her shoulders and announced, "Babs will do nothing of the sort. If the fact that the residents enjoy the animals means nothing to you, then they're coming with me."

That's why she was now on her way home with Furball in a box bitching in the back seat and the canaries in their cage singing happily in the front. And why she was thinking there is a downside to being assertive.

*Just what the hell are Kit Kat and Hershey going to think about this?*

\* \* \*

217

"So the Bergeron Bitch gave Furball and the birds the boot, huh? I'll probably be next," Bear said.

The Cognitive Corner membership was arranged in the parlor blockading the way to the stereo system to keep bored young aides from turning it up to earsplitting. Lily had seen Bear look down in the dumps before, but not like this.

Charlie asked, "What do you mean, Bear?"

"Mark my words. They'll let their government contract run out. Then you won't see any more Medicaid patients allowed in here. And the ones who are here already? We'll start disappearing, too."

Eunice's bright little face fell like a deflating soufflé. "But I...you...this is your home."

Lily shot a frown at Bear. "You don't know that, Bear. You're scaring us."

Eunice shivered. "I'm scared all the time anyway after what happened with Mrs. Car...you know."

Bear looked as sheepish as *ursus horribilis* can manage. "Lily's right, Eunice. I got bounced out of Madrona Park because I was too big to handle. Hell, I'm a lot smaller now. Don't need special care."

Now that he mentioned it, Lily noticed that his love handles no longer lopped over the arms of his wheelchair. And she'd seen him in the halls at night walking laps behind his chair, pushing it ahead of him for support.

"I'm sure that's true, Eunice. Bear is pretty smart," Charlie said. Lily knew Charlie from the days he'd managed the appliance store in town. It was in his nature to be as conciliatory now as then.

"And we're all on the alert against shenanigans like that bastard pulled. You don't have to be afraid of that anymore," Lily said.

After a sniff and a blink or two, Eunice gave them a watery smile. "I don't want any of my friends to disappear."

Lily thought about her own situation. She didn't have the money that Eunice had. She was private pay at the moment, but that wouldn't last much longer. Even with money from the sale of her house, by the time she paid off her mortgage and the home equity loan, the remains wouldn't go more than three months, maybe four. Then she'd be counting on Medicaid, too. *If Soundside drops the contract...*

For the first time she felt rising panic that Soundside might not be the end of the line for her. Bergeron didn't like her —*whose fault was that?* — and would do nothing to save her. Lily might have to move again, now that she was just learning to handle the Fun House. Things could get much worse. *Jesus! Will it never end?*

Nurse Mary Beth scuttled in. It was the first time Lily had seen her look anything but unflappable. "I've been looking for you guys. Actually, I was ordered to find you."

*This can't be good.* The nurses were the aristocracy in a place like this. Management usually wore kid gloves. But Mary Beth looked furious. Her ears were a burning red that matched her cheeks. "Bergeron is aware of your night watch program. It is to stop as of now."

"Why...the hell...can't be...what the fuck?" The voices of Cognitive Corner overlapped like angry horns in a traffic jam.

"She says that it demeans our hiring policy, undercuts the nurses on duty, and may well be bad for your health."

"Worse that being attacked?"

"She can't make me stop."

"Me either."

But Lily could see that worse was to come from the disgust on Mary Beth's face. "If you don't stop, she'll take it out on the staff. We'll be accused of poor floor management for allowing patients to feel unsafe. The nurse on duty will be fired the next time Bergeron hears you've been keeping watch."

"You have to be kidding," Charlie said. All the others had dropped their jaws too far to speak.

"I'm so, so sorry guys, but I think she means it. The nurses have valued your help. But jobs are hard to come by now, so please…"

"What's her real reason, Mary Beth?" Bear asked.

Lily nodded. Leave it to the PI to figure there's more to a story than meets the eye.

"My guess? She doesn't like residents who fight back any more than staffers who do." The discouraged nurse shook her head and walked away.

Cognitive Corner mourned. Finally Charlie asked, "Is there anything we can do?"

"You mean short of ordering a hit on the bitch? Nothing that won't hurt the staff," Bear said.

Eunice agreed. "It's the staff that's already catching the worst from Bergeron. Rick told me there'll be no more bonuses for referring people to the CNA classes –"

"What bullshit. A system like that helps bring in good people," Bear observed.

"– and she's not letting aides work four long days instead of five short anymore."

"Like they say, new brooms sweep clean." Charlie shrugged.

Bear growled, "She can take her new broom and ride it into the goddamn sunset."

None of them seemed to notice that Lily had dropped out of the conversation. *What can we do? Will anything keep us safe now?*

\* \* \*

Jessica drove into the Gilbert driveway. Lily had wanted to see her house now that it was staged and on the market.

"Sylvia is meeting us here," Lily said.

"She is?" Jessica thought that Lily was acting a little secretive. Or anxious. Jumpy for sure. Something was up.

They sat in the Toyota for a moment while Lily scrutinized the front yard. The shrubs had been trimmed, the lawn raked, and an embarrassingly cute mailbox with a nautical motif replaced her rusty regulation model.

"Dear God," Lily moaned.

"It's cute. Sort of."

"And you know how I feel about that."

"Then I imagine you're really going to hate the welcome plaque at the front door." Jessica was right. Lily cringed at the *Ahoy!* sign with its sailboat art.

They went into the house through the garage, the best route for Lily's wheelchair. "Now be prepared. It looks different," Jessica warned. Lily and her daughter had been getting along better recently, but the new décor could end that détente.

Lily surprised her. As she looked around, her lovely face went from repose to genuine pleasure. "My daughter has a real talent for this."

Jessica wished Sylvia was there to see her mother's pride.

The living room and dining ell were all one space. Lily's sofa and chairs were still there, clustered around the fireplace. But the television had been removed. So had her dinette set and in its place, Sylvia had brought in her own teak dining table and chairs. The table was set with Sylvia's china, and a bowl of fresh cut flowers graced the center. New translucent curtains at the patio door brightened the room, as did colorful pillows artfully tossed along the hearth.

Lily even approved of the granite counter and fresh paint in the kitchen. "Wonder why she didn't do this while I lived here?"

Sylvia, just coming through the front door, asked, "Would you have let me?"

"Probably not."

"Well there you go."

Sylvia kissed the top of her mother's head when Lily pronounced her daughter's efforts to be spectacular. Then they continued the tour. New linens spruced up the master bedroom, and Sylvia had put a brass daybed in the guest room. Bright floral art prints added splashes of color to the walls. There was absolutely no clutter, even in the closets, so the little house seemed almost spacious.

Everywhere the scent of Lily's favorite potpourri kept the air fresh and inviting. "It's just wonderful," Lily praised. "Now let me peek at my garden."

And there it was, as well tended as ever. Jessica had prepared it for autumn, removing debris and mulching all the beds. "You've been keeping it safe and sound," Lily said, reaching for Jessica's hand.

"I admit I've grown attached to it."

"It's a great gift to new owners. And to me. Thank you, Jessica. And Sylvia, there's only one tiny change I'd like to make."

"Okay. Here it comes." Sylvia rolled her eyes. "What's wrong?"

"I want to take that *Ahoy!* sign down."

"But it will make people feel welcome."

"I'm sure Kyle will do that without the sign."

"Well, if that's the only thing," Sylvia nodded, giving in fairly gracefully.

Jessica was pleasantly surprised. *Has she learned to choose her battles with Lily?*

Lily spun her wheelchair around to face them both. She indicated the patio chairs. "Now, take a seat. I have something serious to talk with you about. It's really why I wanted the three of us to get together where we wouldn't be overheard."

*Well, well. Yet another surprise?* Jessica and Sylvia exchanged a shrug, then they sat.

"You know things are changing at the nursing home. The new regime threatens us all. We need to prepare." Lily outlined a plan she had concocted. For the next hour, the three women went through every emotion in the book, kicking the idea around, rejecting and accepting, finally beginning to bring it to life.

Jessica wheeled Lily back into the nursing home, just in time for afternoon meds.

"Now you two think about it in detail," Lily cautioned as she got into her bed. "Only do it if it really works for you."

Just then Nurse Baby Talk bustled in. "Have we had a nice nap?" she asked, administering Lily's insulin.

"We've had a busy day," answered Lily.

"Go to hell," said Gladys, smiling at the new *Ahoy!* sign hanging on the wall over her bed.

\* \* \*

The next day, Sylvia invited Jessica for lunch at an upscale little bistro to discuss what they began to call Lily's Plan. "To be completely honest, I really don't like field greens," Sylvia said raking through her salad to find the edible bits.

"My horses do, but give me old fashioned iceberg lettuce any day," Jessica agreed.

Over coffee, Sylvia said, "Lily's Plan would be scads of work, especially for you. I mean it's a lot more complicated than 'Gramps has a barn, let's put on a play.'"

"Trust me, I know."

Things went quiet for a moment, but Sylvia could tell that Jessica had more to say. She tried to help her get started. "There's so much to consider."

"That's just it. It challenges everything. My business… my time…my relationship with Ben. How involved I really want to get. Whether I would actually be any good at it."

"From my point of view, I need to be absolutely sure Lily would be safe. And, of course, I need to work out the expenses with Kyle to see if we can swing it. Let's talk again in a week and make our final decision."

But in a week, Sylvia was thinking about anything but Lily's Plan.

## NINETEEN

FUN HOUSE CHRONICLE
# The Phlebotomist

*She is a lovely sprite of a girl. A phlebotomist by trade, she never has difficulty finding the vein. Chronically ill patients are pleased when she does the job. "She never hurts you," they say.*

*She is too young to know she must be on the alert at all times. So when her mate said, "I just can't do this anymore," she was caught unaware, having failed to see any signs. The blow came as a preemptive strike, felling her as surely as a raptor downs prey.*

*It was the crushing weight of his words that caused her the greatest pain. Shock and anger, to be sure, but mostly the staggering effort it took to suck air in and expel it in an approximation of breathing. She did not argue once he had his say. It was not in her nature to plead. He packed his things, leaving behind only unanswered questions.*

*To her coworkers she seems a little less fun, looks a little more tired. She continues on her way, taking samples, making patients glad she is working this shift. She draws blood so gently; his technique was so cruel.*

*In time she will breathe deeply again. She'll hear love songs without sighing, and she'll recover her self worth. But today, she is too young to know.*

AFTER THE fact, Sylvia realized that Kyle's death might have been prevented if it weren't for the series of incidents that slowed everyone's response time, including her own. They were at Sahib, their favorite Indian restaurant, celebrating the sale of Lily's house. It had only taken a week. "I'm thrilled a young couple is buying the old place," Sylvia enthused. "Maybe they'll hire me to decorate it."

"I'll certainly suggest you," Kyle said, setting down his fork and frowning. "I don't know. This tikka masala just doesn't seem to agree with me." Sylvia noticed that his forehead was sweating, but the room was very warm, so she discounted anything more dramatic than foreign spices.

"Do they have kids?"

"In the tikka masala? Surely not."

"No, silly. The young couple."

"No. But a big dog already dug two holes in the garden while they were inspecting the house."

"Oh my God. Don't tell Mother. What could be worse?" she said, not realizing she was about to find out. She excused herself to go powder her nose, as she coyly called it. Days later, she pieced together the story of what happened while she was gone.

Doctors told her that the demise of Kyle's heart muscle tissue spurred chaotic electrical impulses that stopped it from beating. Within four minutes brain death had begun. They agreed that, yes, he was very young for such a thing and it was all very sad although not unheard of.

He was alone cradled into a small booth, so she could find no one who noticed whether he gasped or floundered before he went still. When Sylvia returned from the restroom, she patted his shoulder, causing his body to slump forward, knocking the basket of roti onto the floor. Her horrified cry brought the waiter and then the manager. In retrospect, Sylvia thought if the solemn young man had not been new himself, he might have known how to use the restaurant's defibrillator. He ordered the waiter to call 911, but one of the ambulance crew told Sylvia that the dispatcher had trouble deciphering the man's thick accent, and that had held them up.

Another dinner guest was administering CPR when the ambulance finally arrived. Later, Sylvia realized the EMTs must have known Kyle was already dead but had chosen not to tell her. That painful chore was someone else's job.

She could not drive in her current state, so the restaurant manager took her to the hospital. *He's no doubt worried about his restaurant's reputation,* she thought in that way the shocked mind flits wildly about when it can't deal with the real facts at hand. She shivered with cold in the hot car. *I'll wake up soon and Kyle will tell me it was just a dream and go back to sleep, my love. It's bad, but it's going to end.*

At the hospital, the restaurant manager asked if there was anyone he could call to stay with her.

"Yes, my mother…" Sylvia began, then realized there was no one to come. And that the nightmare was not going to end any time soon.

* * *

Lily was called on to be the protector once again, seeing to her daughter's needs while Sylvia struggled to tread water in the emotional flash flood. "We are all caregivers to each other at one time or another," Lily mourned to Chrissie. "That pendulum just keeps swinging back and forth."

She hired the funeral home and made sure a notice of Kyle's death was in the paper. She had Jessica do the legwork for her, quite literally, of setting up the memorial service, following Sylvia's wishes. The service was well attended because, while Sylvia did not have close friends, Kyle had been surrounded by business associates and well wishers.

Jessica made sure that both Lily and Sylvia were at the service, sitting side by side. Lily was nearly overwhelmed to see Chrissie, Clarice and Ernie wheel in Bear, Eunice and Charlie. The service was non-religious; Sylvia told Lily that enough smiting had been done.

Everyone paid their respects to the widow as they left, including one remarkably handsome man that Lily didn't recognize. Nor did she hear what Sylvia whispered in his ear as he leaned toward her and handed her a business card.

\* \* \*

The night of Kyle's death, and each night for the first week, Jessica stayed with Sylvia, making sure the shattered woman swallowed the Ativan her doctor had prescribed. The first night Sylvia told her that she now knew how Lucy felt when she lost her head. It took Jessica a while to recall the broken doll.

A couple days later, Jessica found Sylvia on the floor in front of Kyle's bureau, her arms around a clutch of his sweaters. The beautiful wool was soaked with her tears. Jessica put her own arms around the new widow and held tight until her blouse was also soaked, and Sylvia had exhausted herself with the terrified sounds an animal might make caught in a trap.

Ed the Evil had put Jessica through grief like this not so long ago. She had always seen Sylvia as an employer more than a friend, someone she valued because she was important to Lily. Now she cradled her until Sylvia at last straightened and pulled away. "Thank you, Jessica. My goodness, I'm so sorry. I'm sure you have better places to be."

Jessica realized Sylvia was embarrassed by her outpouring. *She doesn't have a clue how much we share.* "Sylvia," she said, "I've had those same swollen eyes. I am here because there is no place better for me to be."

On the first day of the second week, Sylvia told her it was time for her to go home and get on with her life. She, Sylvia, was going back to work and would be fine on her own. Henderson Interiors had clients and jobs that had waited too long. "Besides, we must start working on Lily's Plan," Sylvia added.

Jessica was not so sure that Sylvia could yet endure the loss of the load bearing wall in her perfectly constructed design. But she also understood that a new widow needed to explore the loss of him, to poke at it the way your tongue explores a tooth that has been pulled. This exploration took a certain amount of solitude.

*I remember every rotten bit of it.* Suddenly, the thought brought her up short. *It is getting to be just a memory!* Seeing Sylvia grapple with such loss made Jess realize how far she herself had come out of the darkness. While she wasn't watching, her love for Ed had been busy morphing into something far more pleasant than painful. Life had kick started in for her once again.

She clung a little tighter to Ben that evening. "Have you had a physical lately?" she asked while they sat in front of the TV.

"As a matter of fact, yes," Ben answered, obviously surprised. "Why? Are you thinking of buying me? Like one of your horses? Care to examine my teeth?"

"Just wanted to know." She cuddled closer and said no more about it.

\* \* \*

Sylvia drifted through the first weeks in a haze. Kyle had lawyers and accountants that efficiently shut his business down, handled his finances, debts, receivables, and insurance. When all was said and done, the lawyer consoled her by claiming she was now well off.

*Well off,* Sylvia considered the term. *I've been gutted like a trout, and I have to remind myself to breath, but I am now well off.*

She maintained her composure and her clients for a brief time until the day a man entered a meeting wearing a sweater very like Kyle would have chosen. She began to cry inconsolably, all the while apologizing by saying, "I can't imagine why I'm acting this way when I'm so well off."

After that, Sylvia closed Henderson Interiors indefinitely. Clients were all so sorry, but they soon moved on to other firms. During this time, her shock at Kyle's demise wore thin, only to be replaced by something infinitely more thorough at evisceration.

She could think of nothing to do with herself, so she began to visit her mother more often. But she found no relief when she got there so the visits were short and unsuccessful. At night, all pretense of normalcy was swept away. Without Jessica in the house, she could roam each room, searching for traces of Kyle everywhere. She would sit at his desk, calling repeatedly to hear his recorded message on voice mail.

She knew she had to protect herself from too many of the drugs that could ease the pain, and at times she could manage sleep from simple exhaustion instead of chemistry. She was not suicidal because it never occurred to her to be. For Sylvia, imagination ended at a well appointed home. But her dreams had the imagination her conscious hours lacked:

*One night a morgue team was performing an autopsy on her as she watched from above.*

*"Look at the size of this grief sack,"* the coroner said, *staring into her chest cavity.*

*"Why it's smashed the living daylights out of the joy organs and funny bones,"* said his assistant.

*"Yes. Mark this cause of death as swollen sorrow."*

Finally, on a rainy morning, Sylvia realized there was only one person she really wanted to see. She made the call.

That afternoon she sat at a miniscule table farthest from the baristas. Her grande decaf skinny vanilla latte was on the table in front of her, as yet untouched. *Why is it that the chairs in all Starbucks are so uncomfortable? And why am I wondering about that?* Her thoughts were so scattered left on their own that she got through each day most successfully by linear concentration. *I will now rise. I will now dress. I will now pretend I can eat a breakfast.* Some mornings the simplest of decisions was beyond her. What shoes with what bag with what outfit with what jewelry. So she had worn the same pair of black flats for days.

It was unusual for her to be inside a Starbucks, as opposed to strafing the drive-thru on the way to some design job. She had never visited this particular one in Seattle at all. But it was the one that he had suggested for their meeting when she had called him. *Our get-together. Our assignation. Our confrontation.* Her mind reeled through words like a thesaurus.

She saw him park the Acura and look in the rear view mirror to be sure his hair was orderly. She imagined that the mop of tight dark curls was never completely under control, and that the five o'clock shadow started a couple hours early for him. She was staring at him as intently as she might a blind date.

He wore a suede jacket, cut like a sports coat, over an open necked shirt. She thought the jacket might hide a couple extra pounds around the mid section. He was not as tall as Kyle had been, but outweighed him with the kind of husky build she'd expect from a man who had at one time played a muscle sport like hockey or football. His steps as he crossed the parking lot were confident, but he slowed once he entered the coffee shop, located her and nodded. He placed an order with the barista, and when his coffee was ready, he came over to her tiny table. His size diminished it all the more.

Now that he was here, Sylvia's mind went blank. She literally could think of nothing to say.

"I'm Tony Sapienza," he began, and tried to cup his hand over hers, but she pulled it back off the table and onto her lap. After a moment, he continued, "I was Kyle's friend. I'm sorry for your loss. And for mine." His voice cracked the least little bit.

"Yes. I know who you are. Well, at least what you were. To Kyle." Time passed, as she watched customers order four-adjective coffees with pastries she considered dangerous to your health. Eventually, she started again. "I knew Kyle was gay, of course, although we didn't discuss it. Oh, I didn't know at first. At first, I don't know that he even knew it for sure. Our sex life was always, well, gentle. I never liked it all that much, and he was never terribly demanding."

She used her fingers to make quote marks around the word lucky. "I was always one of the lucky women who had a man who enjoyed romance and a good cuddle. Sex, yes, sometimes and it was sweet. There was always love. And kindness. We shared a lot, interests in design and real estate, a liking for a civilized lifestyle, laughter. I respected him and loved him, and I think he did the same for me."

"There's no doubt of that," Tony interjected. "Love and respect for you were the deal breakers that kept him from committing to me. I surely tried to break that bond. But he didn't want to go public, and you gave him the reason he needed not to."

"I would have expected no less of him."

"So what do you expect from me?"

"I don't want to be your friend or your enemy. I don't want to be your confidante. I don't want to know the secrets you and my husband shared." She paused to sigh, then put her hand gently on top of his. "I just want to know someone else's sorrow is as insurmountable as mine."

They sat and held hands until long after their coffee had grown cold. Neither mentioned the things about Kyle that they didn't share. But they reminisced about the things they did. They swapped stories about his vanity over thinning hair, his love of all things French, his addiction to sweets and the other peculiarities that made him unique. They tapped into each other's misery, lightening each other's load.

From then on they called each other when one of them wanted to wallow in sorrow, neither feeling responsible for uplifting the other, but in the process helping themselves through the night. In so doing, Sylvia began her long journey through the stages of grief.

* * *

Sylvia continued to visit, but Lily could tell she was as disconnected as the undead. "I know she's just going through the motions of her days. Keeping to appointed rounds. It's the only way she's controlling herself right now."

"Nothing wrong with that," Jessica answered. "Seems to me you once told me never to underestimate the importance of a daily grind."

For the brief periods she would stay, Sylvia appeared so detached that she didn't even straighten this and that with ever busy hands. Instead, she sat in near complete stillness. Just once she pulled a chair close to Lily's bed and rested her own head next to her mother. Lily stroked her hair, thinking that living through the death of a spouse was the one thing she would have never chosen to share with her daughter.

That night, Nurse Mary Beth had heard Lily crying and brought her a cool cloth and a cup of tea. "Black and red and green," the nurse soothed. "Whatever the color, teas have been used as restoratives by most every culture for generations." She was the best of the nurses, to Lily's way of thinking. She knew that just the murmur of the human voice and a calming touch could often help her old charges through long, bleak nights.

"You may not want to go through all this sorrow, Lily," Nurse Mary Beth said. "But you're old enough to know that you can. That's the only advantage old folks have over the young."

**TWENTY**

**FUN HOUSE CHRONICLE**
## The Hotel

*H*$e'd$ *loved his daughters all their lives; he just didn't know who they were anymore. When they brought him to the care center, Glenn believed he was checking into a hotel. These unknown women seemed nice enough, so he went along peacefully.*

*He did not have a private room, and this he resented no end. "Get him out of here," he ordered the bellman, an aide who was not a bellman at all. His anger increased when the other resident showed no inclination to leave, and even smelled of bodily functions that best remained private to Glenn's way of thinking. And where the hell had his wife gone, come to think of it? Why hadn't she joined him on this particular trip?*

*"Bring my car around," he said to the room service attendant who brought in an evening meal Glenn did not remember ordering. "I'm checking out."*

*And, sure enough, after a brief stint of declining health, that's exactly what he did.*

FALL ARRIVED in the Northwest, blown in along with torrential rains. *No sitting outside in the courtyard today,* Lily thought as she wheeled herself excitedly into the activities room. Too many people were there for her to tell

Cognitive Corner her news. Her leg began to jiggle as she stifled her secret.

"Morning, Lily," Eunice greeted in her sweet voice, the closest thing to singsong now that the canaries were gone. Lily returned the greeting then noticed Bear had beaten her to the crossword again. *Dammit.*

"Another one bites the dust," he said, his heavy jaw fixed in a scowl. "Glenn checked out last night."

"And he had to do it without help from Furball," Eunice added.

"Oh, dear. I'm sorry about Glenn, for his daughters. At least they don't have to witness his confusion anymore," Lily said while she swiveled her wheelchair, looking around the room. Babs had moved even closer in order to restack the board games on the shelving near their table, so Lily couldn't bring up the subject most on her mind.

Instead she turned to Eunice. "What was all that hooey about the cat helping people cross the Great Divide?"

"Oh, it wasn't hooey," Eunice declared. "All the time the Mister was a patient here before me, I heard how Furball helped with the ones dying all alone. He'd curl up next to the poor soul, and purr. Help calm then. It was the only time he ever got near anybody."

"So we've heard, but how'd he know?" Bear's eyebrows scrunched in a look of disbelief.

Babs interrupted. "I asked Nurse Mary Beth just that," she said as she placed Yahtzee on top of Risk. "She thought the cat could detect the odors surrounding death, the chemicals released then. Or maybe it could tell when respiration became difficult."

"Or maybe Furball picked up cues from the nurses when their day-to-day routine changed," Bear grunted, still sounding skeptical.

"Whatever, the Bergeron Bitch was a little too hasty," Eunice said hotly. "Furball was sensitive to death. He comforted more than a few old bags of bones around here. He might have helped Glenn."

"Oh dear. I wouldn't call Patricia that," Babs said, shaking her head. She bent closer and lowered her voice to add, "But I'm really glad you did." Then she scurried away.

Lily checked the room again. No staff was in sight. Gladys was swearing at the television, and Charlie was involved with a couple other residents putting together a jigsaw. They'd just have to tell him later. She had to spill the beans, or she'd burst.

She leaned forward and whispered to Eunice and Bear, "Listen up, you two. You know I talked to Sylvia and Jessica, right before Kyle died."

"Yeah, but it's okay, Lily. We understand Sylvia has more important things to do now," Eunice said.

"Maybe. But Jessica just called. According to her, she's in."

"Holy crap!" Bear bellowed until Lily shushed him.

"Hot damn!" Eunice trilled.

Lily high fived a huge paw and a bony little hand covered with gold and gemstone rings.

* * *

Jessica did not tell Ben about Lily's Plan right away. She needed to mull it over by herself, roll around the pros and cons. She waited until after she'd met Sylvia for lunch. Just days, in fact, before Kyle died.

When she finally decided to give it a go, Jessica was

excited and maybe a little less than sensitive when she told Ben. In retrospect, she realized he needed time to assimilate, too, just like she had. But she chose a time when she felt comfortable to reveal her secrets. Unfortunately, it was also a time when Ben was, well, pretty excited, too.

They were in bed between episodes of afternoon sex, lying on their backs balancing wine glasses on naked bellies that had been pressed together just moments before. "Lily says Soundside is under siege," Jessica began. Ben was lazily stroking her breast. If he kept that up, it wouldn't be long before she set her shiraz aside. "She says the residents on Medicaid are afraid they'll be kicked out by the new regime. It would affect Bear first. But if Soundside drops the contract completely, then Lily goes, too."

"You're kidding. That's terrible," Ben mumbled leaning over to nuzzle her neck.

"Lily and Patricia Bergeron never got along, so Lily doesn't expect any favors. Wouldn't take one from her anyway."

"I'm sorry, Jess. I know how much Lily matters to you." Ben set his glass on the nightstand and turned toward her.

"But Lily has a plan. A plan that depends on Sylvia and me. If we don't agree, they don't know what will become of them."

"No pressure there," Ben snickered, slowly trailing his fingertips from her breast, down her rib cage to her hip bone.

"She said I'm a great caregiver and need money, and that Sylvia knows the ins and outs of real estate rehabs. So she wants us to convert my house into an Adult Family Home."

Ben's fingers stopped their southward journey. "She wants you to do what?"

If Jessica hadn't been so involved in telling her story, she might have realized he'd gone as still as stone.

"She's been thinking about it ever since I brought her out here to meet Marisol. She saw how big the house was then. She figures it this way. Eunice has money for the rehab and would float a loan. Sylvia can invest, too. They'd pay me to take classes the state requires to run a home and to buy a license. Eunice would get her money back by living here free until the debt is paid, then she'd go private pay. Bear and Lily would be on Medicaid from the beginning. And they'll ask Charlie to come. There'd still be room for a couple more. That would give me enough monthly income to run the place, hire staff and make a profit."

When Jessica paused, Ben remained silent, and she finally noticed. An afternoon rain drummed on the window, and one of the horses in the barn whinnied. Seconds clicked by. *Maybe he's just thinking about it.* "Sylvia told me she was embarrassed that her mother plotted with her pals before even asking us about it. Lily can be very manipulative. But we agreed we'd think about it."

Finally, Ben made a guttural noise that sounded like he'd been hit. "Manipulative? Sylvia allowed that Lily is manipulative? How about dictatorial? A tyrant? A fucking control freak? I can't believe you're actually thinking about this."

Jessica had never heard him angry before. She saw the line of his jaw tighten.

"Well, of course there were questions for me to answer for myself, Ben," Jessica said as soothingly as if she were speaking to an irate horse. As much as she loved Lily, she

wouldn't make such a life change without a lot of exploration. She had to be convinced there would still be time for
her horse business. She needed to know the requirements
of running an Adult Family Home, how to qualify for
receiving Medicaid payments, what schooling she needed. Did she really want the responsibility of caring for so
many in such fragile condition? Was this for herself or just
for the money? Would there really be any money?

"Sounds to me like you've already made up your mind."
Ben's pronouncement was flat, not at all happy.

His tone made Jessica shiver. *Is it getting cold in here?*
"I've been doing some homework. Research online. Plus
conversations with Clarice and with Jeff Parkinson about
the possibility of such a thing."

"So it's a done deal," said the man who'd turned to
stone.

"I admit that it sounded crazy at first. But the more
I've thought about it, the more right it feels. I have the
room, and if I really work at it, the time. Heaven knows I
have the financial need. This could save my ass, Ben, and
let me keep the ranch up and running. I wouldn't have to
sell Marisol."

Ben rolled slowly away from her, and sat up on his side
of the bed. She reached for him, but he pulled away. "So
you found it important to consult with everyone but me."

"Ben, I'm consulting you now."

"Then don't do it." His first arguments involved what
was good for her. "They're using you...it's too risky...
you're already too busy...I can provide for us both."

Then the arguments shifted to what was good for him.
"What about us...need more, not less...make some damn
commitment."

It escalated from bicker to bitter to Ben storming out. Jessica had no idea what he would do, whether he would be back, how he blew off steam. Ed the Evil would have gone to a shooting range. Chopped wood. Rebuilt a motorcycle. Ben, he told her later, exhausted himself in the gym. He bought all new power tools. He went on a strenuous hike into the Cascades. To really wallow in self pity, he'd even driven the streets of Seattle looking for his daughter.

*Different actions but the same way to heal.* Jessica realized that men lick their wounds in private, work things out for themselves. But while Ben was gone, she realized something about herself, too. She had changed.

She would never again be as compliant as she was with Ed. Even though she felt desolate at the idea that Ben might leave her, she wanted what was best for her. She would move forward with her plans, not willing to depend solely on Ben or his money. With her whole heart she wanted him to move forward with her. But that was his craziness to grapple with, not hers. The decision was up to him.

He appeared on the third night, holding a large soup pot and a grocery bag. "It's Wednesday. I've brought dinner," he said. She opened the door, and he came into the foyer and walked to the kitchen. He set the grocery bag on the counter and the pot of old-fashioned chicken soup on the stove. He turned to her and said, "This is just one of the recipes that old people will really like. A pot this size would be enough for everybody."

That night, she wanted more than make-up sex. She wanted love. She begged him not to frighten her again, and told him there was more and more room in her heart for him all the time. They made promises to each other about consideration and trust and never just walking away.

In bed, he was different than anyone she had known. He was beefier than Ed to begin with, not all lanky and smooth. He took his time start to finish, was less athletic but more tender. Watching him sleep in the early morning hours, Jessica understood that Lily had been right about loss. Ed was a chapter in her story, but not the final one. In fact, she no longer had to think of him as Ed the Evil.

He was just Ed again.

* * *

After Kyle died, Jessica kept Sylvia involved with Lily's Plan whether she wanted to be or not. "You need to keep active, get started with the preparations," Jessica ordered.

Her mission was to rehabilitate Sylvia along with the house. Sylvia was becoming important to her, not only as Lily's daughter but as her…what? Business partner? Coworker? Friend? One thing she had learned from Lily was that if you didn't have the family you were born into, you got yourself another one. So maybe Sylvia was becoming an older – if not wiser – sister, one that she would learn to love for their differences more than like for their similarities.

Now Jessica and Ben stood with Sylvia in the downstairs bedroom of Jessica's farmhouse, staring in a variety of directions like a colony of meerkats on the alert. Ben was using enough body English to direct traffic as he explained their plans. "We thought we could knock out this west wall to build a second big bedroom and another bathroom. Then we'd put in handicap accessible showers. There'd be a hall at the south end for a smaller private room and to connect to the living room."

Jessica couldn't help but cut in. "And along the north wall, we'll have patio doors for exits. That would keep us in code. We'll have a patio all along the back for a container garden. For you know who." Jessica beamed at Sylvia.

"The kitchen, living room and dining room stay where they are so no major changes except in appliances and furnishings."

"What about a staff room?" Sylvia asked. Jessica could tell from the fit of her slacks that she'd lost weight. But the outfit was clean and pressed. Sylvia's hair looked nice. She was at least keeping up her personal standards. *A good sign.*

"This way," Ben said. They went up the stairs that led from the kitchen.

There was a guest room and a bathroom that Ed and Jessica had put in, but the rest of the floor was still unfinished. "We thought we'd expand up here as our family grew. And that's just what I'm doing, but not in the way I thought." Jessica said. She'd never expected to do it with oldsters instead of youngsters.

Ben said, "We'll, I mean Jessica, will move up here. We'll frame in a staff room over the downstairs bedroom, then the rest will be Jess's personal living and office space. She's discovered there are a shitload of docs to keep on each resident."

"So what do you think?" Jessica cut in. Sylvia's approval was key. Without it, Lily wouldn't be able to move here. And there wouldn't be enough money to move forward.

He'd been slow to get with the plan, but now Ben seemed too excited to stop selling. "You're more expert with this stuff than we are. But I'm not a bad craftsman...."

"...neither am I..."

"...and Sam says he'll help..."

"...while I go to school." Jessica said, ending the ping-pong conversation.

Sylvia looked deep in thought, as if she were considering the open space and the ideas they'd presented. They followed her back downstairs, trailing along as she walked through the house one more time. Speaking almost to herself, Sylvia said, "If we framed in the back porch and added a bath, we'd have another private room. Someone with the resources will pay well for the best."

Finally she turned toward them. "Kyle had a home inspector he trusted. Real estate is so slow I'm sure the guy could use some work. He knows how to do all we'll need. And the tradesmen to hire. Of course, I know a lot of tricks to make it look great without a lot of cash." She nodded with the ghost of a smile, the first one Jessica had seen on her face in days. "I think we can make this happen."

It must have surprised Sylvia when Ben enfolded her in a big hug. But afterwards, she held out her arms, and Jessica embraced her as well.

\* \* \*

*I have animals out the ass.* Clarice separated Furball from Kit Kat once again. The two of them would never see eye to eye, so she shut Furball in her son Cole's room, put the canaries in her bedroom, and gave Kit Kat and Hershey the rest of the house. It was a temporary arrangement at best, and she visited them each in turn, like a chaplain going cell to cell in the big house. Sometimes, like now, Furball jetted through the door then had to be corralled again.

She'd been worried about what to do with them all. But now that she'd been told about Lily's Plan, she knew that the first three residents in the new Adult Family Home would be two canaries and a really pissed off cat. Not to mention how surprised Jessica's dog Folly would be.

She'd agreed to help get the new Adult Family Home up and running. It was a godsend for Lily and the rest of her Cognitive Corner buddies. It might just pull Jessica back from the financial brink, as well. And all this freelance money was becoming a tidy sum in her own coffers.

With input from Eunice, Sylvia and Jessica, Clarice developed an initial budget. Eunice would put up a lump sum to pre-pay a year. After that, she would pay monthly. Sylvia invested the lion's share toward the upfront costs. She included some of the life insurance money from Kyle, saying he would have been proud of the gesture. She would begin to earn a healthy percent starting in year two.

They counted on Medicaid income from Charlie, Lily and Bear. They hoped to hire three aides, with Jessica performing the duties of a fourth one. In addition, they required one housekeeper, a cook and visiting nurse support for two hours each day. Clarice rolled the numbers and made a recommendation to Jessica that they prepare for six residents. They'd be in the hole until a fifth came along, and six was the limit that the state allowed. The more the merrier from a bookkeeper's point of view.

"We must move quickly," Clarice confided to Jessica. Things at Soundside were getting worse. At the last staff meeting Babs was desolate when Patricia Bergeron reneged on the $20 matching grant from Soundside for the staff holiday party.

"But I've promised everyone," Babs pleaded.

"Then you'll just have to lose a little face," the Bergeron Bitch answered.

Clarice thought about it at home as she gave the canaries fresh water. *Guess that put us all in our place.*

She'd looked up the Medicaid contract, and it terminated at the end of the year, not much more than three months away. She figured CompreCare would probably renew it, but start dumping the more expensive people. Bear would be among the first to go either way which would break Lily's heart. Sometimes Clarice wondered how she'd let herself get involved with these old souls. Other times she wondered what had taken her so long.

Clarice tried to keep a low profile at work in case her anger overflowed. In the meantime, her relationship with Jeff's wife, Terri, thrived, becoming a real friendship. They began having lunch together each Wednesday. Clarice roughed out Lily's Plan for Terri, and Terri provided hints from Jeff on how to proceed.

Wherever they went for lunch, it had to be close enough to Soundside that Clarice could get there and back in an hour, but far enough away that she wasn't likely to be seen with the former boss's wife. If the meal was heavier than their favorite Thai food, Clarice had learned a trick from Terri. She asked for a doggy bag to be delivered at the same time the meal was served. She cut her portion in half right then and put half away; if it stayed on her plate too long, she would eat it all. At long last, Clarice was developing instincts for weight control.

*Weight loss isn't rocket science. It's harder.*

**TWENTY-ONE**

**FUN HOUSE CHRONICLE**
## The Hospice Room

*There is a hospice room next to the nurse's station. When a resident is a breath from deceased, she is moved here so the family can have privacy to mourn and so nurses can be close at hand to monitor and minister. Life expectancy is a matter of hours or, at most, days. Drugs are turned up to minimize pain. Worry is now more about comfort than addiction.*

*After a lengthy stint in the nursing home, a favorite old grandmother from a Northwest tribe is moved to this final chamber. She is beloved by her community. Several of her extended family even work here, providing her care.*

*A night comes when tribal officials and friends gather together in the parlor. Several wear ceremonial garb and carry traditional instruments. They plan a sing for the elder. In their songs they will pay respect and celebrate the beautiful trail she will leave when she passes.*

*Although their message is one of solace, the atmosphere is solemn. The woman's eldest son quietly enters her room to awaken her and let her know the singers are here to lighten her journey. The respectful hush in the parlor is suddenly shattered by her voice, ringing out loud and true. "Tell them to get out of here."*

*No more is said as the singers and their instruments quietly slip away.*

*The old woman dies that night, an unsung soul on her own silent path to points unknown. Not all people are crazy about tradition.*

WHILE THE Adult Family Home was under construction, Soundside was as rife with intrigue as a room full of politicians. There wasn't really need for all the secrecy, but Bear was a cloak-and-dagger junkie, and he loved it.

He'd been surprised that Charlie hadn't immediately leapt at the idea of leaving Soundside for greener pastures. He actually had to sell the idea. And he was relentless. At night when the two were alone in their sterile digs on opposite sides of their curtain, Bear would spin tales about the house and grounds he'd never seen, embroidering on Lily's report about them. "A two-story mansion set deep in the country with old-growth forest and the Cascade Mountains as a backdrop. Lush green fields with herds of horses that we can watch all day, patios with all the planters we want, staff as gentle as lambs. All managed by Lily's friend Jessica, a genuine nurturing goddess." He could almost hear the crescendos of *Morning Mood* accompany his pitch.

Charlie's biggest concern was about leaving Nurse Mary Beth and her particular ministrations with the most private part of his anatomy. "If you got these sores behind your balls, you'd understand," he said to Bear. "She doesn't hurt me so much when she attends to them."

"Yeah? Well, Mary Beth will train a new nurse with your nuts in mind. Or even come with us herself. Then you'd be left here all alone." Bear knew he should be ashamed

249

of himself. "All your friends will be gone. You'll be alone with a bunch of demented travelers for company. And the Bergeron Bitch to answer to. Scary shit, dude."

Finally, Bear's badgering developed a chink in Charlie's armor. Maybe he'd be willing to move if someone would help him with all the paperwork and if the new place promised he could keep feeding birds, an activity he'd come to enjoy.

*Hook, line and fucking sinker.* Bear gave himself an imaginary pat on the back. He justified his promises by assuring himself that Charlie would be a lot better off, even if it frightened him now. Since his so-called better half never visited anymore, Charlie really should stay with the friends that wanted him.

Jessica met with Cognitive Corner and told them that, while she was taking classes, they should start thinking about staff or another resident or two. "I'm not willing to raid Soundside myself, but what you do isn't my business."

While Lily and Eunice developed a list of staff they'd like to see at the Adult Family Home, Bear took on a different job for Jessica. He offered to run background checks. Since it was so much like detective work again, he was proud to contact his old buddies still on the police force. He could search for convictions online, but the cops could search for actual charges. Bear took it as a personal mission that Jessica would never have to deal with a sumbitch pervert like the one who'd terrified Eunice and brought Jeff down.

\* \* \*

Lily and Eunice decided that, of all the aides, there were only two worth inviting to the new Adult Family

Home. Chrissie and Rick. Whether they'd go was an entirely different matter. After all, there'd be fewer benefits like health insurance. Jessica could not promise everything from the first day. But she could offer a better salary and more flexibility in hours.

Lily said, "If we could convince Alita to come as the housekeeper, maybe Rick would follow."

"Like a bee to a blossom."

Try as they might, they could think of no other aides so they moved on to other functions. "Nobody from this kitchen," Eunice said crinkling her nose. "Burnt toast won't be a required skill." She thought for a moment and added, "And we can lose our own stuff without the assistance of anyone from this laundry."

"No money for a physical therapist on staff," Lily said imagining the final loss of Ernie. There'd be others they'd miss, too. "No Lia or Babs or Belly Dancing Grannies."

The twosome worked to avoid a funk.

"No pain, no gain."

"No guts, no glory."

"No give, no take."

But a funk descended nonetheless when Eunice asked, "Wait a minute! What about our Clarice?"

Lily said, "She's helping Jessica and Sylvia now. But over the long haul? I just don't know how much we'll see her."

\* \* \*

Once Charlie was in the boat, Cognitive Corner reviewed the rest of the residents and decided that each offered the new Adult Family Home too much difficulty.

Either their minds were drifting away or the nature of their disabilities was such that they would be a liability to themselves and the other residents. But one decision caused them actual pain.

"We can't handle her," Jessica said.

"We can't handle her," Sylvia said.

"They can't handle her," Bear and Eunice and Charlie said.

"But how can I leave Gladys behind? Nobody understands the old salt like I do. Who will help the nurses get what she wants without me to translate?" Lily realized that being a member of Cognitive Corner came with a price. She had placed herself in loco parentis and now intended to turn her back.

"Well, okay. Maybe we could try," Bear, Eunice, Sylvia and Jessica relented. But Gladys didn't understand well enough to agree. Clarice checked records and found that Gladys had no family left to authorize a move. Chrissie said nobody had visited her in the years she'd worked there. Finally, Jessica put her foot down.

"Lily, we've tried but we're road blocked. And there is so much else to do right now. But once you have moved, I'll try again to convince Gladys. Maybe she'll understand once you're gone that she can follow, too."

Lily agreed and tried to put it out of her mind. She had more time now that Sylvia and Jessica had less of it, and she found her new computer was the best way to keep herself out of their hair. Bear had helped her order the Toshiba laptop on his netbook, and now that it had arrived, he taught her the fundamentals of an internet search and email and just plain word processing.

"I love this!" Lily enthused. Even Bear was impressed

by the speed with which she was learning.

"You're pretty cool for an old lady," Rick said with admiration, watching over her shoulder as she surfed in the parlor.

"Old?" Eunice sniped at him. "On a cruise ship she'd be considered young."

The online news sites fascinated Lily throughout the day. She began quoting articles to the staff and watching YouTube. She even decided to find out what had become of her blood relatives, if any still existed. "Probably all horse thieves and deserters," she said as she searched ancestor. com.

"I myself am related to the Barrymores and Bernhardts," Eunice claimed, with a theatrical flip of her hair. The effect was diminished when the orange spikes refused to budge.

"If I can find anyone, maybe Sylvia would get interested in contacting them. Give her something new to think about."

"Look up Harmon's family, too."

"If his relatives are the big pricks his parents were I'll only find them on porn sites."

"Oooo, let me help with that."

* * *

Four people were Sylvia's building blocks to begin again. She was aware of it as the frozen tundra of grief melted enough for her to be aware of anything.

Jessica kept her involved in the Adult Family Care project. "You pick out the floor coverings, the color scheme, the furniture, the other stuff the home will need," Jessica said. "I have too much to do with school and construction." She even asked Sylvia to name the place and get an ad in the phone book.

"Okay, but Heartbreak Hotel is already taken," Sylvia had responded.

Of course, Lily was another building block who had always been available in times of need. That used to work for a skinned knee or a math problem. Now Sylvia was sensitive to her mother's burdens and tried to contain her own sorrow during their visits. She turned the naming detail over to Cognitive Corner and sat back to listen in. Eunice liked anything with alliteration like Happy House or Content Cottage.

"Excuse me, Eunice, but that makes me want to puke," Bear growled.

Charlie swore it had to be a bird-ish name like Jessica's Nest or Final Migration. Bear growled even louder.

Finally, Lily pronounced, "Let's name it exactly what it is." They agreed Sylvia should have a plaque made for the front door:

*Latin's Ranch – An Adult Family Home*

Of course, Sylvia couldn't really hide her grieving from her mother. "You must not cancel your activities of daily living," Lily said. "Go shopping. Buy me a new nightie. One without bunnies. And a slipper." Once Lily had Jessica pick her up, then go get Sylvia. They went to Latin's Ranch so they could see the progress on the house. "The only thing you really need is time," Lily counseled, and Jessica agreed. "You won't stay in mourning forever." It was kind of them to offer that hope, but Sylvia didn't really believe it.

The day came when she received an email from her third building block. Trai, her half brother, wrote from Vietnam. He said Lily had sent him an email with her contact information.

*Mother? An email?*

His message sent condolences, then in stilted English he talked about himself and his family. His son, Dinh, worked on the Lido deck of a cruise ship, and had actually seen some American ports. Trai closed, saying he was very curious about his American sister and would she please tell him all about herself.

*Nothing to tell. Except I'm so well off.* But she saved the email, and thought about it through the day. In the night, she rose, put on her slippers, padded down to her work room and booted up the computer.

*Dear Trai: When I was a child I wanted a sibling. I thought I would have somebody to play with who came along with us each time we moved. I didn't know about you. Maybe Mother was right not to tell me, I'm not sure. I might have been easier on her if she had been more open with me. Either way, I've met you now.*

*I grew up isolated, having learned not to bother making friends because we soon left them behind. Mother was company enough until I married Kyle. And then I needed nobody else to be really close to.*

*It appears that was a mistake. Now that he's gone, I feel pulled out by the roots. I need a place to plant myself again. So I will try to become your sibling. It may be some time before I get beyond sounding rather formal, little brother, but I will try.*

*I'm glad that you made it through the war and that you live happily today. Regards to your wife (my sister) and your children (my nieces and nephew). Your big sister, Sylvia*

The fourth building block in her life was Kyle's lover,

Tony. "You can't just get me up and running like some kind of fancy new spark plug," Sylvia complained. "Our friendship is weird enough as it is, don't you think?"

"That's bullshit. We could go in January," Tony said, stirring his coffee, while his dark eyes stared lasers at her. Sylvia averted her gaze down at the travel brochures he had spread out on the table. She tidied them into a neat fan.

He marched on. "Air France has a great rate if we book now, and I reserved a hotel in Paris for six nights. Just in case you say yes." He added in a lower tone, "Two beds, of course, or if you prefer, we can get two rooms. But it is spendy."

Sylvia had said no, absolutely not, when Tony first mentioned it. He must be joking. His plan was that they should go together to Paris, to visit the places that Kyle had wanted to see. Kyle, who had been a first rate Francophile when it came to art, fashion, food, wine, and snobbery, had never actually seen the country.

"He'd never take the time to go with me," Tony said, looking wistful.

"Me either," Sylvia said. "Maybe he couldn't decide which one of us to ask."

Thinking about Kyle's dilemma, she felt something within her shift. Her shell began to crack as if a chick inside was finding its way out. She began to giggle. It grew into an actual laugh, and Tony joined in. They guffawed until tears were forced from their eyes.

"He'd make us go to every tourist thing, Arc de Triomphe to the Louvre." Tony sputtered.

"Shop the Champs-Elysées," Sylvia said with drama.

"Take a bateau mouche along the Seine. Visit each choco-laterie we passed, to soothe that sweet tooth."

"And, of course, cast aspersions at the passersby from sidewalk cafés," Tony said, then corrected himself, "Well, maybe from inside in January."

"You know, a Parisian café surely would be a damn site more rewarding than one more Starbucks latte." Sylvia found herself wondering just why she thought she couldn't go. *Why not?*

Why not celebrate Kyle's spirit with this delightful man if it helped her relieve the ache? Who said she couldn't do the unexpected thing if she jolly well wanted to? Maybe she had inherited a little of her mother's wanderlust after all. And so, much to her own surprise and against what she perceived as society's norms, Sylvia found herself agreeing to accompany the memory of Kyle to Paris, along with his handsome lover.

TWENTY-TWO

FUN HOUSE CHRONICLE
# Belle

*B*elle *is nearly a hundred years old, sweet as cotton candy and just as airy. Befuddlement has not left her suspicious or afraid. She has drifted gently into madness.*

*Go back four decades and Belle was a nurse. To this day, she maintains a sense of the rightness of things, and she chooses to position herself smack dab in the middle of the intersecting halls at the nurse's station. Nothing much gets past her there. Today she greets visitors with a heartfelt smile, offering each a piece of her cheese sandwich. She has no idea who they are, but she's glad they're here.*

*She likes a good tight perm, does Belle, so her snowy white hair is curly as a karakul lamb. Her wrinkled pink skin is baby soft, and though it must have suffered hard use, stress lines have been eased years ago. Belle has managed to find a little gold in her golden years. She is at peace.*

*"Where you going, Belle?" asks an aide sorting linen when Belle trundles past in her chair.*

*She stops, cocks her head, considers and answers, "Well... I don't know." Then off she goes on down the hall.*

*Wherever she's heading, they will be delighted when she arrives.*

Jessica was grappling with sleep-deprived days caused by wakeful nights of worry. Ben provided a wall of strength to huddle beside, but he had the audacity to snore softly while she thrashed.

*What the hell have I agreed to? Can I do it all?* Fretting each step of the way, she was nonetheless working her way through all the chores. To begin, she made sure her basic business was secure. She let all her boarding and riding customers know they could still count on her, and of course, on Sam. In fact, she'd even be home more of the time now. It would be business as usual for Gina Lola and the Marin's pony and all the rest of the herd. Latin's Ranch was just taking in a few human boarders along with horses.

Jessica completed her management course and purchased her license. Building inspectors peered at this and shoved at that during the rehab process while Ben trailed them in eager anticipation. Official reports were written, approved and filed. Now Jessica was waiting for the arrival of medical equipment and for the final go-ahead from the State. The whole process exhilarated, exhausted, infuriated and frustrated her.

"You've done very well to be near completion of construction so soon and with your mind and budget still more or less intact," Sylvia told her.

Hiring staff took another bite out of Jessica's time. Clarice committed to staying involved on a freelance basis, and Chrissie, Rick and Alita all accepted jobs at Latin's Ranch. Jessica didn't know the exact start date, but she'd give them at least two weeks warning so they could leave Soundside with clean records.

A nursing service agreed to provide a registered nurse for two hours each day. Jessica was going to approach Mary Beth about it but decided to wait until after the Ranch had a little work history. No reason to antagonize Soundside more than necessary.

Jessica thought that finding a cook might be her toughest task, but one found her. Aurora announced she'd like the job. "Heavy cleaning is too hard on my bones these days, but I love to cook," the Latina said patting her well padded tummy. "And I love to eat, *qué lástima*." She'd make breakfast and lunch for the aides to serve. The mid-day meal would usually be the main one, but she could also leave easy dishes for Jessica to heat for the evening.

"You think maybe this Ben would be my assistant cook? *Muy guapo*."

"Back off, you old *puma*," Jessica laughed. "*Es mio*."

\* \* \*

Jessica hoped to be open by the first of November, but realistically, it was going to be some weeks later. Ben suggested they aim at Thanksgiving as their first official meal together. "What a lovely idea," Jessica agreed.

At the moment they were sitting on the new dining room floor, sharing a pizza. The room was void of furniture, gleamed with newness, and smelled of fresh paint, lacquer and lemony cleaning fluids.

"Looks full of promise and ready to go," Ben commented.

"Yeah. They promise to deliver the tables and chairs tomorrow," Jessica said. "Just like they promised to deliver them today." She took a look around as she picked onions off her slice. *I didn't order onions, did I?* But she was mostly occupied with how proud she was of the work they'd done. "It's even pretty, don't you think? Sylvia's done a terrific job."

Sylvia had chosen the non-skid laminate flooring in a sunny wood tone she called Butternut. It would make easy going for wheelchairs and walkers, plus be simple to clean. The walls of the dining and living rooms were a light shade of turquoise with coral accent walls.

"I read that aqua is the one color that looks good on everybody," Ben observed.

"It's not aqua. It's Desert Gemstone."

"Excuse me. I'll keep that in mind." He shoved the pizza box aside and stretched his back. He and Sam had worked alongside Jessica almost every evening, doing the heavy lifting to complete the house. He moved closer, nudging her until she began massaging his shoulders. "I should never have fallen for a younger woman. They are slave drivers."

"Oh? Tell me, would an old lady do this?"

Sometime later Ben answered, once he had caught his breath, "Dear God, an old woman might. But I'm not sure we could call her a lady."

* * *

Before Latin's Ranch was ready, the Bergeron Bitch kicked Bear out of Soundside. He made it easy for her to do it.

The big man was walking the halls after dinner, as was his habit. He'd lost enough weight and built back enough muscle that he could circle the halls without breaking into a sweat. He pushed his wheelchair ahead of him to keep his balance as he exercised. If he exhausted himself with increased speed or distance, he could always sit back down.

He was singing about a highwayman who'd always be around and around. He rounded a corner himself and smacked into two travelers who were blocking the hall. His wheelchair bowled theirs apart, slamming to an abrupt stop. He pitched sideways and down, the wheelchair toppling back on top of him.

* * *

Lily heard the clatter from the parlor. She wheeled herself out and saw Bear lying in the hall, blood spurting from his face. Her heart faltered…everything but Bear lost focus. "Bear!" Lily yelled then shrieked even louder when he did not react, "Help, help!" Only in a haze was she aware of one traveler crying, another going on down the hall, and Violet lurking nearby.

Lily leaned forward and reached for his chair, trying to haul it off him. Bear was so very still. She stretched out to pull up on the wheels, but it was too much strain for her, and she cried out again. That's when Violet must have thought Lily was attacking Bear instead of helping him. The confused old warrior lifted her walker and brought it down on Lily's extended arm.

Lily heard a brittle crack right before the tidal wave of pain. She screamed again. The Fun House floor buckled, tumbling her upside down. Blackness followed.

When Lily came to, she was in the hospital. She had always known another infection would cause her return, but she was wrong. An intern explained it was the kind of broken arm that a youngster could have weathered with aplomb but would be much harder for her. It was a fairly clean single break that required no pins, so the possibility of infection was not as great as it could have been. But the muscles assaulted by Violet's walker were hyper flexed and greatly abused. They would likely be even more painful than the break itself.

Drugs put her under for a time, but the throbbing pain was so intolerable that it soon broke through. This time, Sylvia was sitting beside her. Lily looked from her daughter's haggard face down to the fiberglass cast on her own right arm. Only the tips of her fingers showed. She tried to move them and gasped. Sylvia leaped up to find a nurse, but Lily stopped her. "Wait...tell me. Bear."

Sylvia told her that Bear and one of the travelers had also been brought to the hospital for x-rays and observation. The traveler was already back at Soundside, and Bear was down the hall recovering from a sprained ankle, a broken nose and massive bruising. "He looks like a retired palooka more than ever."

Lily was in too much agony to smile, but she was grateful Sylvia was there to tell her the news. Then, for the first time in her life, she asked the nurse to give her more pain medication, and she went under again.

The hospital kept her overnight, then released her back to Soundside. She was drugged even deeper than her first trip there all those weeks ago, but this time the meds couldn't keep the pain at bay. Nurses Baby Talk and Happy Face told her they had increased dosages as much as the doctor would allow. Lily slept for short bursts between shots. As she occasionally surfaced, she became aware of Gladys at her side.

"Goddamn, son of a bitch," the old sailor crooned as she stroked Lily's uninjured hand.

\* \* \*

Bear was told he'd be ready to leave the hospital the following day, although for the life of him he couldn't imagine how his beat up old carcass could handle any more jostling. Sam Spade or Lew Archer could take far more of a pounding than he could. He was goddamned humiliated to have been kayoed by a couple of nutburgers on wheels. He despaired that his old buddies would ever hear such a sorry tale.

Then things got worse. Apparently the Bergeron Bitch exercised her power behind the scenes. The hospital's social worker told Bear he could not return to Soundside. "They've had so many admissions, that they simply have no more beds for male residents," the effete young man said. "Do you have anywhere else you could go? A relative perhaps?"

Bear had nobody but Lily, Eunice and Charlie. His wife was long gone, who the hell knew about his brother, and any old squeezes had stopped answering his calls long ago. He had a choice. Take paratransit to the nearest dump. Or call Jessica.

\* \* \*

"Oh, God. Oh, I'm so sorry," Jessica sputtered. "But you can't come here yet, Bear. The state could close me down before I open. Hell, I don't even have any beds yet. But don't lose heart…I'll find something…it won't be for very long…keep your eyes on the good things ahead."

Bear was Jessica's first lesson in how the owner of Latin's Ranch had to be resourceful and positive when things leaped aboard a handcart to hell. Jessica was terrified for Bear and even more so for how Lily would react to his exile. *Better to not tell her, not until she's improved.* The owner of an adult care home apparently had to be duplicitous, too.

She called the hospital's social worker, and together they began to work the system. He contacted other nursing facilities, but the only one that would take Bear was rated so low by the State that the social worker wouldn't recommend it. He finally confessed to Jessica. "If we have no other choice, we sometimes release patients to the parking lot. Then a local mission might take them. Or a homeless shelter."

"What?" Jessica was appalled. She knew things were bad, but how could this be true? *What are we doing to our old people?*

"I know it sounds cold. But the hospital isn't responsible. We need to make a living too, you know," the social worker justified with frustration.

"Do missions even have equipment for somebody in Bear's shape? Hospital beds? Commodes?"

"Maybe. Probably not."

Jessica shuddered. She refused to call on Ben at work. This problem was hers to solve. So she recruited Sam, making him go check out two Adult Family Homes. She dropped in on two more. One had no room, and two did not take Medicaid patients. The fourth smelled of urine the minute she walked through the front door.

Dead end.

In desperation, Jessica thrashed her brain for another plan. Finally, she called the cheap non-chain motels in the area, working her way alphabetically through the Yellow Pages. The Roadside Rest appeared to offer what she needed. She called the social worker and then Bear to explain what was going to happen.

* * *

In its earlier life, the Roadside Rest would have served families seeing the U.S.A. in their Chevrolets. Mom and the kids would have waited out front while Dad went in to be sure it was clean. Now it looked like a place where out-of-work families were spending their last dimes on fast food. Drug buys were going down in some rooms. In others, hookers…but, no, the dive hadn't slid that low quite yet.

Bear had all these thoughts when the team of EMTs extracted him from the ambulance. They wheeled him to room 128 in the back, where street noise was not so loud. Bear watched greasy wrappers and sheets of a newspaper blow by the row of rooms like urban tumbleweeds.

Jessica was waiting for him in the room. "I paid the motel to take out one of the twin beds, and I rented a hospital bed. They moved Norman Bates out of the shower, too."

The female EMT chuckled approvingly.

"Smart thinking, doll," Bear whimpered. As the team transferred him gurney to bed, his bruises yelped even though hydrocodone dulled the worst of it.

"Call me doll again, and I'll really make you whimper," Jessica warned.

"Nurses, caregivers, aides…the world's being overrun by touchy broads."

The female EMT added, "Don't you forget it, Mister."

"Holy shit, they're ganging up."

"Don't you know it, Mister," the male EMT echoed in a weary tone. "You do what they say, and you won't get hurt."

After the ambulance crew left, Bear closed his eyes and took a deep breath. He tried to keep up the act, but he was feeling damn weak. When he opened his eyes, Jessica was staring at him. She smiled and said, "You look more like a panda than a grizzly."

"Fucking black eyes make me look like I lost the fight."

"You did. The travelers are both fine."

"Figures. But how's Lily?"

"Weak. In pain. Worried about you when she's not too hopped up to worry about anything."

"When you can, tell her I'm fine. I am fine, right? You're not dropping me here like last week's leftovers?" He was desperate for her reassurance. After such high hopes for life at Latin's Ranch, he couldn't stand it if Jessica refused to take him in his fragile condition.

"You are absolutely fine. You'll be here a couple of weeks at most. By then the Ranch will be ready, and you'll be my first homesteader." She smiled and lightly patted his chest.

He listened gratefully as she explained what they had in store. He should pay the motel from his disability money. "Soundside doesn't get to keep another nickel of it. But Clarice says since Medicaid pays them direct, we need to wait until they return it for us to claim it. Eunice is putting up the cash you'll need in the meantime."

"Sounds like you dames got my back." Bear looked around the room as much as a stiff neck would allow. He felt another niggle of fear. "I don't know if I can make it here alone."

"You won't have to. We'll see you through this. I know this place is no Taj Mahal, but it has some features that newer places don't. To start, your clothes are there." She pointed to an alcove with a rod. "Motel NoTells don't always have real closets." Bear was impressed she'd realized he couldn't easily battle with a closet door to reach his things.

"Chrissie brought everything here. And she put your computer under your pillow." Bear felt for it, and there it was. "But there's no wifi, so I'll take it home with me if you want."

She indicated the bathroom and continued the room tour. "We removed the bathroom door to be easier with your wheelchair. This is a retrofitted handicap room so there are handrails around the toilet. But don't try the shower on your own. Chrissie or I will give you bed baths. One of us will be here every day, as often as we can.

"If you can handle your own meds, I'll leave your blood pressure and cholesterol pills here on the nightstand along with the water pitcher. And there are four more painkillers."

"I can be trusted with that."

"Good." She frowned at him, apparently trying to look tough. "Now here are the rules for the next couple weeks. We're doing a lot for you so you have to promise to do one thing for us. Don't make us worry. If there's nobody here to help you pee, don't get up. Use the urinal I've stored in the nightstand drawer." She opened the drawer to show him the device.

"I'm supposed to stick my dick in that?"

"It's that or pee in the bed. But don't get up on your own. If you drop the TV remote on the floor, don't pick it up. Read until one of us can get here. Don't try to get in your chair by yourself to wheel down to Reggie's Tavern. In short, don't be stupid. Is that a promise?"

"Yes, ma'am."

"Say the word."

"Promise."

"In your time here, you'll be meeting some new family members. A bunch of us are taking turns. A lady named Aurora may bring your meals. She may also hit on you. Chrissie and I will do body care this week. Rick will be on call to help out when he can.

"Sam is my barn manager, and Ben is my lover. Either man might fill in some of the time when I can't be here. If you do anything that makes either of them leave me, I will shred all your clothing. Otherwise, I'll just wash it."

Bear wanted to laugh, but he wondered if she just might do it.

"One more thing. I bought you a pre-paid phone." She handed the little instrument to him. "My number, Ben's and Soundside's are all programmed in here. Anything you need, just call. When you feel up to it, call and reassure Charlie. He's nervous. Any questions?"

Bear looked at the lovely woman standing in front of him, her streaked hair in wild curls, the freckles on the bridge of her nose making her look younger than her years, and her hands on slim, athletic hips. "Just one. This Ben guy?" Bear asked.

"What about him?"

"Does he have any idea what he's getting himself into?"

Jessica laughed, and Bear liked the sound of it. "He's a lucky SOB, and so are you. Many fine women give a damn about you, Bear."

And what the hell would he do without them? He was a lucky SOB. He hadn't cried since he'd burned himself with a cherry bomb when he was seven. This time, it wasn't pain that caused the tears.

\* \* \*

Drugs blunted the ache but blurred her thinking, lowering her resolve. Lily felt dizzy at times and floated at others. Her resources diminished. The depression she tried so hard to hold at bay was now a predator on the loose. The Grim Jokester was winning.

She became paranoid and confused. She couldn't always remember Latin's Ranch and the brighter days ahead that she had planned. She became convinced that Bear was dead, that everyone was hiding it from her. She collapsed into herself, giving up all the fight that was in her. Somewhere deep inside, she was aware of how hopeless she must appear, slumped in her chair, no longer well enough to care.

With her broken arm, she could not do the simplest tasks much less take care of herself. She was trapped by the dreadful sights and noise of her old nemesis, the dining room. Nurse Happy Face explained and seemed genuinely sorry. "We just don't have time to go room to room, feeding everyone who needs help. You have to come to us now." Lily was rolled down the hall whether she wanted to go or not. She was parked next to a table with two others who needed help with their meals. And she was told to open wide for the overcooked peas.

Jessica tried, Clarice tried, Charlie tried, but Lily didn't.

Eunice sat with her and spun long sagas about how wonderful things would be at Latin's Ranch. "We'll both saddle up and ride like the wind," Eunice promised. "Nothing and no one bad will catch us at the Ranch."

"The Ranch?" Lily asked.

When Bear was well enough, he called her from the motel. Nurse Baby Talk placed the phone next to Lily's ear, and Bear talked a long time, telling her about every little thing from the hospital through today. Before saying good-bye, he got serious. "Jessica is a minor miracle," he said to Lily. "And she loves you. Don't let her down. You must come to the Ranch with us."

"The Ranch?" Lily asked.

Still, Lily might have battled her way back, defeating the Fun House one more time. But that was before the night Gladys died, ripping a wider hole in her heart. Lily had heard the old pirate's last words. "Fucking cat?" she'd rasped.

Nurse Mary Beth had to tell her Furball didn't live there anymore.

\* \* \*

When Chrissie called to tell her what had happened, Sylvia closed down her decorating programs and rushed to Soundside. She found Lily parked in the parlor, mouth agape and drooling on her food-stained robe. Sylvia wheeled her to the shower room and, assisted by Chrissie, undressed her mother and placed her tenderly in the step-in tub. The aide found a plastic trash bag to wrap Lily's arm so it wouldn't get wet, and they turned on the water until she was ribs high in warmth.

Slowly Sylvia washed her mother in gentle suds starting with her hair. She spoke of love and loss, of Trai and her father. She said Lily never had to worry about abandonment, not like her family had done to her. She admonished Lily to reject joining the travelers, to fight such a suicidal slide. Sylvia then quietly held Lily there in the enormous tub, while the old woman mourned so violently it was as though gremlins clawed her innards and ghouls battled for her very essence.

As Chrissie put Lily to bed, Sylvia called the nurses together and pleaded that pain killers be minimized. "She needs clarity now more than ever if we are to save her from despair. The real Lily is slipping away." Then Sylvia sat with her through the night as her mother thrashed and wept.

In the early hours, Lily calmed. Sylvia did not know if her mother slept or just lay still in exhaustion. But she did know it was time to release her own anger, exasperation and fear. Sylvia said, "I can't talk you back just by saying I need you. If that could happen, mothers would never die. You raised me to be strong and accept what comes. But don't you agree that losing both Kyle and you just weeks apart is asking too much?

"Even if you don't agree, this isn't about you and me anymore. You started the idea of Latin's Ranch. You introduced hope where there was none. Damn it to hell, you made us all believe. Don't you dare turn your back on us now. You are obligated to keep us moving on the road you showed us, even if you have lost belief in it for yourself.

"This isn't about painkillers, not the kind that come in a bottle. Your mind is as strong as it ever was. You come back to yourself now. Damn it, you fight. You owe me that."

* * *

Lily was was floating like a parched castaway, one too exhausted to yell for help any longer. She was ready to slip slowly into the deep. Sylvia's voice merely soothed her, at least until her daughter began to sound angry. "Damn it to hell…you are obligated…don't you dare…"

*I'm old, and I'm sad. How dare she speak to me this way?* The simple thing was to ignore it, to peacefully float…

*Wait. Just wait. A daughter doesn't talk to a mother like that. I must speak with her. I must…*

Then Lily was awake. Pain rushed back, along with desolation.

*But why? I can't walk, but I can think. I feel misery but also love. I can't give in to despair when I've provided hope. I've made promises.*

* * *

Morning came, bringing Jessica with it. Sylvia was glad of the company as she held vigil next to Lily's bed. She listened as Jessica described the move in hushed tones, now just six days away. There seemed to be no joy in it anymore.

"We'll do it next week," Jessica said. "Bear will be at the Ranch by then. I'll get Charlie and Eunice in my Toyota. I'll come back for Lily. Somebody here will help me load her because she won't be able to do the transfer without it."

"No." A weak voice disagreed.

Sylvia and Jessica stared at each other, then at the bed.

"No?" Sylvia asked.

"No." The invalid turned her head and stared at them.
"Eunice and I will go together."

Lily was back.

## FUN HOUSE CHRONICLE
# Lily

*I* have a Will which is not your bee's wax, but you can call this my last Testament if you've a mind to. You might have guessed I'm the one who composed these Chronicles. They're what I've seen, what I've learned, what I've surmised. It just makes sense to write this stuff all down in case you're facing a Fun House of your own. Once Bear taught me the computer it got a bunch easier, especially since I started working mostly left handed. What with breaking my right arm and all.

Anyhoo, this last Chronicle is about Latin's Ranch and what's happened to all of us since we escaped the Fun House walls.

Those last few days at Soundside, Charlie, Eunice and I were as excited as pups adopted at the pound, waiting to go to our new digs. We passed the time making Indian bonnets and pilgrim hats for Jessica's Thanksgiving dinner. Eunice glued multi-colored glitter to feathers she cut from construction paper. Charlie said he didn't really think the First People wore parrot feathers, but Eunice told him to lighten up. We even added some sparkle to the buckles on the black felt pilgrim hats. I should take a moment here to apologize to Babs for making the activities room look like it was hit by taggers armed with glitter.

*Jessica picked us up at Soundside in a van she'd rented just for that purpose. It had a lift for Charlie and me. Eunice was able to skitter into the front seat like a goddamned monkey. Everyone turned out to say good-bye to us. Babs, of course, Lia and Clarice. Nurses Mary Beth and Baby Talk and Happy Face. And Ernie, my beloved Ernie. All of them saw us through our suffering and added to our joy.*

*Bear was on the porch along with Chrissie and Aurora when we arrived at Latin's Ranch, all of them waving their arms like an aerobics class. An episode of The Waltons couldn't have made a better homecoming...except I don't remember any of that bunch looking as beat to crap as Bear and me. His eyes had gone from black to chartreuse by then. And I could barely wipe my own nose.*

*Thanksgiving was one for the record books. Everybody contributed something, including Sam who brought weed so everyone could share a peace pipe of brotherly love. It's legal here in Washington. It wasn't his fault Jessica wouldn't let him pass it around.*

*Ben cooked outdoors, a ham in the Char-Broil and a turkey in a fryer. Aurora handled everything else to serve buffet style on the enormous counter they built in the kitchen. The two of them bickered about everything. Should there be oysters or chestnuts in genuine stuffing...which was better, cranberry sauce or jelly...butter for the pumpkin bread or just the Parker House rolls...when to decant the snooty French wine Sylvia had brought along to toast Kyle.*

*Speaking of Sylvia, she made the dessert. She's not been cooking much since Kyle died, and I know she loves to do it. She made a gorgeous torte of light sugar-free cream and fresh fruits, something even us diabetics can enjoy. She served it on a lovely lacquered tray with mother of pearl inlay around the rim. It was a gift to her from Trai.*

*Clarice's son stayed away at school, but she came. She didn't contribute to the menu for which we can all be grateful since pilgrims didn't celebrate with reduced fat Triscuits. Instead, she made a centerpiece with a little guidance from Babs. By the time they finished up with all the grape vines, dried grasses, silk flowers, bittersweet, candles, and those little imitation song birds with wire feet to stick into the vines, it was too damn big for the table. Clarice said she didn't know how to make anything that wasn't Queen-sized.*

*Furball destroyed one of the imitation birds and hacked up a sparkly glob of feathers between the Ed the Evil memorial football recliner and the game on TV. Sam was in the recliner at the time – he claimed it was his own personal Plymouth Rock until turkey time – and Bear was parked next to him. The language of those two over a little cat puke? Well, it takes a lot to turn these old ears blue.*

*Chrissie worked as aide and server that day, so she brought along her children. Otherwise, we'd be just about the only house in America without a kids' table. Alita and Rick missed the meal because she was off introducing him to her parents. His wild oat days may have been harvested.*

*I know Jessica held out hope that Ben's daughter Rachel would put in an appearance. That didn't happen, and nothing was said. It's not a story that will have a happy ending, I'm afraid. But Ben's not the kind of man to give up on things or I guess he wouldn't still be walking Gina Lola and Latin Dancer. Hope he's up to it if and when the worst happens. I know Jessica can handle it.*

*I thought the guests of honor were Jeff and Terri Parkinson when they arrived. He announced he'd taken a job with an assisted care facility in Olympia to begin in the New Year. Terri will keep coming to birder meetings with Clarice, so that friendship seems to be cast in cement.*

*Then Ernie showed up. Jessica must have invited him as my own personal guest of honor. But I noticed he was spending a fair amount of time with Clarice. Hope something's afoot there.*

*I'll tell you who the real guest of honor turned out to be. My daughter brought along a gorgeous hunk of manhood named Tony Sapienza. Eunice took one look and chirped, "Oooo, Sylvia, he's a looker! Is he your new fancy man?" My Sylvia wanted to crawl under the brand new flooring, but the Italian Stallion loved it.*

*Sylvia and Tony pulled two dining room chairs over to my wheelchair. She gave me a hug and a kiss, but I kept my sights on him. I figured it's way too soon for her to be stepping out with another guy. Then she said he had been a friend of Kyle. He says to me, "Kyle always described his mother-in-law as a real firecracker. Said you were beautiful, like Sylvia. He didn't lie."*

*Okay, he's a charmer, but I'm no fool. I can see that Sylvia is a nervous Nelly so I say, "What's up, you two?"*

*"Mom, I don't want to shock you, but I want you to know the truth. Tony was more than Kyle's friend." She was never going to get it said. So I did it for her.*

*"You mean you were his lover?" I say to Tony.*

*"You knew Kyle was gay?" Sylvia says to me, all surprised.*

*"You knew he was gay?" I say to her, pretty surprised myself.*

*"I certainly knew Kyle was gay," Tony says in delight.*

*"You never said," says Sylvia.*

*"You never said," says me.*

*"I never said, either," says Tony. "Isn't this fun?"*

*That's when Sylvia sent him to join Clarice, Ernie, Sam and Bear watching the football game. She asked how long I'd known, and I told her I never knew for sure until I hired Kyle to sell my house. I asked him about it then. "He said that it was something you two didn't talk about. So I figured you didn't know."*

*"Of course I knew," she told me. "It just wasn't something that needed dissected. Our relationship was based on a lot of things as well as sex, for crying out loud."*

*"But isn't it why you never had children?"*

*"Of course not. Kids weren't a priority for us."*

*Well, that nearly shut my mouth. But it was Truth or Consequences time. "I always thought you didn't want a child because you were so unhappy as one." Cost me some pride to say that right out loud. And wouldn't you know I'd been wrong all these years? Sylvia never dreamed that's what I was thinking. "Children just weren't right for me. You know that I'm too controlling for that. Kyle knew it, too."*

*I could have saved myself a lot of guilt if I'd just opened my yap and asked. Then she says she wanted me to meet Tony because he's been such a help to her. I said it took guts for him to come here. She was about to tell me something else but that's when Eunice bellowed, "Now this is a damn fine looking bunch of the thankful. But when do we eat?" Shades of Gladys.*

*So we ate. I pigged out on the first real mashed potatoes I've had since I entered the Fun House. They were smooth and creamy, with almost no lumps. Comfort food, indeed.*

* * *

*That was all a couple months and a couple of holidays back. Here's an update, and then I'll say good-bye.*

*The Soundside staff had its own unsanctioned holiday party. It was deemed a great success by most who attended even though it was not as grand as Babs had hoped.*

*Chrissie dropped in, and reported that she'd seen Clarice dancing more than once with Ernie. She's doing enough freelance now that she's planning on leaving Soundside in the spring.*

*Rumor has it Nurse Mary Beth went directly to Compre-Care with complaints about Patricia Bergeron. A nurse is the diva of a nursing home so her say would carry a lot of weight. Maybe that's why they didn't give Bergeron the administrator job on a permanent basis. Or maybe they never intended to. They might have just used her until they could find the person they really wanted.*

*Sylvia continues to write to Trai and she's making noises about going to visit him one day. In the meantime, his son, Dinh, works on a cruise ship that makes the Seattle/Alaska roundtrip all summer. Sylvia plans to meet him when he can get a few hours off. She's in Paris now with Tony. I think that Kyle is slowly releasing his hold, and she intends to start up Henderson Interiors once again. She keeps Tony's number on speed dial, but I'm sure her need for him will subside as time passes.*

*And if not, well, he's family here now, too. He likes the place enough to have had his grandfather move into one of the private rooms. Frankie's got every bit of Tony's charm. And a lot of hair for an old guy, too. Eunice hopes he's mob, and Bear is afraid he is. All I care is that Clarice has told me*

*Latin's Ranch is now in the black. Maybe my moving days are finally done.*

*Jessica is too busy for many long chats just now. I guess I'm jealous because she's no longer just mine. She's ours. But she looks radiant. And she says that if Ben and she ever do marry, they want me to be matron of honor. So I need to get this arm strong enough to roll a wheelchair down the aisle.*

*None of us misses the Fun House although Eunice would like a few entertainers to laugh at. Bear has found Sam to be a great audience for his stories. They've become buddies. I believe there might be poker nights in Sam's mobile home now and then. Charlie seems fine here...turns out other nurses can handle his balls. My only souvenir is the Ahoy! sign which reminds me of my old roommate. Not much else I want to remember.*

*Fortunately nobody around here is allergic to animals. There's usually a horse neighing or canaries singing or a dog rolling on a rug. Charlie holds the bird feeders upright for me to fill, and I can manage a scoop with my left hand. Furball hasn't curled up in anyone's bed. At least not yet.*

*Meals together are mostly fun unless one of us is feeling poorly which happens a lot when old folks gather. Since none of us is a traveler or as demented as The Creature, it's not so noisy here. The only shrieking is at the movies. I must say I don't have the tolerance for spooky films that Jessica does. I've had my fill of scary stuff.*

*There are little niceties here. Sylvia brought over my old silver set. Jessica allows us tea that is actually hot because she knows we won't burn ourselves. She uses gentle soap to wash our unmentionables. She doesn't tattle to Sylvia about a stash of dry roasted peanuts. These small freedoms are huge.*

*I'm sorry the residents we left behind do not share in them. I know all this won't last, of course. Some damn thing will happen, and I will have to fight off the Grim Jokester once again. But it's worth the fight because life continues in surprising ways if you just let it.*

— THE END —

**If you enjoyed *Fun House Chronicles*,
you can follow Bear, Lily and the gang in these
Bear Jacobs mysteries, available as ebooks
from amazon.com:**

## Bear in Mind

In the first of the PI Bear Jacobs series, the residents of Latin's Ranch investigate the case of Charlie's missing wife. At first they think she's a heart breaking bitch who abandoned her hubby. But Bear learns that women in the community are disappearing at an alarming rate…and to no place good. It's a dangerous and twisted trail that Bear follows toward a surprising conclusion. Bear in Mind is a cozy with bite.

## Hard to Bear

Life at Latin's Ranch adult care home is anything but restful. A vicious gang is producing old-fashioned snuff films with a violent new twist: custom ordered murder for sale. Bear and friends are in grave danger as they join forces with a mob family, a special forces soldier with PTSD, and a pack of mad dogs to seek out the evil that has taken root in the Pacific Northwest woods. Meanwhile, back at Latin's Ranch, Lily's daughter draws a bead on a hot new lover, and Jessica takes in a baby to protect.

## Bear Claus

A novella to add to your holiday cheer. Somebody is charging Eunice's account for too many fancy pants at the My Fair Pair lingerie shop. Bear and his gang follow a suspect on a merry chase through a local casino. Then all turns serious as the trail leads to more dangerous places beyond.

## Bear at Sea

Cruises are supposed to be more fun than this! Watch for the third novel in the Bear Jacobs series, coming soon.

## Author's Acknowledgments

This novel does not belong just to me. First and foremost, I salute many of the administrators, nurses, aides and staff who work with our loved ones in their final days. It is an impossibly difficult job. If you believe in angels, look for them inside the Fun House walls.

My sister, Donna Whichello, never let me give up on this novel even when it came too close to my own Grim Jokester. She has been the most excellent of editors. Thanks to my friends Jan Shamberg, Carol Richards, Mindy Mailman, Renee Rosen and Ellen Green who saw me through many hard days while my husband was ill. Thanks also to Adrianne Lee and Orysia Earhart, the members of my critique group who had the courage to say, "It sucks," when it did.

Thanks, too, to Max, my own 'cockadock' who was the model for Folly, the cocker spaniel/dachshund mix that is never very far from Jessica.

And finally, my endless gratitude to readers of my blog who convinced me that I could do this writer stuff.

## About the Author

LINDA B. MYERS won her first creative contest in the sixth grade for her *Clean Up Fix Up Paint Up* poster. This led to a career as a copywriter in Chicago. A few years back, she turned in her stilettos for rain boots and moved to the Pacific Northwest. You can visit with Linda online at www.LindaBMyers.com

10003518R00164

Made in the USA
San Bernardino, CA
04 December 2018